Voices of Medieval England, Scotland, Ireland, and Wales

Recent Titles in Voices of an Era

Voices of Civil War America: Contemporary Accounts of Daily Life
Lawrence A. Kreiser, Jr. and Ray B. Browne, editors

Voices of Early Christianity: Documents from the Origins of Christianity
Kevin W. Kaatz, editor

Voices of Early Modern Japan: Contemporary Accounts of Daily Life during the Age of the Shoguns
Constantine Vaporis, editor

Voices of Revolutionary America: Contemporary Accounts of Daily Life
Carol Sue Humphrey, editor

Voices of Shakespeare's England: Contemporary Accounts of Elizabethan Daily Life
John A. Wagner, editor

Voices of Victorian England: Contemporary Accounts of Daily Life
John A. Wagner, editor

Voices of World War II: Contemporary Accounts of Daily Life
Priscilla Mary Roberts, editor

Voices of Ancient Egypt: Contemporary Accounts of Daily Life
Rosalie David, editor

Voices of the Reformation: Contemporary Accounts of Daily Life
John A. Wagner, editor

Voices of the Iraq War: Contemporary Accounts of Daily Life
Brian L. Steed, editor

Voices of Medieval England, Scotland, Ireland, and Wales

Contemporary Accounts of Daily Life

Linda E. Mitchell, Editor

VOICES OF AN ERA

GREENWOOD™

An Imprint of ABC-CLIO, LLC
Santa Barbara, California • Denver, Colorado

Library of Congress Cataloging-in-Publication Data

Names: Mitchell, Linda Elizabeth, editor.
Title: Voices of medieval England, Scotland, Ireland, and Wales : contemporary accounts of daily
    life / Linda E. Mitchell, editor.
Description: Santa Barbara, California : Greenwood, an Imprint of ABC-CLIO, LLC, [2016] | Series:
    Voices of an Era | Includes bibliographical references and index.
Identifiers: LCCN 2016011259 (print) | LCCN 2016016430 (ebook) | ISBN 9781610697873
    (hardcopy : alk. paper) | ISBN 9781610697880 (ebook)
Subjects: LCSH: Great Britain—Social life and customs—1066–1485—Sources. | Great Britain—
    Social life and customs—To 1066—Sources. | England—Social life and customs—Sources. |
    Scotland—Social life and customs—Sources. | Ireland—Social life and customs—Sources. |
    Wales—Social life and customs—Sources.
Classification: LCC DA170 .V65 2016 (print) | LCC DA170 (ebook) | DDC 941.03—dc23
LC record available at https://lccn.loc.gov/2016011259

ISBN: 978–1–61069–787–3
EISBN: 978–1–61069–788–0

20 19 18 17 16   1 2 3 4 5

This book is also available as an eBook.

Greenwood
An Imprint of ABC-CLIO, LLC

ABC-CLIO, LLC
130 Cremona Drive, P.O. Box 1911
Santa Barbara, California 93116-1911
www.abc-clio.com

This book is printed on acid-free paper ∞

Manufactured in the United States of America

CONTENTS

DOCUMENTS OF MEDIEVAL ENGLAND, SCOTLAND, IRELAND, AND WALES

Contents

PREFACE

Voices of Medieval England, Ireland, Scotland, and Wales contains excerpts from some 63 unique sources, arranged into 8 topical sections and 50 subsections. The sources range in date from the 600s to the late 1400s and cover the multiple and diverse cultures of England both before and after the Norman Conquest (1066); early and later medieval Ireland and the "Lordship" of Ireland that resulted from the English conquest of the twelfth century; the Scotland of the early medieval Scots and Picts as well as the unified kingdom of Scots that developed after the year 1000; and the region of Wales from the early native principalities to the English conquest of the thirteenth century and the establishment of the English Principality. This is a very long time frame, and a widely diverse collection of peoples and cultures; as a result, not all cultures are treated equally or consistently, but the reader will find all cultures represented on some level in every section.

The history of the British Isles in the Middle Ages—a period that covers a thousand years (from 500 to 1500) and includes many different cultures, from Celtic peoples, to the Anglo-Saxons, Vikings from Scandinavia, Normans (who had been Vikings) and French—is significant for a number of reasons, both for the people of the time and those of later eras who now live in English-speaking countries all over the globe because of Britain's imperial conquests of the seventeenth and eighteenth centuries. First, Britain and Ireland and the small islands that surround their coasts had a long history of interaction with each other and also the European continent. Indeed, all the people living in the British Isles throughout the Middle Ages were immigrants, from the Celtic groups that arrived before recorded history, to the Germanic groups that traversed the English Channel and the North Sea between the sixth and eleventh centuries, and occupied territories throughout the islands. This diversity and the retention of continental ties affected the development of the islands' cultures. Irish missionaries converted Anglo-Saxon kings in the sixth century, and continental Europeans in the eighth and ninth centuries; Norse kings occupied the northern isles of Scotland until the fourteenth century; Anglo-Saxon kings married Merovingian and Carolingian princesses; Normans—descended from Vikings who occupied the region around the mouth of the Seine River—covered the British Isles, establishing lordships and building castles in Britain, Wales, and Ireland; they married local women, creating hybrid medieval cultures that have endured into the modern age. Second, the peoples of the British Isles during and after the medieval period also carried their cultures all over the world, through crusade, settlement, and conquest. The seeds of the British Empire lie in the planting of Anglo-Norman people and governance in Ireland and Wales; the kings of Scotland in the twelfth century embraced Norman culture as well, inviting Norman barons to become a new magnate class north of the border and building their royal administration on the framework of Anglo-Norman systems. Thus, any country all over the world touched by British imperialism has a connection to Britain and Ireland in the medieval period.

PRIMARY SOURCES, MEDIEVAL CULTURE, AND THE MODERN RESEARCHER

Primary sources—materials that were created at the time under study—are an essential component to historical research and form the foundation of what historians of every era and geographical region use as the basis for research and the writing of historical texts. For the Middle Ages, "primary" sources are complicated, because historians have to choose between the kinds of sources all historians would consider "primary"—the public and private documents created by individuals or institutions that record their daily lives, practices, thoughts, and ideas—and those that some historians might consider "secondary"—works of interpretive history written by people of the era but not quite contemporary with the events being discussed. Recognizing that both components comprise the essential materials needed to understand the medieval world, this sourcebook incorporates both kinds of written medieval sources. In addition, I recognize that medieval sources can also be unwritten: they can comprise the material remains of cultures of the medieval world, such as archaeological remains, buildings, art and artifacts, and the physical material of the documents themselves: the animal skins, ink, glue, and thread that were used to create books; and many other forms of written texts. Sources can also be, in some way, immaterial, such as music that has been reconstructed from arcane notation in manuscripts, performed on instruments built not at the time, but through interpretations of images of musical instruments depicted in books and on the facades of churches. All these comprise potential sources for study of the Middle Ages.

The medieval sources for the different regions of the British Isles vary considerably in quantity, quality, and aspect. England's collection of sources is vast and diverse—possibly the most comprehensive collection of medieval sources in all of Europe—because of the early introduction of written documentation of the royal administration, finance, and courts of law. In contrast, documentation of the kingdom of Scotland's administration began relatively late and reached the level of that of England only in the early modern period. The multitude of small principalities and kingdoms in Wales created almost no written documentation until confronted with the Anglo-Norman barons intent on conquering them. This was much the case as well in Ireland, but the conquest of the island's eastern half resulted in an incredibly rich and diverse collection of sources for what came to be known as the "Lordship of Ireland." This document cache was tragically lost when the Public Record Office, housed at the central government building called The Four Courts, was burned down in the 1922 Irish Revolution. Thus, while it is relatively easy to find adequate documentary sources for many aspects of medieval English life, it can be far more difficult to produce parallel levels of detail for the rest of the British Isles.

The languages of medieval sources can also problematize the work of the modern researcher. The overwhelming majority of written texts in the Middle Ages were written in Latin; this was not the classical Latin of Virgil or Ovid, but rather the Latin of the chancery clerk, the university professor, the steward of the manor. In many cases, this Latin—localized, living, influenced by vernacular languages—can be highly formulaic but it can also be difficult to translate. In England, before the Norman Conquest, the royal administration used both Latin and Old English, or "Anglo-Saxon," in its official documents. Wales, Ireland, and Scotland had few written sources before the twelfth century, but some of these were also written in vernacular tongues—Welsh, Irish, Gaelic, Pictish—as well as in Latin. After the Norman Conquest, the English chancery created documents not only in Latin but also in French, the language of the court, until the very end of the medieval period. Old English ceased to be a written language, but the vernacular reappeared beginning in the thirteenth century in a new guise: Middle English, influenced profoundly by French. This gradually filtered into the language of the English chancery and courts of law but English did not replace French as an official language of royal and local government until the end of the Middle Ages—and did not replace Latin in many official documents until considerably later. Household account lists of items in the "buttery" of St. James's Palace during the reign of Queen Anne (r. 1702–1714) were still written in Latin! English became far more pervasive in popular culture, however, with poems, ballads, and other kinds of popular texts appearing in English in the century before the courtier-turned-poet Geoffrey Chaucer (ca. 1343–1400) revolutionized the use of English as a literary language of the highest caliber.

The form of writing of many documents, manuscripts, and letters in the Middle Ages looks nothing like the texts modern researchers use today. In the centuries before the printing press (and, indeed, for many centuries thereafter before the invention of the typewriter) all written documents and books were copied by hand using specific forms of the Roman alphabet that were considered appropriate to the context of the writing. Documents of the British Isles were written in various forms of "court" or "chancery" hands, which evolved over the centuries and changed according to the dictates of the document, the language, and the purpose of the writing. Books also had forms of the alphabet that were specific to the purpose or format of the book. In Anglo-Saxon England, a "round-hand" based on Irish uncial and Carolingian or "Insular" minuscule developed for the writing of books; after the conquest, different forms of "Gothic" script developed. In both books and documents, most written texts were also heavily abbreviated, to save both space on the page and the time it took the copyist to write them. The medieval researcher of original languages must master these different forms of writing by studying the "paleography" (literally, "old writing") appropriate to the documents she or he reads.

RATIONALE FOR CHOOSING SOURCES FOR THIS COLLECTION

The rationale for the materials chosen to be included in this sourcebook revolves around two fundamental issues: the desire to present a picture of the medieval British Isles that is inclusive of the Celtic regions, rather than exclusive only of England; and the desire to present sources that have not appeared in other sourcebooks before. These two goals required a rather different process of compilation, editing, and production because many of the sources included in this collection had never been translated before, let alone printed in other collections. In addition, sources that can be found in numerous other sourcebooks, or online, have been replaced by other sources that are far less frequently excerpted. Thus, although Magna Carta is not included here, two documents from fourteenth-century Ireland and Scotland—the *Remonstrance of the Irish Chiefs* (1317) and *The Declaration of Arbroath* (1320), respectively—are, because they reflect the values presented in Magna Carta as they filtered from the field of Runnymede in 1215 to more peripheral regions over the course of one hundred years.

The idea of recreating the "voices" of people of the past has also influenced the choices made for this sourcebook. Instead of presenting the standard documents of royal proclamation and official church doctrine, you will find the recording of disputes between individuals as they were resolved in the royal court, or the reports of investigations of unnatural death, or the letters of an aggrieved Cistercian abbot sent to Ireland to quell disturbances between Cistercian monastic houses. It can be very difficult to recreate the voices of common people of long ago but their words can be heard as an echo in the dry reports of accidental death, disputes over land, and religious dissent.

It is easiest to identify the lives and activities of elite people of the past because they leave more records and figure more prominently in the institutions of government, church, and military. The actors in the majority of documents and the subjects of medieval chronicles are overwhelmingly members of the elite; thus, kings and queens, earls and countesses, abbots and bishops occupy many more pages than do peasants, merchants, and the urban poor who comprised the vast majority of the population. Nevertheless, some documents do provide windows into activities and lives below the elites: children's activities can be determined by descriptions of their deaths in coroners' inquests; urban courts oversaw the making of bread and ale and the activities of food vendors, prostitutes, and laborers; common people who engaged in political and religious dissent are described in unflattering terms by monastic chroniclers, but their activities are recorded and can be analyzed. Myths, legends, political satire, and religious drama were all consumed by people throughout medieval society and these kinds of entertainments can provide access to the state of mind of people both elite and common. These kinds of sources, that illuminate medieval nonelite lives, are important components to this collection.

ORGANIZATION OF SECTIONS

The excerpts from about 63 separate sources are organized into eight thematic sections: domestic life; education and training; economics; religious life; politics, law, and administration; war and diplomacy; crime and deviance; and popular culture. Subsections within each theme often comprise more than one source, or several extracts from a single source. For example, some of the richest sources for the medieval researcher come from the records of the English royal administration: records of litigation, coroners' inquests, royal letters, and so on. These records contain thousands of small entries and extracting a few from each of these kinds of sources provides a small window into understanding both how people interacted and also how the royal administration worked. When possible, two or more different perspectives on an important event are presented for the purpose of comparison. For example, Anglo-Saxon and Norman views of the battle of Hastings (1066) appear in order for the views of both the conquerors and the conquered can be analyzed.

In addition to the extracts themselves, each subsection incorporates an historical introduction; a suggestion of issues to keep in mind as you read; a brief description of the aftermath to the issues discussed in the source(s); a series of questions to ask yourself; a number of topics to consider for further analysis; and a few suggestions for further information should you want to pursue the topic in more depth. Sidebars provide specific information on issues raised within the sources themselves, or provide additional information on essential components. Specific terms that might be confusing to the reader are also defined in fact boxes within the sources.

OTHER FEATURES OF THIS VOLUME

Other useful features include a section on Evaluating and Interpreting Primary Documents, which includes a series of questions to consider and suggestions on how to assess medieval sources; a biographical appendix outlining brief histories of people mentioned in the sources, introductions, and aftermath sections; a glossary of terms; a parallel chronology of events in the British Isles from 500 to 1500; and a bibliography of both general sources for medieval British history and useful websites to explore. An index provides easy access to the contents of the volume.

ACKNOWLEDGMENTS

The completion of this sourcebook would have been impossible without the assistance and generosity of many people. A number of publishers, authors, and website creators have allowed excerpts of their materials without requiring to pay permission fees. These include the Anglo-Norman Text Society; A. Cynfael Lake, who is the creator of the website on Dafydd ap Gwilym; and the Cistercian Society. I am also indebted to the organization that maintains the Internet Archive (archive.org), which has provided a tremendous service in scanning public-domain books that would have been unavailable without its efforts. Many medieval documents and chronicles would be completely inaccessible without this service. The National Archives of the United Kingdom and the British Library maintain vast collections of documents in manuscript that I have used repeatedly over the last three decades and I am fortunate to have been able to utilize this research in some of the materials I translated for this collection.

The process of creating this sourcebook would have been difficult, indeed, without the hard work of two of my graduate research assistants, Kimberly Fogarty Palmer and Rachael Hazell; they labored long and hard, transcribing sources for me to edit and translate. In addition, Kimberly Fogarty Palmer practiced her skills in translating texts from Middle to Modern English: she is the official translator of several sources in this collection. She also contributed to the timelines I have used to compile the historical trajectory of medieval England, Ireland, Scotland, and Wales.

Finally, my family has had to endure my absence—mental and physical—as I worked on the completion of this book. This project required a significant amount of time, energy, and thought, which I had to squeeze in-between teaching, research, writing, editing, and administrative duties. Their patience, especially that of my spouse, Neal Lewis, has been—as always—infinite, and I am very grateful for their—his—forbearance.

INTRODUCTION

The British Isles—comprising the main islands of Ireland and Britain; smaller islands of the English Channel, the Irish Sea, and the North Sea; and the medieval kingdoms, principalities, and lordships of England, Ireland, Scotland, and Wales—might not be large in land mass, but they were one of the most diverse regions—physically, as well as ethnically—of Europe in the medieval period. Originally populated by Stone-Age people whose artifacts have been dated to as early as 8000 BCE, the monument of Stonehenge has been dated to between 3100 and 2000 BCE—these peoples were also probably related to the prehistoric populations of western Europe known as the "Bell-Beaker Culture" (ca. 2800–1800 BCE). Sometime during the ninth century BCE, migrations of Celtic peoples connected to the Hallstatt and La Tène cultures of continental Europe moved into the islands. The resulting Celtic subgroups—the "Britons," the "Scots" or "Gaels" (who originally settled in Ireland and then moved to the western regions of modern-day Scotland), and the "Picts"—eventually absorbed any previous residents of the islands and their culture and thoroughly replaced the earlier Neolithic and Bronze Age cultures that had existed.

The invasion of Britain by the Romans in the first century CE represented the first of a wave of conquests that further diversified the population of the British Isles. The early medieval British Isles experienced several waves of invasion from different Germanic groups ranging from Angles, Saxons, and Jutes in the fifth and sixth centuries to Vikings—Norse and Danes—in the eighth through the eleventh centuries. This changed the composition of the islands in fundamental ways: even Celtic strongholds such as Ireland and Scotland were affected by Viking raids and settlements. The last of these invasions was the Norman Conquest of DUKE WILLIAM OF NORMANDY in 1066, which replaced the Germanic political culture of "Anglo-Saxon" England with a Norman French one. The Normans then spread throughout the British Isles, conquering portions of Wales and Ireland and settling, at the invitation of the Scottish kings, in Scotland.

Throughout the Middle Ages, the British Isles was not a unified whole of large, centralized kingdoms: this was the case only for the kingdom of England after about 930 CE. The Celtic regions of Ireland, Scotland, and Wales were divided into competing independent principalities, lordships, or—in the case of Scotland—"**mormaer**-ships," which jockeyed for power and position even when faced with invasion by Normans or consolidation by ambitious kings. After the Norman Conquest, the growth in power of the kings of England led to conquests of Wales (beginning soon after 1066 and more or less completed by about 1300) and Ireland (beginning in 1177 but never fully complete even by 1500). In Scotland before the year 1000, the kings of Dál Riata, the western Gaelic region north of the independent kingdom of Strathclyde, and those of the Picts in the east competed for dominance, until the semilegendary king KENNETH MACALPIN (Cináed mac Ailpein) conquered the Picts sometime around 843 CE and united the two southern parts of the region of Scotland, known eventually as the "Kingdom of Alba." Even at this juncture, Scotland was far from united, as the mormaers (also known as "earls" or "thanes") of the northwest regions remained independent, and the northern part of Scotland, as well as the Hebrides and Orkneys and the islands of Man and Skye in the Irish Sea, were all invaded and conquered by Norse and Danish Vikings, who also established independent lordships and kingdoms on the eastern coast of Ireland. Indeed, the main cities of medieval Ireland—Dublin, Wexford, Waterford, Limerick, and Cork—were all founded by the Vikings.

England was originally broken into seven small Anglo-Saxon kingdoms until the era of the Viking invasions (beginning in the early eighth century), when the southern region was unified under the kings of Wessex and the northern region comprised the "Danelaw"—a region of Viking dominance ruled by the kings of Norway and Denmark (usually these were the same person). KING ATHELSTAN OF WESSEX (r. 924–939) is usually regarded as the unifier of the two halves of England, which were ruled as a single kingdom from that point on. After the Norman Conquest of 1066, although the northern border between England and Scotland wavered for the next 300 years and more, the two main kingdoms began to stabilize in both territory and authority, with England being the dominant polity in the British Isles.

Wales and Ireland had very distinct Celtic cultures and retained them for a very long time, even after they were invaded by the Normans and conquered. The tiny region of Wales had always shared a volatile border with England—the reason for King Offa of Mercia (r. 757–796) to build his famous Offa's Dyke along the border of his kingdom and that of the Welsh Principality of Powys—but this was invaded soon after 1066 by Norman barons interested in amassing territory that was independent of the king of England's jurisdiction. Soon the entire north–south border between Wales and England—the March of Wales—as well as the southern portion of the country were conquered and organized into "marcher" lordships—from Pembroke in the west to Cardiff Bay and the Severn River's estuary in the east. The princes of Wales, consolidated into three main polities of Deheubarth in the south- and central-west, Powys in the central-east, and Gwynedd in the north, then competed with the marcher barons and each other for dominance until the conquests of KING EDWARD I (r. 1272–1307) effectively obliterated the Welsh principalities.

Ireland had a long history of resisting invasion. Indeed, the Romans were unable to establish even a beachhead on the island, although there is evidence of significant trade between the eastern Irish kingdom of Leinster and Roman Britain. Ireland's relative stability was shattered by the Viking invasions and the establishment of a Viking kingdom based in Dublin. The kings of Leinster ceded the coastal territory to the Norse kings of "Dubh Linn" (in Irish Gaelic, meaning Black Water) or "Dublinia" (the Viking name) but retained their control over the eastern region, competing with the kings of Connacht (west-central), Munster (south), Meath (the "Southern Ui Neill"—east-central), Northern Ui Neill (northwest), and the small principalities of Breifne, Oriel, and Ulidia (north-central and northeast) that eventually made up the province of Ulster. The extreme lack of unity in Ireland and the intense competition for the position of "high king" (Ard Rí) made the Irish kingdoms fairly easy targets for both Viking and, eventually, Anglo-Norman conquest, but the regionalism and intense competition of the Irish warrior class also made it difficult for invaders to retain consistent control over the island.

After the Norman Conquest, the political, economic, and social cultures of the British Isles—whether ruled over by Norman, Angevin, or English kings or by native princes and kings—entered the European milieu in very significant ways. After all, the kings of England after 1066 were also the dukes of Normandy. Beginning with the reign of HENRY II (r. 1155–1189), the kings were also the counts of Anjou and Maine as well as dukes of Aquitaine. When Henry invaded and conquered Ireland and expanded Anglo-Norman dominance over Wales and Scotland by claiming suzerainty over both regions, it seemed that the kings of England would achieve the status of emperors in the western portions of Europe. This ambition went unrealized because of the territorial losses of King JOHN (r. 1199–1216), but it was a dream that reappeared in the reigns of Edward I (r. 1272–1307), EDWARD III (r. 1327–1377), and HENRY V (r. 1413–1422) with significant effects on the British Isles and France.

The temperate climate—despite being very far north—of the British Isles, the varied terrain throughout the islands, the numerous navigable water systems, and the abundance of raw materials—especially metals and high-quality stone—encouraged a diverse economic system based on agriculture, exploitation of raw materials, manufacturing, and commercial exchange. Primary to the economic success of the kingdoms was sheep farming. British sheep produced the highest quality wool in Europe—estimates are that there were ten sheep for every person living in England!—and England dominated the trade, exporting raw wool and thread to Flanders, the major producer of high-quality textiles in medieval Europe. Agricultural production of wheat and other grains, cattle and dairy products, and other kinds of food for human consumption often took a backseat to sheep farming and wool production, except in areas where the soil was particularly fertile, such as in East Anglia and the Midlands, in the eastern and central portions of England. Mining of tin, iron, and small amounts of silver and gold competed with sheep pasturage in Cornwall and mid-Wales. The many rivers, lakes, and salt water harbors produced an abundance of fish and eels that were marketed throughout the island. The production of salt was a significant occupation in the marshy areas of Kent and coastal East Anglia. The presence of veins of fine quality clay and silica in the West Midlands made it a manufacturing center for pottery and glassworks. Finally, the efficient system of county towns, known as "burhs" in the Anglo-Saxon period, which had been largely invented by King ALFRED of Wessex (r. 871–899) as part of what was known as the "burghal defense system," linked by road and water to each other and to the great metropolis of London, encouraged trade and localized manufacturing centers throughout Britain and, after the conquest, Ireland. England was considered a wealthy country in the Middle Ages. Although Scotland, Wales, and Ireland were somewhat more marginal economically in comparison to England, they contributed significantly to the British and European economies through raising sheep and processing wool, arable farming in areas that could sustain the growth of wheat, and exploitation of raw materials, especially wood and stone. There was a reason, however, for people living in Scotland and northern Ireland to consume far more oats than wheat: the climate was more conducive to oat production than to wheat.

According to some medieval theologians, society was best divided into three "orders": those who prayed occupied the top tier, those who fought were just below, and those who labored occupied the bottom rung. In reality, the social organization of medieval Britain and Ireland was far more complex and fluid. Not only were the elites—members of the nobility, aristocracy, and knightly classes—the most politically enfranchised, but they also dominated the membership of the clergy. Urban dwellers, ranging from elite merchants and manufacturers to domestic servants, apprentices, and the subaltern poor, grew in number and prominence over the centuries, but those at the highest level usually dreamed of entering the landed elite rather than retaining a position among the merchant classes. The peasantry—both free and unfree (serfs or, in legal terms, **villein**s)—varied widely in levels of wealth and prominence, from those who assumed local political authority on manors and in villages to day laborers and itinerant workers. Social mobility—both up and down—was common among the higher levels of the peasantry and lower levels of the knightly class, who came to be known as the "gentry" in the later Middle Ages. While it is true that status was often inherited, landed and monetary wealth could influence social and political standing in significant ways.

The legal status of people living in the British Isles also varied widely. In the early Middle Ages, the Anglo-Saxon kingdoms each maintained separate law codes which, while similar, nonetheless reflected each kingdom's particular development of custom and precedent. As the seven kingdoms coalesced into two, and then one, these law codes also were blended, along with Scandinavian customs derived from the Viking inhabitants of the Danelaw. Under Anglo-Saxon law, free people were divided into classes that were determined by the *mundium* (man-price) that would be assessed in case of violent death. Women as well as men were evaluated along this scale; indeed, women's *mundia* were often larger than those of men because of their childbearing abilities.

After the Norman Conquest, England developed a far more detailed, specific, and complex legal system that ranked people as free or unfree but did not significantly differentiate between them beyond that point, at least under the theory of the law. The one exception to this was the legal status of married women, in that they had no independent status and their legal "personality" was subsumed under that of their husbands. Single women—either unmarried or widowed—however, retained full legal independent status and, with a few exceptions such as not being permitted to serve on juries or act as justices (they could represent people as attorneys, however), they had access to the elaborate legal structure that evolved over the period between 1066 and 1500.

The systems of law in the Celtic and Gaelic regions differed significantly from each other and from English Common Law. Based entirely on custom and precedent, and largely unwritten until the twelfth century, Celtic law tended to group people into kinship units that operated corporately, rather than identifying them as individuals. After the conquests of Ireland and Wales, communities were differentiated as "Englishry," "Welshry," and "Irishry" and were assigned legal status based on the system of law they traditionally maintained. Thus, for the conquered territories of the British Isles, multiple systems of law and identity under law operated simultaneously. This was even more complicated in Scotland, where Scottish kings, influenced by the development of English Common Law in the twelfth century, introduced many similar precepts into their written law codes but nonetheless also honored local, regional, and ethnic legal systems that abounded in the various regions of the kingdom.

The British Isles were rather densely populated, especially in the southern halves of the kingdoms and territories, where urban development occurred earlier and more energetically. Current estimates are that about 2–3 million people lived in Britain and Ireland around the year 1100 and that the population exploded between that time and the devastation of the **Black Death** of 1347–1350, to around 6–7 million. Over 100,000 lived in London alone, and numerous communities and county towns achieved populations of 10,000 or more. The century following the first major outbreak of plague saw the population plummet to perhaps as low as 2–3 million. The city of London lost 80 percent of its population, sustaining only about 20,000 people in 1450. Population numbers in the British Isles did not recover to preplague levels until the early eighteenth century. The effects of both the population explosion and its dramatic decline were significant. Land values skyrocketed in the thirteenth century as the scarcity of land and the abundance of labor encouraged land-lords to convert their villeins to wage laborers and to retain arable land in their own hands whenever possible. After the Black Death, the opposite was true: land was relatively abundant and labor was very scarce. Wages began to rise, which led the king and royal administration to try, unsuccessfully, to limit wages through the legislation of the Statute of Laborers (1351). The only result was a growing restiveness among the peasantry and the explosion of the commons into a series of increasingly violent revolts: the Great Rising of 1381 and Jack Cade's Rebellion of 1450 are but two examples of common responses to royal pressure on wages.

One positive benefit of the dramatic loss of population was a significant rise in the quality and quantity of food consumed by common people. With abundant land resources and a tight labor market, British landlords turned increasingly to sheep and wool production and expanded dairy production as well. This led to a change in the diet of the typical peasant living in the British Isles from being largely grain based to one in which about a quarter of the calories consumed were in the form of high-quality animal proteins—meat and dairy.

Like the rest of western Europe, the peoples of Britain and Ireland were, at least after the ninth century, mostly Christian in orientation and owed allegiance to the Church of Rome and the papacy. Christianity had many faces, however, especially in Ireland and regions of England and Scotland evangelized by Irish missionaries as early as the third and fourth centuries, before the Germanic invasions. Irish forms of Christian observance proved difficult to erase, despite concerted efforts—and armed with **papal bull**s that mimicked crusades rhetoric—on the part of the kings of England and Scotland to subsume all their territories under Roman orthodoxy. One result of the English conquest of Ireland and Wales was the development of a more systematic diocesan and parish organization in both regions, with a separation between the work of the "secular" clergy (those who served the lay population) and the "regular" clergy (those who occupied monasteries and priories) that had not really occurred before the twelfth-century invasions. All regions of the British Isles eventually developed a dense network of cathedrals and parishes and of a wide variety of religious orders, from Benedictine and Cistercian to Dominican, Franciscan, and Augustinian. Several indigenous monastic orders also developed, such as the Gilbertines founded by St Gilbert of Sempringham, and both the Templars and the Hospitallers—two crusading orders—established themselves in England, Scotland, and Ireland as well. Lay piety was expressed through patronage—the donation of lands and benefices to monastic houses and to the building of chantries and chapels in major cathedral and parish churches—and voluntary renunciation of secular life: the removal of individuals to "anchorholds" (to live as anchorites and anchoresses) was one of the more unusual aspects of lay piety in the later Middle Ages in England, for example, but it had a long tradition in Ireland.

After the Norman Conquest, Jews who had been living in Normandy and other territories controlled by the dukes of Normandy and Aquitaine began to migrate to England under service of the Norman and Angevin kings. They settled in major metropolitan areas —London, Norwich, Lincoln, Oxford, and York—where significant trade economies had developed. Jews were highly educated and skilled laborers, especially in the working of gold and silver, in leatherwork, and in certain kinds of textile manufacture. They were also highly skilled scribes and physicians and maintained trading and commercial networks throughout Europe. Because of their status as essentially royal servants, Jews were unable to own land, and the kings of England used them mercilessly as bankers for their military, building, and administrative projects. Edward I (r. 1272–1307) and his wife Eleanor of Castile were particularly determined to wrest all the wealth from the Jewish communities. By the time Queen Eleanor died in 1290, the royal couple had largely succeeded, and this fact was used by Edward to justify the expulsion of the Jews from England in that year. The Jews did not return officially until the establishment of Cromwell's Commonwealth in the seventeenth century. The Jews of England scattered, some going back to the continent, and some traveling to Scotland, where there were no laws against their settlement, and to Ireland, where native resentment against English authority encouraged the Irish to welcome the small population of Jews who managed to cross the Irish Sea and join the community of Jews living in Dublin and along the south coast. There is no indication that the 1290 Edict of Expulsion was honored even in those parts of Ireland under direct English control.

The principal aspect of medieval life in the British Isles that tied together all of the disparate parts and populations after the year 1000 was the ubiquity of the royal administration—of England or of Scotland—expressed in law, statute, **writ**, **charter**, and court. England's administration, in particular, was heavily dependent on the maintenance of an elaborate chancery that produced thousands of written documents every year. This was reflected in the growth of public records recorded not only in the main administrative centers of Westminster and Dublin but also in the county boroughs and incorporated cities and towns (those with royal charters), and even in private baronial estates. The richness of the public records, combined with the parallel development of record-keeping by monastic houses and dioceses, beginning at a relatively early period in comparison to kingdoms on the continent, provides the researcher of medieval Britain and Ireland with a plethora of sources from which to draw. The administration of the realms touched every person living in the British Isles at some point in their lives and this defines, in many ways, the cultures of the region.

Evaluating and Interpreting Primary Documents

Primary sources, even when they seem to be neutral reports of events or ideas, are never neutral. Historians must always take into consideration the fact that all texts are "mediated" in some way: they are circumscribed by the motives of the author, the context in which the document was created, and the purpose or use to which it was put. This is particularly true of medieval sources because the vast majority of medieval people were not literate—not in their own vernacular languages and certainly not in the Latin of the chancery, law court, or religious institution. In addition, some documents that might seem to be neutral are not because of the process by which they came to be created. A good example is an entry from a "plea roll"—a document recording the process of litigation between two parties. The entry of a suit on a plea roll records all the parties involved (or does it?), the particulars of the case (or does it?), and the resolution of the case (or does it?). The plea rolls are all written in Latin, using highly formulaic prose and utilizing a standardized system of abbreviation to speed up the writing process as the clerk in charge of the roll had to write while the court case was proceeding. On the face of it, this seems to be a fairly straightforward system and one not prone to subjective manipulation. In fact, it is not straightforward at all. First, the litigation was initiated by the purchase of a "writ": a fill-in-the-blank style of form that could be purchased for a few pence (or a few shillings for a more complicated plea) that was completed by a clerk through the dictation of the litigant. However, the writ is written in Latin—and the people doing the talking are speaking in English or French (or, perhaps, Welsh or Irish at times). The clerk might have trouble with spelling names of Welsh or Irish people in Latin forms, he might not write down the names of the litigants correctly, or he might leave off some people for the sake of brevity. After the writ is "enrolled"—registered so that the litigation can commence—the sheriff is required to summon the litigants to court. The clerk in charge of the plea roll receives a copy of the writ and writes, in highly abbreviated form, the particulars of the case into the roll, leaving some space to write down the arguments that will be made in court. This, too, is written in Latin—but all the public proceedings of the court are made in French (before 1362) or in English (after 1362), so the clerk is simultaneously translating and writing down the arguments of the case. What if the clerk runs out of room on the roll? Sometimes he will simply stop writing. Sometimes he will flip the page over and continue the transcription of the arguments, with a line or arrow indicating the continuation. What if there are words the clerk cannot translate? Sometimes he makes up a word, or tacks a Latin ending onto an English or French word.

What if the argument is very complicated, with many questions from the justices of the Bench? The clerk might choose not to include any of the detail in the roll. Therefore, the clerk has made numerous choices, from translation to wording to how much detail he is willing to write down: all of these are forms of "mediated" text, and the researcher has to be aware of the potential absences as well as the information presented.

Different kinds of sources are often read in different ways, but there are several standard questions every researcher must ask—and answer to the best of his or her ability—in order to gain an understanding of the document.

- What kind of source or document is this? Is this a legal document? A literary source? A chronicle entry? A letter?
- Who or what organization is the author of this document? A named author, such as found in a literary text or letter? A government official or clerk? A monk or other professional religious?
- Who is the intended audience for the document? Is it an individual, such as the receiver of a letter? Is it a government organization, such as the royal chancery or exchequer, that is charged with maintaining archives of all documents they produce? Is it a community of people, such as the receivers of a statute or law code?
- When and where was the document written? This is a particularly thorny issue when dealing with orally transmitted sources that are written down centuries later, as often occurred with early medieval sources, whose earliest manuscripts could appear long after the creation of the "text."
- What is the purpose of the document? Is it a literary text designed to be read aloud to a mixed audience? Is it a text designed to be read by a specific person? Is it an official document designed to be read in the market square by the sheriff? Is it a record of a legal transaction, such as a deed, charter, or contract? The purpose of the document often determined its form and this is a vitally important component to understanding how to read and understand the text.
- Is there an unstated purpose or "subtext" that motivated the author of the document? This is an important question to ask, especially when dealing with literary texts and other creative works. No matter how "neutral" a text might seem, if it is created by someone for a specific purpose, there is an agenda or motive behind its creation. Teasing this motive out can be difficult, but it is an essential component to understanding the text.

It is also important to be aware that the fundamental motives of the person or persons involved in the making of a particular document or text are ultimately unknowable. For example, the bequests a person makes in a last will and testament might seem straightforward, but we in the modern world will never know exactly why those particular bequests were made to those particular people or institutions.

Finally, because none of the sources available to most student researchers of medieval history are in their original languages, but are instead translated into modern English, the student has to be aware that translations themselves are sometimes not straightforward. Translations are also mediated and edited texts in which the translator makes specific choices as to how to render the original text. Literal translations can be unreadable—especially if they mimic the style of Latin and French used in medieval court documents—but loose translations can be highly subjective. Sometimes words and phrases are so mangled that they are untranslatable. Sometimes abbreviations in the original manuscript documents leave off so much of the word that the translator has to make a decision as to what the intention of the author was, from a wide variety of possibilities. A student unfamiliar with Latin or

French cannot really assess the accuracy of a translation but can form conclusions about the "authenticity" of the translator's process if the syntax makes little sense, the translation is difficult to follow, or the interpretation or meaning is difficult to make out. Ultimately, though, the student has little choice but to trust the translator's skill in producing an accurate interpretation of a given document or source. It can be instructive to look at multiple translations, especially of literary texts, in order to assess the accuracy of a particular translator's efforts.

CHRONOLOGY OF BRITISH HISTORY, 500–1500

500–600   England   Germanic invasions; establishment of Anglo-Saxon kingdoms

Ethelbert of Kent (r. 558–616) converts to Christianity

Establishment of archdiocese of Canterbury by Augustine

Other Anglo-Saxon kings, except kings of Mercia, convert to Christianity

Ireland   First church founded by St. Patrick in Armagh (ca. 450); development of Irish monasticism

Clonmacnoise monastery, Offaly, founded by St. Cíaran (ca. 544)

Glendalough monastery, Wicklow, founded by St. Kevin (late sixth century)

Scotland   The kindom of Dál Riata controls the western region of Scotland and also northeastern Ulster, Ireland

Consolidation of Pictish lands into kingdom

Iona monastery founded by St. Columba (ca. 563)

King Aedán mac Gabráin (r. 574–608) expands influence of Dál Riata

Wales   Wales broken into small kingdoms and principalities; Powys and Gwynedd dominate

600–700   England   King Penda of Mercia (r. 628–655), last pagan king, dominates England

King Oswald (r. 634–642) unifies Northumbria; Lindisfarne Priory founded by monks from Iona (634)

Synod of Whitby (664) establishes Roman practice over Irish in Northumbria

Bede, historian and teacher, born (672–735)

	Ireland	St. Mullins monastery, Carlow, founded by St. Moling (mid-seventh century)
	Scotland	Expansion of Picts kingdom into Dál Riata and the south
		Dál Riata subject to Pictish and Northumbrian kings for most of seventh century
	Wales	Alliance of Cadwallon ap Cadfan of Gwynedd (d. 634) with Penda of Mercia; brief control of Northumbria
700–800	England	King Offa of Mercia (r. 757–796) builds dyke between Mercia and Wales
		First Viking invasions into England; sack of Lindisfarne (793)
	Ireland	First Viking incursions into Ireland
	Scotland	Picts control much of Dál Riata not conquered by Vikings
		Viking raids along west coast of Scotland and the northern and western isles
	Wales	Powys loses territories originally controlled after building of Offa's Dyke
800–900	England	Rise of kingdom of Wessex
		Vikings invade and establish Danelaw in north; end of Northumbrian kingdom
		Alfred the Great, king of Wessex (r. 871–899), unifies southern England; defeats Viking army at Edington
		Beginning of Anglo-Saxon Chronicle; Burghal defense system; Alfred's education reforms
	Ireland	Conflict between kings of Munster and the Uí Néill for position of High King of Tara
		First Viking settlements in Ireland; founding of Dublin (ca. 840)
		Kells Abbey founded by monks from Iona fleeing Viking incursions
	Scotland	Supposed revival of Dál Riata under King Aed Find (r. 736–738)
		Viking conquests of Dál Riata lead to creation of Viking kingdoms in the western regions
		Consolidation of Pictish and Gaelic regions against Viking incursions leads to reign of Kenneth
		MacAlpin (ca. 843–858); his house formed the origins of all later royal lineages of "Kingdom of Alba"
	Wales	Rhodri Mawr of Gwynedd (r. 844–878) consolidates rule over most of Wales

900–1000	England	King Athelstan (r. 924–939) of Wessex defeats northern alliance at Brunanburh
		Kings of Norway reestablish dominance in Danelaw after Athelstan's death
		Battle of Maldon (991): Viking victory over Anglo-Saxons; 1st payment of Danegeld
	Ireland	Brian Bóruma [Brian Boru] becomes king of Munster
	Scotland	King Constantine II (r. 900–943) joins northern alliance against Wessex; defeated at Brunanburh
		Malcolm I (r. 943–954) establishes alliance with English kings; gains Strathclyde
	Wales	Hywel Dda, grandson of Rhodri Mawr, creates kingdom of Deheubarth (r. 920–949)
		Viking raids take toll on Wales (950–1000); breakup of consolidated territories into smaller polities
1000–1100	England	King Ethelred II and son Edmund Ironside killed in battle (1016)
		Cnut, king of Norway and Denmark, becomes king of England (r. 1016–1035)
		Cnut's sons Harold Harefoot and Harthacnut share rule (1035–1040)
		Harthacnut rules alone (1040–1042)
		Ethelred II's son, Edward the Confessor, reestablishes the House of Wessex (1043–1066)
		Harold Godwinson becomes king of England (1066); defeats Harald Hardrada, at battle of Stamford Bridge
		Invasion of Duke William of Normandy; defeats King Harold II at battle of Hastings (1066)
		Duke William crowned king (r. 1066–1087)
		Feudalization of England; Normans begin to invade Wales
		Domesday Book survey completed (1086)
		William II "Rufus" crowned (r. 1087–1100)
		First Crusade (1096–1100); William II seizes Normandy from Duke Robert when he is on crusade
	Ireland	Brian Bóruma ousts the Uí Níell as High Kings of Tara (r. 1002–1014)
		Battle of Clontarf first Irish victory over Vikings (1014), but Brian Bóruma killed

		Position of high king contested and disempowered
		The kings of Leinster gain control of Viking kingdom of Dublin (1050s)
		Reforms of the Irish church; development of diocesan structures
		Muirchertach Ua Briain, king of Munster (r. 1086–1119), consolidates rule over Ireland
	Scotland	King Duncan I (r. 1034–1040) killed by Macbeth (r. 1040–1057)
		Malcolm III kills Macbeth's stepson Lulach and rules Scotland (r. 1058–1093); marries Margaret of Wessex
		Conflicts between Malcolm III and William I of England lead to invasions and border raids
		Malcolm III dies in border skirmish: battle of Alnwick in Northumberland (1094)
		William II of England supports Duncan II (r. 1094) and Edgar (r. 1097–1107) as kings
	Wales	Gruffudd ap Llywelyn of Gwynedd (r. 1039–1063) consolidates rule over Wales
		Gruffudd ap Llywelyn defeated in battle by Earl Harold Godwinson (1063); killed by his own men
		Bleddyn ap Cynfyn, king of Gwynedd (1063–1075) and Powys (1069–1075), creates alliance with King Edward
		Normans begin to invade Wales; establish marcher baronies along border and southeast
		Death of Bleddyn ap Cynfyn leads to civil war and further Norman expansion
		Rhys ap Tewdwr of Deheubarth killed (1093); Normans invade as far as St. David
		Welsh resistance to Normans slowly reclaims territory; Gruffudd ap Cynan rules Gwynedd (1081–1137)
1100–1200	England	William II killed in hunting accident; Henry I is crowned (r. 1100–1135); coronation oath serves as model
		Henry I creates exchequer and chancery departments; creation of Pipe Rolls
		Marriage of Henry I and Edith [Matilda] of Scotland unites Norman and Wessex houses
		Death of Prince William (1120) establishes Empress Matilda as heir to throne

At death of Henry I, barons renege on agreement to crown Empress Matilda; elect Stephen of Blois

Civil war during reign of Stephen (r. 1135–1155) between his allies and those of Empress Matilda

Second Crusade to the Holy Land (1145–1149)

Henry, count of Anjou and duke of Normandy, claims throne for his mother, Empress Matilda

Treaty of Winchester (1153) establishes Henry as heir to Stephen

Reign of Henry II (1155–1189); expansion of royal administration and system of law

Constitutions of Clarendon (1164), designed to regulate legal status of clerics, sparks conflict with Thomas Becket

Becket controversy leads to his murder (1170); many elements of Constitutions of Clarendon remain in effect

Assize of Clarendon (1166); Assize of Northampton (1176) create petty assizes: primacy of royal courts

Revolt of "Young" King Henry, brothers, and Queen Eleanor of Aquitaine against Henry II (1173–74)

Invasion and conquest of Ireland (1171–1175); Leinster ceded to Strongbow and Aiofe by her father

Death of Henry II; succession of Richard I (r. 1189–1199)

Third Crusade to Holy Land (1189–1192) led by Richard I and King Philip II Augustus of France

Richard I captured and imprisoned on return from crusade; held to ransom of 150,000 marks (1192–94)

Philip Augustus invades Normandy during Richard I's captivity; Prince John revolts

Richard I regains Normandy; dies from wound received in siege of vassal's castle; John succeeds him

Ireland   Muichertach Ua Briain gives his fortress of Cashel to the church (ca. 1101)

Competing coalitions among Irish kings leads to political disarray: "High King with Opposition"

Diarmid Mac Murchada, deposed king of Leinster, arrives in Bristol to secure help from Norman barons

First Norman invasion of Ireland (1167–1169)

Invasion and conquest of Ireland (1171–1175); Leinster ceded to Strongbow and Aiofe by her father

		Establishment of the lordship of Ireland by Prince John (1185); expansion of Norman holdings
		William Marshal marries Isabella de Clare, heir to Leinster
	Scotland	David I (r. 1124–1153) succeeds brother Alexander I (r. 1107–1124); beginning of Normanization of Scots court
		Expansion of influence of Scots kings through most of Scotland; subjection of mormaers of Moray
		David I initiates reforms of the church; feudalization of lordships; establishes Norman-style administration
		David I supports Empress Matilda against King Stephen
		David I dies; succeeded by Malcolm IV, his grandson (r. 1153–1165)
		Malcolm succeeds in putting down revolts of mormaers; gains earldom of Huntingdon from Henry II of England
		William I (r. 1165–1214) succeeds his brother, Malcolm IV
		William I supports Young King Henry in revolt; captured and in Treaty of Falaise (1174) declares Henry II overlord of Scotland; swears fealty to Henry II (1175)
		Richard I of England agrees to revoke Treaty of Falaise for 10,000 marks (1189)
		Once rule was consolidated, William I continued the plan of his grandfather, extending feudalization of lands; founding burghs; expanding royal jurisdiction in law and administration; expanding royal officials' reach
	Wales	Battle of Crug Mawr (1136): Owain Gwynedd and Gruffudd ap Rhys of Deheubarth defeat Normans
		Welsh rulers take advantage of civil war in England to consolidate their claims over Norman settlers
		Owain Gwynedd (r. 1137–1170) rules Gwynedd
		Powys divided into two parts; Rhys ap Gruffudd of Deheubarth (r. 1155–1197) dominates Wales
		Rhys ap Gruffudd named justiciar of south Wales by Henry II
		Death of Owain Gwynedd (1170) results in division of kingdom
		William Marshal marries Isabella de Clare, heir to Striguil and Pembroke
1200–1300	England	Rule of King John (1199–1216)
		John's loss at battle of Bouvines results in forfeiture of Normandy (1214)

First Barons' War and battle of Runneymede lead to Magna Carta (1215)

John grants England as a fief to papacy in exchange for protection from barons

John dies (1216) succeeded by Henry III (r. 1216–1272)

Minority of Henry III (1216–1230): William Marshal reissues Magna Carta as regent (1217)

Henry III issues Magna Carta under his own seal (1225)

Failed military campaigns in 1230 and 1246 lead to unrest; arrival of Lusignan siblings (1248)

Second Barons' War and Provisions of Oxford (1258); Simon de Montfort controls government

Battles of Lewes (1264) and Evesham (1265) end Barons' War with royalist victory; death of Simon de Montfort

Dictum of Kenilworth (1266) establishes basis for former rebels to regain their lands

Lord Edward joins Louis IX of France's crusade (1270); death of Louis IX in Tunis

Death of Henry III (1272); succession of Edward I (r. 1272–1307): he returns from crusade (1274)

Edward I revamps legal system: Statutes of Westminster I (1275) & II (1285); Mortmain (1279)

Conquest of Wales and establishment of the Principality (1277–1283); Statute of Wales (1284)

Edward I claims authority to determine successor to Scottish throne after death of Margaret of Norway

Death of Queen Eleanor of Castile (1290); Jews expelled from England

Edwardian war in Scotland begins; battles of Dunbar, Stirling Bridge, and Falkirk (1296–1298)

Threatened baronial revolt leads to final reissue of Magna Carta (1297)

Ireland   John travels to Ireland to shore up rule (1210)

Lacys of Meath embroiled in conflict between King John and the Braoses of Bergavenny

Revolt of Earl Richard Marshal in Ireland (1233–34)

Division of Marshal lordship of Leinster among thirteen coheirs (1248)

		Reestablishment of traditional Irish kings in Leinster, if only in title
		Establishment of a consistent appointment of justiciars to govern Ireland
		Geoffrey de Geneville appointed justiciar of Ireland (1273–76); military defeats against Irish of Leinster
		Roger Mortimer, earl of March, appointed justiciar of Ireland (1285–1327)
		Parliament of Ireland established (1297)
1200–1300	Scotland	Alexander II (r. 1214–1249) succeeds his father, William I
		Puts down revolt of the MacWilliam and MacHeth clans; supports barons against King John
		Alexander makes peace with Henry III
		Alexander marries Joan of England, daughter of King John (1221)
		Alexander crushes revolts in Argyll and Galloway
		Treaty of York (1237) settles border between England and Scotland
		Alexander III (r. 1249–1286) succeeds father (mother: second wife Marie de Coucy); age 7
		Marries Margaret of England (1251); attains majority in 1262
		Treaty of Perth (1266): king of Norway cedes Western Isles and Isle of Man to Scotland
		Death of Alexander III (1286); only heir is Margaret of Norway, age 3; guardians of Scotland chosen
		Death of Margaret of Norway (1290) begins the Great Cause; King Edward I intervenes
		John Balliol crowned (1292–1296); promotes alliance with France; deposed by Edward I
		Edwardian war in Scotland begins; battles of Dunbar, Stirling Bridge, and Falkirk (1296–1298)
	Wales	Llywelyn ab Iorwerth sole ruler of Gwynedd (r. 1200–1240); alliance with King John leads to rule of Wales
		Llywelyn annexes southern Powys with John's help (1208); marries Joan, John's illegitimate daughter
		Relations between Llywelyn and John sour; Llywelyn supports barons against him
		Llywelyn concludes Treaty of Worcester (1218) with Henry III's regents (William Marshal)

Llywelyn makes Peace of Middle (1234) with England; Dafydd ap Llywelyn succeeds (r. 1240–1246)

Division of Marshal estates to coheirs (1248); war between Henry III and Dafydd

Gwynedd divided between Dafydd's nephews Owain and Llywelyn ap Gruffudd (1258–1282)

Llewelyn supports the barons in the Barons' War; makes princes of Powys his vassals; conquers other territories held by marcher barons; pushes the Powys princes into alliance with England

Conquest of Wales and establishment of the Principality (1277–1283); Statute of Wales (1284)

Welsh archers make up prominent portion of English army

1300–1400	England	Invasion of Scotland after murder of John III Comyn (1306); death of Edward I (1307)

Reign of Edward II (1307–27); barons force exile of Piers Gaveston, royal favorite (1308)

Revolt by Lords Ordainer (1311) and enforcement of Ordinances; death of Piers Gaveston (1312)

English defeat at battle of Bannockburn (1314); Great Famine (1315–1317)

Revolt of Thomas, earl of Lancaster; his capture and execution (1322); rise of the Despensers

Revolt led by Queen Isabella and Roger Mortimer; deposition and death of Edward II (1327)

Reign of Edward III (1327–1377)

Minority (1327–1330) ends; arrest and execution of Roger Mortimer; Queen Isabella confined to Castle Acre

Beginning of Hundred Years' War (1337–1453); battles: Sluys (1340), Crécy (1346), Poitiers (1356)

Scottish invasion of England; battle of Neville's Cross (1346) results in capture of King David II

Founding of the Order of the Garter (1348)

Black Death (1348–1350)

Statute of Laborers (1351); Peace Justice Statute (1361); "Good" Parliament (1376); Edward III suffers stroke

Death of Prince Edward of Wales and Edward III (1377)

Succession of Richard II at age 10 (r. 1377–1399); regency headed by John of Gaunt

Poll tax exactions lead to Great Rising (1381); popularity of Wyclif's teachings enhance revolt

Concerns over court favorites and war with France leads to demands of Lords Appellant (1387)

"Merciless" Parliament (1388) executes almost all court favorites in attempt to control king

Richard II regains control of government; first expedition to Ireland (1394–1395)

Richard moves against the former Lords Appellant; exiles Henry Bolingbroke and executes other magnates

John of Gaunt dies (1399); Henry, his son, returns from exile and deposes Richard; crowned Henry IV (1399)

Ireland   Resurgence and expansion of native Irish princes in western Ireland

Invasion of Ireland by Edward Bruce, welcomed by native princes (1315)

Remonstrance of the Irish Chiefs written and sent to Pope John XXII (1317)

Murder of William Donn de Burgh, earl of Ulster (1333); lands split among Irish and Anglo-Irish heirs

Resurgence of Irish native rule leads to alliances with "Old English" barons (1350–onwards)

Black Death (1348–1350)

Lionel, duke of Clarence, appointed governor of Ireland; Statutes of Kilkenny (1366)

Art Mór Machadha Caomhánach [Art MacMurrogh-Kavanagh] becomes king of Leinster (r. 1375–1416); his lengthy reign results in a significant expansion of the territory of Leinster returning to Irish control and the Anglo-Irish residents of his lands reduced to vassalage

King Richard's expedition to Ireland results in securing of the lordship, although not for long (1394–1395)

Second expedition to Ireland of Richard II (1399)

Scotland   Murder of John III Comyn of Badenoch by Robert Bruce (1306); coronation of Robert; war with England

Robert I Bruce reigns (1306–1329)

Encourages revolt of Irish against English rule

Battle of Bannockburn (1314): Scottish victory

Declaration of Arbroath (1320); papal acceptance of Scottish sovereignty

Robert I dies; succeeded by David II (r. 1329–1371), age 5; guardians struggle with renewed claim of Balliols

Second Scottish War of Independence; Edward Balliol fails to regain throne

David II in exile in France; returns (1341)

Scottish invasion of England; battle of Neville's Cross (1346) results in capture of King David II

Robert Stewart (his cousin) guardian of the Realm while David II in captivity (until 1357)

Black Death (1348–1350)

David II dies (1371); succeeded by Robert II Stewart (r. 1371–1390)

Sons of Robert II govern as lord lieutenants: John, earl of Carrick, and Robert, earl of Fife

Robert II dies (1390); succeeded by son John, who calls himself Robert III (r. 1390–1406)

	Wales	Black Death (1348–1350)
1400–1500	England	Reign of Henry IV (1399–1413); death of Richard II (1400)

Multiple rebellions, including the Epiphany Uprising (1400) and the revolt of the Percys (1402–1408)

Illness leads to Prince Henry taking control of government (1410–1413)

Death of Henry IV; succession of Henry V (r. 1413–1422)

Council of Constance (1414–1418) condemns teachings of John Wyclif

Resurgence of war in France; siege of Harfleur and battle of Agincourt (1415)

Treaty of Troyes declares Henry V heir to throne of France; marriage to Catherine of Valois (1420)

Death of Henry V (1422); succession of Henry VI, aged 9 months (r. 1422–1461, 1470–1471)

Catherine, dowager queen, forms relationship with Owen Tudor; they have six children but never marry

John, duke of Bedford, led regency council; competition among Henry's uncles

Henry comes of age (1437) and assumes governing at age 16; resumption of Lollard religious dissent

Competition within family (dukes of Gloucester and York; Beauforts) promotes instability in kingdom

Jack Cade's Rebellion (1450) reflects popular discontent with royal government

Gascony, last English-held French province, surrenders to Charles VII (1451); end of Hundred Years War (1453)

War of the Roses begins (1454); battle of Northampton (1459) results in capture of Henry VI

Richard, duke of York, named Protector of England; killed in battle of Wakefield (1460); Henry VI freed

Edward of York victorious over Lancastrians at battle of Towton (1460); crowned Edward IV (1461–1483)

Earl of Warwick rebels; Henry VI restored (1470–1471); Yorkist victories at Barnet and Tewkesbury (1471)

Edward IV restored (1471) but unrest continues; dies (1483); succeeded by son, Edward V, age 13 (1483)

Richard, duke of Gloucester becomes regent; then takes throne as Richard III (1483–1485)

Henry, son of Jasper Tudor (son of Owen Tudor and Catherine of Valois) and Margaret Beaufort, invades (1485)

Battle of Bosworth Field (1485); Richard III killed; Henry Tudor crowned Henry VII (1485–1509)

Henry VII marries Elizabeth of York, daughter of Edward IV and Elizabeth Woodville (1486)

Ireland
Lordship of Ireland recedes to Pale immediately around Dublin

English rule in Ireland assumed by Fitzgerald earls of Kildare; further decline of English overlordship

Although essentially freed from oversight by the English administration in Dublin, the native Irish kings' own conflicts with each other lead to a fracturing of their lands and centers of authority; this discourages development of political institutions that would have prevented the invasions and reconquest of Ireland by the Tudors

Richard, duke of York, appointed lieutenant of Ireland (1447); Irish chiefs of Leinster and Ulster submit to his rule (1449)

Richard, duke of York, leaves Ireland and returns to England (1450)

Resurgence of Irish chiefs of Leinster (MacMurrough) and Ulster (O'Neill)

Residents of the Pale build defenses around the borders of the territory against Irish and Anglo-Irish incursions

Richard of York flees to Ireland (1459) after being declared a traitor by Parliament; remains until 1450

Revolt against Tudors; Lambert Simnel crowned Edward VI in Dublin (1487)

Scotland   James, son of Robert III, captured by English en route to France; spends 18 years as prisoner

Robert III dies (1406); his brother Robert, duke of Albany rules as guardian (till 1420)

Murdoch, duke of Albany replaces father as Guardian (untill 1424)

Ransom of James I finally paid; he returns to Scotland (r. 1424–1437); executes Murdoch for treason

Battle of Roxburgh: defeat (1436); James I murdered (1437)

James II (r. 1437–1460) succeeds, age 7; guardianship falls to earls of Douglas

James II declared of age (1449) but competition between Crown and Douglas family continues

Battle of Arkinholm (1455): Douglas defeated by royal forces

James II reforms laws and administration

James II killed by artillery shell in taking Roxburgh (1460); succeeded by James III (r. 1460–1488), age 9

Regency until 1469; considerable political unrest both before and after

Conflict within Stewart family between brothers and James III

Invasion by Richard, duke of Gloucester (1480); James III imprisoned by his own barons in Edinburgh Castle

James III re-establishes control of government but conflict with barons continues

Army of barons supporting son James (IV); James III is defeated and killed in the battle of Sauchieburn (1488)

James IV succeeds (r. 1488–1513); establishes peace with England; annexes Lordship of the Isles

Wales   Revolt of Owain Glyndwr (1400–1409)

Penal laws against Welsh enacted (1402) to disrupt potential rebels

Council of the Marches established (1472) to consolidate rule of the Principality and the Marches

DOMESTIC LIFE AND THE MEDIEVAL HOUSEHOLD

1. ANGLO-SAXON WILLS

INTRODUCTION

Unlike the British Isles after the Norman Conquest, when land was transmitted through so-called **feudal tenures**, Anglo-Saxon England's land law permitted estates to be transmitted to the next generation through wills. The survival of wills from the tenth and eleventh centuries make these documents nearly unique, because no other early medieval Germanic society has similar documents that survived in the vernacular (that is, in Old English, not Latin) and at such a high level of complexity.

Only wills from elite English people have survived, but they tell us quite a lot about the material items they valued, the family relationships and friendships they honored, and the importance of making bequests that honored the king as well as the social interactions of the persons making the bequests.

KEEP IN MIND AS YOU READ

Wills were usually presented orally, dictated to whoever was available, and on one's death-bed. Only rarely were wills written before the immediate expectation of death. Therefore, these documents have a more informal feel than other kinds of legal documents, which were standardized and maintained by professional scribes. Nevertheless, there were certain conventions to the writing of wills, including the requirement to make bequests to the church, to acknowledge the need to pay the **heriot**, the death duties owed to the king, and the conventional pleas for survivors to pray for the souls of the deceased.

Document 1: Anglo-Saxon Wills

The Will of Wynflæd

Wynflæd declares how she wishes to dispose of what she possesses, after her death. She bequeaths to the church . . . the better of her offering-cloths, and her cross . . . And she bequeaths to her daughter Æthelflæd her engraved bracelet and her brooch, and the estate at Ebbesborne and the title-deed as a perpetual inheritance to dispose of as she pleases . . . And to Eadmær [she grants] the estates at Coleshill and Inglesham, and she grants to him also the estate at Faccombe, which was her **marriage-gift**, for his lifetime, and then after his death, if Æthelflæd survive him, she is to succeed to the estate at

Faccombe, and after her death it is to revert to Eadwold's possession. . . . [Wynflæd frees a large number of slaves and requests that, if any others are found that they be freed as well]

And [she grants] to Ælfwold her two buffalo-horns and a horse and her red tent. And she bequeaths to Eadmær a cup with a lid, and another to Æthelflæd, and prays that between them they will furnish two fair goblets to the refectory for her sake, or augment her own ornamented cups . . . And she bequeaths to [Eadwold] her gold-adorned wooden cup in order that he may enlarge his armlet with the gold . . . And she bequeaths to him two chests and in them a set of bed-clothing, all that belongs to one bed. . . .

And she bequeaths to Æthelflæd, daughter of Ealhhelm, Ælfhere's younger daughter, and her double badger-skin gown, and another of linen or else some linen cloth. And to Eadgifu two chests and in them her best bed-curtain and a linen covering . . . and her best dun tunic, and the better of her cloaks, and her two wooden cups ornamented with dots, and her old filigree brooch . . . And she grants to Ceolthryth whichever she prefers of her black tunics and her best holy veil and her best headband . . . [more bequests follow for some vowed nuns who are given vestments from among her clothing].

Then she makes a gift to Æthelflæd of everything which is unbequeathed, books and such small things . . . and the utensils and all the useful things that are inside, and also the homestead if the king grant it to her as King Edward granted it to Brihtwyn her mother.

The Will of Wulfgeat

This is the will of Wulfgeat of Donington; namely that he grants to God his burial fee, namely, one **hide** at Tardebigge and one pound of pence, and twenty-six freedmen, for his soul; and to Worcester a brewing of malt, half from Donington and half from Kilsall; and to St Ethelbert's the equivalent of half a pound; . . . and to Leominster four full-grown bullocks; and to Bromyard one bullock; and another to Clifton; and four bullocks to Wolverhampton; and two bullocks to Penkridge; and two bullocks to Tong. . . .

And he grants to his lord two horses and two swords and four shields and four spears and ten mares with ten colts. . . . And he grants to his wife the estates at Kilsall and Evenlode and Roden for as long as her life lasts, and after her death the land is to revert to my kindred, those who are nearest. And to my daughter Wulfgifu [I grant] the estate at Donington . . . and the estate at Thornbury which was bought from Leonoth with her mother's gold; and to the son of my daughter Wulfgifu the estate at Ingwardine; and to my daughter Wilflæd the other hide at Tardebigge; and to my kinswoman Ælfhild the hide below the wood . . . and if I live longer than she, then I am to have the estate at Wrottesley. . . .

The Will of Wulfwaru

I, Wulfwaru, pray my dear lord KING ETHELRED [II], of his charity, that I may be entitled to make my will. I make known to you, Sire, here in this document, what I grant to St Peter's monastery at Bath for my poor soul and for the souls of my ancestors . . . namely then, that I grant to that holy place there an armlet . . . and a bowl . . . and two gold crucifixes, and a set of mass-vestments with everything that belongs to it, and the best mantle that I have, and a set of bed-clothing with tapestry and curtain and with everything that belongs to it. . . .

And I grant to my elder son Wulfmær the estate at Claverton . . . and the estate at Compton . . . and I grant him half the estate at Butcombe . . . and half of it I grant to my younger daughter Ælfwaru . . . And they are to share the principal residence between them as evenly as they can, so that each of them shall have a just portion of it.

And to my younger son Ælfwine I grant the estate at Leigh, ... and the estate at Holton ... and the estate at Hogston ... And I grant to my elder daughter, Gode, the estate at Winford ... and two cups ... and a band of thirty *mancuses* of gold and two brooches and a woman's attire complete. And to my younger daughter Ælfwaru I grant all the women's clothing which is left.

> *mancus:* a coin similar to the Arab *dinar,* considered an international form of coinage

And to my son Wulfmær and my second son Ælfwine and my daughter Ælfwaru—to each of the three of them—I grant two cups of good value. And I grant to my son Wulfmær a hall-tapestry and a set of bed-clothes. To Ælfwine my second son I grant a tapestry for a hall and tapestry for a chamber, together with a table-cover and with all the cloths which go with it.

And I grant to my four servants Ælfmær, Ælfweard, Wulfric and Wulfstan, a band of twenty mancuses of gold. And I grant to all my household women, in common, a good chest well decorated. ...

Source: *Anglo-Saxon Wills.* Edited and translated by Dorothy Whitelock. Cambridge: Cambridge University Press, 1930. Pp. 10–15, 54–57, 62–65. Reprinted with the permission of Cambridge University Press.

AFTERMATH

Wills operated as documents that identified not only appropriate heirs to the deceased but also their relationship to—and future family members' associations with—elite institutions and figures such as the king and the church. Although disputes undoubtedly occurred between testators and those who felt they were being shortchanged, we have little information on the procedures following the probate of the will in the era before the Norman Conquest.

Under Anglo-Saxon law, like all early medieval Germanic law, all the children of the deceased, both male and female, were potential heirs. Although the main properties usually were bequeathed to a son (not always the eldest), this was not required, and daughters and other women often received substantial bequests in wills. This system changed radically after the Norman Conquest.

ASK YOURSELF

1. What do early medieval wills tell us about family relationships?
2. In what ways did the king and/or the church interact with people making wills?
3. Do wills tell us anything about the status of women in early medieval England and, if so, what?
4. What do wills tell us about what Anglo-Saxon people considered valuable or important?

TOPICS TO CONSIDER

1. Consider the ways in which men and women differed in the kinds of items they bequeathed and what that might tell us about gender roles and status. This is a discussion that can continue through to the modern day.

2. Think about the ways in which modern-day consumption of goods is discussed and compare the concerns about excess consumption with the ways in which Anglo-Saxon people used and consumed goods. Consider the possibility that a love of—even obsession with—"things" might be an element of the human condition, not just a symptom of modern-day decadence.

Further Information

Clarke, Peter A. *The English Nobility under Edward the Confessor.* Oxford: Oxford University Press, 1994.

Crick, Julia and Elisabeth van Houts, eds. *A Social History of England, 900–1200.* Cambridge: Cambridge University Press, 2011.

Fell, Christine. *Women in Anglo-Saxon England.* Bloomington: Indiana University Press, 1984.

Stafford, Pauline. "King and Kin, Lord and Community: England in the Tenth and Eleventh Centuries." In *Gender, Family and the Legitimation of Power,* edited by Pauline Stafford. Aldershot: Ashgate, 2006.

2. Account Rolls and Domestic Activity

INTRODUCTION

We know about the daily activities of noble households from the preservation of accounts written down by the steward or bailiff of the household. Royal account records are numerous; noble and lower household accounts are far more rare, but when they exist, they open a fascinating window on what medieval people ate, who dwelled in their households, and how they organized their daily lives. The annual summary for the household of the KING EDWARD II's cousin THOMAS, EARL OF LANCASTER in 1314–1315 outlines the expenditures made by the earl and countess, ALICE DE LACY, who was Countess of Lincoln and Salisbury in her own right, and their households from September 29, 1314, to September 29, 1315; it shows that the earl's household was both large and focused on military activities. Payments for liveries for the men-at-arms and for Earl Thomas's retainers and associates comprise the bulk of the annual expenditures. The expenses for the countess's household, which was notated separately—indeed the couple did not get along, and they lived apart most of the time—were considerably smaller than those of the earl.

In contrast, a deed that records the monies paid out by Countess of Pembroke, JOAN DE VALENCE, in 1302 describes a much simpler household. The extant daily accounts that survive for Countess Joan's household in the years 1295 to 1297—which straddle the period before and after the death of her husband, WILLIAM DE VALENCE—describe in far more detail the daily activities of the countess and her attendants, as the example below suggests, but also leaves out many of the relationships identified in the receipt.

KEEP IN MIND AS YOU READ

Accounts were written by estate officials, whose command of Latin was not always the most accurate, and who were concerned about keeping their entries brief and concise, in part because parchment, made from sheepskin or calfskin, was very expensive. Therefore, they often left out details we would consider important, such as who was residing in the household with the "lord" and/or "lady"—although visitors were often identified—and how many people were employed by the householder.

Medieval English currency was more complicated than modern-day money. The English pound sterling was literally a pound of silver, divided into 240 parts called pence, which were grouped for accounting purposes into 20 units of 12 pence, which made up the English shilling. The most common coin was the silver penny, which could be cut in half to make an "oblate"—a half penny—or even into quarters, called farthings. Ha'penny and farthing coins were not minted until later. The English penny was common currency throughout the British Isles, although the Scots also minted their own pennies.

Document 1: Accounts of Thomas, Earl of Lancaster, 1314–1315

[A]n account made by H. Leicester, *cofferer* to Thomas, Earl of Lancaster, for one whole year's expenses in the Earl's house, from the day next after Michaelmas in the seventh year of Edward II, until Michaelmas in the eighth year of the same king, amounting to the sum of seven thousand, nine hundred, fifty-seven pounds, thirteen shillings, four pence, half penny, as follows:

To wit,

In the Pantry, Buttery, and Kitchen: £3405 and more

For 184 **tun**s and one **pipe** of red or claret wine, and one tun of white wine bought for the house: £104 17s 6d

For Grocery wares: £180 17s

For six barrels of sturgeon: £19

For 6800 stockfishes, so called, for dried fishes of all sorts, as lings, habardines, and others: £41 6s 7d

For 1714 pounds of wax, with vermillion and turpentine to make red wax: £314 7s 4 ½ d

For 2319 pounds of tallow candles for the household, and 1870 pounds for lights of Paris candles, called perchers, £31 14s 3d

Expenses on the earl's great horses and the keepers' wages: £486 4s 3 ½ d

Linen cloth for the L. and his chaplains, and for the pantry: £43 17d

For 129 dozen [skins] of parchment with ink: £4 8s 3 ½ d

Total: £5230 17s 7 ½ d

Item—for two cloths of scarlet for the earl against [for] Christmas, one cloth of *russet* for the bishop of Anjou, 70 cloths of blue for the knights, 15 cloths of *medley* for the lord's clerks, 28 cloths for the **esquires**, 15 cloths for officers, 19 cloths for grooms, 5 cloths for archers, 4 cloths for minstrels and carpenters, with the sharing and carriage for the earl's **liveries** at Christmas: £460 15d

Item—for 7 furs of variable *miniver* (or powdered ermine), 7 hoods of purple, 395 furs of *budge* for the liveries of barons, knights, and clerks, 123 furs of lamb for esquires, bought at Christmas: £147 17s 8d

Item—65 cloths saffron color, for the barons and knights: in summer, 12 red cloths mixed for clerks, 26 *ray cloths* for esquires, one *ray cloth* for officers' coats in summer, and 4 ray cloths for carpets in the hall, for £345 13s 8d

cofferer: a leading household official
russet: a coarse cloth dyed using woad and madder to create a gray or reddish-brown color
medley: striped or varied-colored
miniver: a pure white fur, highly prized
budge: lamb fur
ray cloth: cloth of a specified width
Paternosters: rosaries

Item—100 pieces of green silk for the knights, 14 budge furs for surcoats, 13 hoods of budge for clerks, and 75 furs of lambs for the lords' liveries in summer, with canvas and cords to truss them: £72 19s

Item—saddles for the lords' liveries in summer: £51 6s 8d

Item—one saddle for the earl of the prince's arms: 40s.

Total: £1079 18s 3d

Item for things bought, whereof cannot be read in my note: £241 14s 1 ½ d

For horses lost in service of the earl: £8 6s 8d

Fees paid to earls, barons, knights, and esquires: £623 15s 5d

In gifts to knights of France, the Queen of England's nurses, to the Countess of Warren [Warenne], esquires, minstrels, messengers, and riders: £92 14s

Item—168 yards of russet cloth, and 24 coats for poor men with money given to the poor on Maundy Thursday: £8 16s 7d

Item—24 silver dishes, so many saucers, and so many cups for the Buttery, one pair of *Paternosters*, and one silver coffin bought this year: £103 5s 6d

To diverse messengers about the earl's business: £34 19s 8d

In the earl's chamber: £5

To diverse men for the earl's old debts: £88 16s ¾ d

Total: £1207 11 ¾ d

The expenses of the Countess at Pickering for the time of this account, as in the pantry, buttery, kitchen, and other places, concerning these offices, 285 pounds, 13 shillings, ½ pence.

In wine, wax, spices, clothes, furs, and other things for the countess's wardrobe, 154 pounds, seven shillings, four and one-half pence.

Total: £439 8s 6 ¼ d

Total sum of whole expenses: £7957 13s 4 ¾ d

This much for this Earl of Lancaster.

Source: Stow, John. *A Survey of London.* Reprinted from the 1603 text. Introduction and notes by Charles Lethbridge Kingsford. Oxford: Clarendon Press, 1908. 1: 85–87. Spelling and syntax modernized by editor.

Document 2: Deed of Receipt, Countess Joan de Valence, 1300

To all those present to peruse this letter, Joan de Valence countess of Pembroke sends greetings in the Lord. Know that Ralph de Sutton, our receiver, for Master Henry [our] esquire [who has represented us] in the prosecution of the suit for the church of Aure in the court of the Archbishop of Canterbury: 13s 4d. And for 16 yards of *fustian* purchased for our use by the hand of Robert of the Wardrobe: 6s 10d. And for the **Preaching Brothers** for their general income, of our gift: 13s 4d. And for the **Friars Minor** for their general income: 13s 4d. And to Lord Matthew the Chaplain for one *tabard* and its repair of our gift: 9s. And for the valet of the household of Lord THOMAS DE BERKELEY for procuring and transporting steel from Paynswick: 40s of our gift. And for John de Lukes, merchant of Gascony for five tuns of wine and transport from that place for our use for the feast of the Nativity of St John the Baptist: £13 6s 8d.

> *fustian:* a durable heavy cloth
> *tabard:* an overcoat

And for Brother Nicholas of Leicester of our gift for one missal and its repair: 16s 4d. And for William de la Ferne, goldsmith of Hereford, for two amulets with rubies made for the feast of the Assumption of the Blessed Virgin Mary: 10s. And for Brother John de Croft of the Order of the Preaching Brothers for one habit and its repair: 8s. And this is the total of all sums: £19 8s 8d which has been allocated to him from the accounts. In testimony of these things we present these letters and append our seal. Dated at Castle Goodrich [Hereford] in the Feast of St Matthew, 30 Edward [I].

Source: British Library, Harley Charter 57 B.45. Translated by editor.

Document 3: Extract from Account Roll of Joan de Valence's Household, 1297

Thursday following [the Feast of the Apostles Simon and Jude], the Lady [Joan de Valence] remains [at Exning] and Lord Aymer and Lord T[homas] de Berkeley and others with them, 20 paupers, and Lady Agnes de Valence [are there for the main meal]

Bread: 6s 6d by purchase. And 3s more also purchased.

Bottle of wine from the stores; beer: 9s purchased

Three cocks, quarter of beef, half a pig, and 2 mutton: 9s 10d; antimony 16d; capons and chickens; 2s 2 ½ d and milk and cheese: 9d; pottage

Total 14s 5d

1 measure salt: 3d

Sauces: 1 ½ d

Lodging: 2s in wood and charcoal

Food for 47 horses [13s 6 ½ d]; iron: 2s 9 ½ d; 2 quarters of oats: [2s 8d]—[total] £7 ½ 6s 10s ½ d. Wages for 22 "garcons": 2s 9d; for the forge: 17d

Candles: 1 ½ d.

Total for the day: 46s

Owing 1d. Item—for the oven [for bread] purchased 10 quarters of wheat: 23d. Item—in earnest money [or good-faith payment] for the hospitality of the lady of Westley for provisioning made for the entire journey of the lady [Joan]: 5d. Item—for the wage of Thomas de Bampton for two days and for his assistants for one day: 5d.

[Total] wages: 2s 10d

Summary total: 48s 10d

> *Lord Aymer [de Valence]*: Joan de Valence's son
> *Lady Agnes de Valence*: Joan de Valence's daughter

Source: National Archives of the UK. Exchequer Records E101/505/26 m. 5. Translated by editor.

AFTERMATH

Accounts were rarely preserved by noble and gentry households beyond a few years, so the existence of non-royal accounts is entirely by happenstance. Nevertheless, the maintaining of accounts was an important part of the job of the steward or bailiff or receiver (depending on the household), and the lord or lady might sue his or her own estate manager for failure to keep accurate accounts in the king's court!

The design of castles in the British Isles followed French and Crusader norms established by the royal castles built by William the Conqueror. These were the typical "motte and bailey" style castles that featured an artificial mound surrounded by a ditch or moat, upon which stood a wooden (later a stone) tower (the keep) surrounded by a wooden palisade called a bailey, from the French word for fortress. In Ireland, any town or region with the word "bally" in the name designates a town or region in which a "bailey" stood. The word "castle," derived from the Latin word castrum, appears in many place names in England especially, but these refer back to Roman-era structures and settlements, just as the Old English word for town—"burgh"—appears in many later place-names.

Eventually, the motte-and-bailey style expanded with the addition of multiple elements: stone walls intersected at the corners by guard towers (this is called a "curtain wall"), massive fortified gates known as barbicans, and numerous buildings within the bailey: the great hall, the keep, chapels, kitchens, latrines, gatehouses, barracks, and assorted outbuildings. Eventually, the greatest castles came to develop even more elaborate fortifications, with two series of curtain walls surrounding an outer bailey and an inner bailey, moats created by diverting rivers or by the creation of artificial lakes, and multiple gates.

ASK YOURSELF

1. It is clear that, although Earl Thomas and Countess Joan are of similar social status, their households were quite different. What issues might account for the differences, and why do you think they occur?
2. What information about household composition and size do these kinds of records tell us and what does this information suggest about noble lifestyles?

TOPICS TO CONSIDER

1. Since accounts can provide both intimate and public information, it is possible to use them—along with other records describing noble households—to illuminate the private lives of medieval elites. Consider how you might make use of these documents in developing such a project.
2. Consider the possibility that even elite households experienced changes in their economic and social status, both growing and shrinking according to political, social, and economic conditions. How might account rolls or account books be useful in tracking such changes over time?

Further Information

Labarge, Margaret Wade. *A Baronial Household of the Thirteenth Century*. Totowa, NJ: Barnes & Noble Books, 1980 [1963].

Mertes, Kate. *The English Noble Household, 1250–1600*. Oxford: Basil Blackwell, 1988.

Ward, Jennifer, ed. *Elizabeth de Burgh, Lady of Clare (1295–1360): Household and Other Records*. Suffolk Records Society, vol. 57. Woodbridge: Boydell Press, 2014.

Woolgar, C. M. *The Great Household in Late Medieval England*. New Haven, CT: Yale University Press, 1999.

3. Information on Domestic Life from Coroners' Rolls

INTRODUCTION

It is almost impossible to discover the exact nature of life in domiciles below the level of the nobility without the assistance of documents that focus on other kinds of issues. One such source is the collection of coroners' inquests compiled beginning in the late thirteenth century. Although the focus of the inquest is to identify how people died, the explanations can involve a wide range of descriptions of nonelite households.

KEEP IN MIND AS YOU READ

Coroners in England and its subject territories of Wales and Ireland were royal officials connected to the sheriff's office in each county. They were in charge of investigating all deaths—whether natural, accidental, or violent—in the county and to determine the manner by which each person died and whether the cause of death was a criminal act. Coroners employed men to go around the countryside conducting these investigations and they then reported their findings at specific scheduled sessions of the coroners' inquest. The "juries" (as these groups of men were called) relied heavily on hearsay and oral evidence in order to determine the manner of death of each victim.

Document 1: Extracts from Coroners' Rolls

Middlesex. Inquest taken at [West Smithfield] before Jordan of Elsing, coroner of Middlesex county, on Tuesday next after Christmas in the thirty-ninth year of Edward III [December 30, 1366], on view of the body of Robert French deceased, on oath of [jurors sent to investigate] . . . They say that on Saturday next after the feast of St. [Stephen] the Martyr the aforesaid year [December 27, 1366] it happened at West Smithfield in the said county that while Robert French lay in his bed in the house of his father, Simon French, a burning coal fell upon the straw of his bed and caused a conflagration . . .

Northamptonshire. It happened at Watford on Wednesday of Whit week in the twenty-ninth year of King Edward [May 24, 1301] that Richard Mandeville and his brother Nicholas were playing *quoits*, and in the course of the game

> *quoits:* checkers

Richard's stone fell upon Nicholas's head, inflicting a slight wound. On the third day following this, as Nicholas lay asleep, he had a stroke of paralysis of which he died on Thursday next before the feast of St. Barnabas the Apostle [June 8, 1301] . . .

Northamptonshire. Sarah Woodward was found dead in a ruined house at Radstone on Saturday the even of Easter in the fifteenth year of King Edward [II] [April 10, 1322] . . . They say that the said Sarah was lodged in a frail and dilapidated house, and on the preceding Sunday it fell in upon her by misadventure and she died forthwith. . . . The fallen wood and stones are appraised at twelve pence . . .

Wiltshire. Inquest was held at Salisbury on Monday next after the feast of All Saints in the fifth year of Richard [II] [November 1, 1381] . . . concerning the death of William Beard . . . [in the town of Salisbury]. [O]n the night after All Saints [of that same year] a fire in the house of the said William Beard was not carefully attended to, and it ignited his bed. Seeing that the fire was harmful and dangerous, William entered the chamber where it was, and was suffocated by the excessive smoke . . .

Source: *Select Cases from the Coroners' Rolls A.D. 1265–1413*. Edited by Charles Gross. Selden Society, v. 9 (1895). London, 1896. Pp. 52, 68–69, 77, 106–107.

AFTERMATH

Statistical studies that have made use of the coroners' inquests from medieval England have determined that men most frequently died when out of doors, and that women and children were more frequently indoors when they died, especially if the death was due to accident. This can tell us a great deal about the division of domestic labor in the Middle Ages—and it is not significantly different than presumptions of domestic life in the Celtic regions of Ireland, Scotland, and Wales.

ASK YOURSELF

1. In what ways were domestic spaces and everyday lives affected by location and economic status?
2. How do you think the determinations were made by the coroners' juries in considering whether a death was accidental or the result of a criminal act?
3. Why was fire such a dangerous situation in medieval buildings?

TOPICS TO CONSIDER

1. Consider using coroners' records from the Middle Ages and those from the modern period and comparing the kinds of information you obtain from them. Is it possible to gain a picture of how people lived from the circumstances of their deaths? Think of ways in which the use of modern coroners' records could help inform the medieval period and vice versa.
2. Consider investigating the varieties of domestic spaces that are described in coroners' records and how these different spaces make up a community. Consider the ways in which you could utilize these records to reconstruct the relationships among residents in these communities.

Further Information

Hanawalt, Barbara A. *The Ties That Bound: Peasant Families in Medieval England*. New York: Oxford University Press, 1986.

Jewell, Helen M. *English Local Administration in the Middle Ages*. Newton Abbot: David & Charles, 1972.

4. HOUSEHOLD GOODS DESCRIBED IN LATER MEDIEVAL WILLS

Although written wills are rare until the early modern period, people of the British Isles after the Norman Conquest began to record wills more frequently in the later Middle Ages. These can help identify the kinds of objects that typically were contained in houses of people from both elite and nonelite domiciles, although such information is almost impossible to determine for peasant families, as they rarely wrote wills, preferring to state their bequests—if any—on their deathbeds. Indeed, most medieval wills until the fifteenth century tended to be what is termed "nuncupative": not written down and orally transmitted from the deathbed to the witnesses in the room.

KEEP IN MIND AS YOU READ

The wills excerpted below are typical of most wills after the Anglo-Saxon period in that the items being bequeathed were the most important goods of the testators, and that these usually included the furnishings of the bedroom—often the only portion of the house that was fully furnished—any tableware that might have belonged to him or her, and the testator's clothing. This is true for elites as well as for members of the middle class. Elite wills tend to be far longer and more elaborate, because they had more goods to distribute.

Document 1: Later Medieval Wills

Excerpt from the Will of Lady Alice West of Hinton Marcel, Hampshire, 1395

On Thursday, that is to say, the 15th day of the month of July, in the year of the incarnation of our lord Jesus Christ, a thousand and three hundred and four score and fifteen, I Alice West, lady of Hinton Marcel, in whole estate of my body and in good mind being, make my testament in the manner as it followeth hereafter. . . . Also I devise to Thomas my son, a bed of tapestry work, with all the tapestries of suit, red of color, decorated with shapes and escutcheons, in the corners, of my ancestors' arms. With that, I bequeath to the same Thomas the stuff belonging thereto, that is to say, my best featherbed, and a blue canvas, and a mattress, and two blankets, and a pair of sheets of Reynes with the head sheet of the same, and six of my best pillows, which that he would choose, and a blue counterpane of miniver and a coverlet of red *sendel* decorated with chevrons . . . Also I bequeath to that same Thomas . . . a pair of matins books and a pair of beads, and a ring with which I was espoused to go, which were . . . his father's. Also I devise to Joan my daughter[-in-law] a bed painted black and white with . . . the stuff of the bed [the bedclothes similar to those listed above] . . . after the choice of . . . Thomas. . . . Also I bequeath to the same Joan a basin of silver with bosses upon the borders and a platter of silver belonging thereto. . . . a mass book and all the books that I have of Latin, English, and French . . . all my vestments of my chapel, with the towels belonging to it, . . . and the tapestries [listed in detail] belonging to the chapel . . . and all other apparel that belongs to my chapel.

[The bequests to her son and daughter-in-law continue]

. . . Also I devise to . . . Alianore my daughter a tawny bed of silk, with . . . four curtains of the suite and a coverlet of silk on one side tawny and [the] . . . other side blue; and the stuff of the bed therewith . . . [a]lso a round basin of silver, which [is engraved with] an escutcheon of my lord's [husband] arms and of mine . . .

A codicil to the will follows:][. . . I would that if it be so that Thomas my son aforesaid, and Joan his wife, will not take the charge to be my executors and to perform the administration of this testament, which is my last will . . . then I would that all the goods which . . . I have devised to the foresaid Thomas my son and Joan his wife in this testament be sold by my executors which would take the charge thereof and truly [distribute] to charitable works for my lord's soul, Sir Thomas West, and for mine, and for all Christian souls. . . .

Will of John Rogerysson of London, 1419–1420

. . . and this is my will if that I die, that Anneys Tukkysworth have the best bedstead, and Richard Gery the next[-best], and Robert Legat 2 pair of sheets, and to the same Robert my blue gown and my hood of red and black; and to Thomas Pykot my white ray gown and my red hood; and to Anneys Tukkysworth my best *boardcloth* and the towels; and Richard Gery the next [best] boardcloth and towel; and Robert Legat three quarters of white and Isabel his wife a boardcloth and a towel; and to William Pertnale a pair of sheets and a red doublet, and a coverlet of blue. And to Anneys Tikkysworth 4 nobles and [the] foresaid chest. And to Thomas Pertenall a pair of sheets and a dagger and a bow without pieces and a pair of green hose; and to Anneys Tukkysworth the best purse and Thomas Pertnale the next, and Isabel Leget the third, and Alson Okenden the fourth. . . . and to Anneys Tukkysworth a silver spoon and my silver girdle [belt] to Thomas Pertnale; and to Robert Leget my pieced bow . . .

sendel: silk fabric
boardcloth: tablecloth

Source: *The Fifty Earliest English Wills in the Court of Probate, London. A.D. 1387–1439.* Early English Text Society. Edited by Frederick J. Furnivall. London: Trübner & Co., 1882. Pp. 4–10, 41–42. Spelling and syntax modernized by editor.

AFTERMATH

Like the Anglo-Saxon wills, it must be expected that disappointed potential heirs were unhappy with some bequests, but because post-conquest wills did not include land, it is more likely that much of the strife between generations was fought in the royal courts over land rights. Wills eventually were recorded and catalogued in county and church archives, much as birth and death records came to be maintained in the same locales.

Under English Common Law, land could not be bequeathed through a last will and testament because all land was officially "owned" by the king, who distributed it through grants to nobles, knights, and others.

ASK YOURSELF

1. What differences occur in the wills of later medieval people in comparison to those of Anglo-Saxon people? In what ways are the wills similar?
2. Is conspicuous consumption a larger problem or issue in the later period than the earlier, and why do you think that might be so?
3. Are family relationships more complex in these wills, and does this complexity reflect a more sophisticated lifestyle in the later period than the earlier?

TOPICS TO CONSIDER

1. Consider making a comparison between the Anglo-Saxon wills and those of later British people. This could lead to a discussion of the changes in noble households and domestic relationships over a long period of time.
2. Consider trying to reconstruct what a noble household might have looked like in the later medieval period based on the information derived from wills.
3. Consider developing a picture of family relations based on the distribution of goods found in these wills.
4. Consider comparing the possible changes in the status of women between the earlier and later periods, based on bequests made in wills.

Further Information

Fleming, Peter. *Family and Household in Medieval England*. New York: Palgrave, 2001.

Kowaleski, Maryanne and P. J. P. Goldberg, eds. *Medieval Domesticity: Home, Housing and Household in Medieval England*. Cambridge: Cambridge University Press, 2008.

Sheehan, Michael M. *Marriage, Family, and Law in Medieval Europe: Collected Studies*. Edited by James K. Farge. Toronto: University of Toronto Press, 1996.

5. Medieval Cookery

INTRODUCTION

Medieval people throughout the period consumed certain particular staples on a regular basis: soups and stews made of vegetables, legumes, grains, or meat called **pottages** (from the Old French word, meaning "pot food"); coarse bread usually made of whole-grain flours, as finely ground wheat flour was very expensive; and proteins derived from eggs, fish, poultry, and meat. The amount of meat-based proteins in the diet depended significantly on both the social class and the liturgical calendar: peasants could rarely afford to slaughter their working animals for meat and were forbidden to hunt game in the king's forests and everyone was supposed to adhere to the rotation of "feasting" and "fasting" periods in the Christian calendar, which forbade the eating of meat on Wednesdays, Fridays, and Saturdays; during Lent; and during Advent.

The writing down of cookery recipes began in the thirteenth century, but the kinds of foods eaten and the forms of cooking go back much farther in time.

KEEP IN MIND AS YOU READ

Medieval cooks were not interested in exact ratios of ingredients, so medieval recipes rarely include them. In addition, the people engaged in food preparation—no matter what the social class of the diner—were far less likely to be literate or to need recipes, so the compilation of cookery books, which began to become popular in the fourteenth century, was more for the edification of the elite classes than for the cooks themselves. Finally, spices such as ginger and saffron and ingredients such as almonds, which were staples of the medieval elite larder, were very, very expensive and so out of reach of most medieval people, who had to rely on onions, garlic, and salt as seasonings.

Document 1: Gourdes in Potage (Fourteenth Century)

Take young *gourds*; pare them and carve them into pieces. Cast [put] them into good *broth*, and do thereto a good part of onions minced. Take pork sodden; grind it and ally it therewith and with yolks of eggs. Do thereto saffron and salt, and messe it forth with *powder douce*.

gourds: hard-shell squashes such as gourds and acorn squash

broth: a soup stock made with chicken and pork

powder douce: a mixture of sugar and ginger, sometimes also mixed with cinnamon and nutmeg

Modern translation (by editor): Winter squash soup. Take young gourds; skin them and cut into pieces. Place in good broth and add a large amount of minced onion. Grind boiled pork and add to the soup mixture, along with egg yolks. Add saffron and salt and serve with powder douce.

Source: Hieatt, Constance B. and Sharon Butler. *Curye on Inglish: English Culinary Manuscripts of the Fourteenth-Century (Including the Forme of Cury).* New York: The Early English Text Society by the Oxford University Press, 1985. Reproduced by the permission of the Council of the Early English Text Society.

AFTERMATH

Medieval cuisine, with its emphasis on sweet spices and flavor profiles that are often not appealing to modern tastes, resembles modern-day cookery from parts of the Middle East and South Asia—in large part because the spices came from those regions. Today's Indian curries, without the addition of "New World" foods such as potatoes, tomatoes, and chili peppers, resemble the flavors and modes of preparation of medieval cooking—which was common not only in the British Isles but all over northwestern Europe. With the introduction of foods from the western hemisphere after 1500, European cooking changed radically, although Europeans never lost their fondness for sweet tastes.

The fireplace and chimney were not invented until the late twelfth century, and even elite houses did not have many of them until a century later. This meant that kitchen staff cooked on open hearths, and the danger of fire meant that kitchens had to be separated from the domestic spaces. When chimneys were invented, kitchens could be moved to the ground floor of the domestic hall, which made it possible to serve food by using pulley systems (dumb waiters) and the food could be served while still hot!

ASK YOURSELF

1. How would medieval people prepare food like this? What might the kitchen look like and what utensils would they have had?
2. Without modern conveniences such as refrigeration and electricity, how well preserved was the food?
3. Did medieval people develop particular taste preferences, and if so, were they similar to modern tastes?
4. Would you find this food appealing? Why or why not?

TOPICS TO CONSIDER

1. There are many different websites that offer variations on medieval cookery. Consider developing a menu for a medieval banquet and seek out information on the kinds of ingredients that would have been most commonly found, and were most desirable; methods of food preparation; and the rituals of food serving.

2. Consider cooking some medieval recipes and serving them to your friends and family. What flavor profiles are different and which are familiar? Discuss the problems medieval people would have had in preparing food without the modern-day conveniences of contemporary kitchens.

3. Develop a comparison of cuisines—medieval and modern. Consider the origins of many of the spices that were used in medieval cuisine—especially those from the East. The procuring of those spices involved a great many people, which led to modern-day trade routes and to imperial conquests of the east by European nations in the early modern and modern periods.

Further Information

Black, Maggie. *The Medieval Cookbook*. 2nd rev. ed. London: British Museum Press, 2012.

Brears, Peter. *Cooking & Dining in Medieval England*. Totnes: Prospect Books, 2012.

Butler, Sharon, Constance B. Hieatt, and Brenda Hosington. *Pleyn Delit: Medieval Cookery for Modern Cooks*. Rev. ed. Toronto: University of Toronto Press, 1996.

"Gode Cookery." http://www.godecookery.com/gcooktoc/gcooktoc.htm

"Medieval Cookery." http://www.medievalcookery.com/

6. Medieval Medical Care

INTRODUCTION

Until the later Middle Ages, medical care for almost everyone was based upon informal and ad hoc treatment of diseases and injuries. This was still the case for the later medieval peasantry, but with the development of "professional" medical training in universities—which very often was inferior in actual success to the home remedies and folklore-based cures commonly used— elite people began to rely on licensed physicians, who based their understanding of disease on ancient Greek and Roman philosophers and theorists, such as Hippocrates and Galen.

What most people relied upon, however, were cures that were often included in general works on cookery, because food and medicine were intimately linked in the minds of medieval practitioners. The two excerpts in this section, from an Anglo-Saxon book of medicinal recipes and from a later medieval collection of medicinal cures, are typical examples of the kinds of treatments commonly used.

KEEP IN MIND AS YOU READ

Most medieval people did not have access to books, so most of the recipes, even when written down—usually by monks for use in the community—come from a long history of oral transmission. Such recipes often operate on the "like cures like" theory of medicine: if you have an illness you treat it by supplying either the opposite of what the illness presents, or you supply something to draw out the illness. The modern sayings "starve a cold, feed a fever" and "feed a cold, starve a fever" are age-old suggestions for curing everyday illnesses, and their contradictions are typical of this kind of method of cure.

Document 1: Cures from **Bald's Leechbook** *(ca. Ninth Century)*

Spider Bites

In case a poisonous spider—that is the stronger one—should bite a man, cut three incisions close to and running away from it; let the blood run into a green hazel-wood spoon, and then throw it away over the road so there will be no injury. Again: cut one incision on the wound, pound a *plantain*, lay it on; no harm will come to him. For the bite of a weaving-spider, take the lower part of *aeferthe* and lichen from a black-thorn; dry it to powder, moisten with honey; treat the wound with that. For the bite of a poisonous spider: black snails fried in a hot pan and ground to powder, and pepper and betony; one is to eat that powder, and drink it and apply it. For the bite of a poisonous spider: take the lower part of mallow; apply it to the wound. Again: cut five incisions, one on the bite and four around about; in silence, cast the blood with a spoon over the wagon-road.

Dog Bites

For the bite of a mad dog: mix agrimony and plantain with honey and the white of an egg; treat the wound with that. For a wound from a dog: boil burdock and groundsel in butter; anoint with that. Again: bruise betony; apply it to the bite. Again: beat plantain; apply it. Again: *seethe* two or three onions; roast them on ashes; mix with fat and honey, apply it. Again: burn a pig's jaw to ashes; sprinkle on. Again: take plantain root; pound it with fat; apply it to the wound so it casts out the poison.

Sexual Health

If a man be over-virile, boil *water of agrimony* in Welsh ale; he is to drink it at night, fasting. If a man is insufficiently virile, boil the same herb in milk; then you will excite it. Again: boil in ewe's milk: water of agrimony, *Alexanders*, the herb called *Fornet's palm*, so it will be as he most desires.

Cures for Sorcery and Magic

[To make] a salve against the race of elves, goblins, and those women with whom the Devil copulates: Take the female hop plant, wormwood, betony, lupin, vervain, henbane, *dittander, viper's bugloss, bilberry* plants, *cropleek*, garlic, madder grains, *corn cockle*, fennel. Put those plants in a vat; place under an alter; sing nine masses over it; boil it in butter and in sheep's grease; add much holy salt; strain through a cloth; throw the herbs into running water. If any evil temptation come to a man, or elf or goblin, anoint his face with this salve, and put it on his eyes and where his body is sore, and *cense* him and frequently sign him with the cross; his condition will soon get better.

Source: "Bald's Leechbook." In *The Anglo-Saxon World: An Anthology*. Translated by Kevin Crossley-Holland. © 1982 Boydell Press. Reprinted with the permission of Boydell and Brewer Ltd.

Document 2: Cures from a Middle English Medical Text (ca. Fourteenth Century)

For Infestations of Vermin

For a sheep's worm or any other living beast that has crept into a man's or woman's ear. Take the juice of wormwood, then of rue, then of *southernwood*, and put it in the ear.

For Skin Infections

For a man or woman who has inflammation of the face, [to take it] away. Take strong vinegar of white wine and anoint the face each day three or four times over the inflammation, it will break out as if it were the measles. When it is so broke out, anoint the sore (as it is said before) for six days, that the filth [infection] may run out, but look: as often as you anoint the face, anoint the back of the head with hot water. After six days, take and break almonds in a cloth and anoint the head therewith. It will be whole soon, but look, when you do the cure for the sickness, do not come out into the wind until it is whole [i.e. healthy].

Cures for Bad Breath

For stinking breath that comes out of the mouth. Take a handful of cumin and crush it in a brass mortar to powder. Steep it into a quarter of good wine from a vessel and let the patient drink thereof first and last, that is at evening and at morning, and [take] each day a pint as hot as he may suffer [tolerate]. He shall be whole [healed] of the sickness within fifteen days.

Also another for the same. Take a quantity of pennyroyal, that is to say, *puliol* and *brodewort*, a good handful, wash it clean and cut it small. Add thereto half an ounce of powder of pepper and an ounce of powder of cumin and mix them together, half to be consumed. Add thereto also a vessel of good wine and then steep it as it is said before. Let the patient use this after meat and not before, one in the afternoon and last in the evening, and always hot. He shall be whole [healed].

For him that has stinking breath through the nose. Take red mint and rue in equal measure. Wring the juice into the affected nose at evening when he goes to bed and he shall be whole.

For Tooth and Gums Care

For the toothache of worms. Take henbane seed, leek seed, and powder of incense in the same quantity. Put them together upon a hot glowing tilestone and make a *latten* pipe, that the nether end be wide that it may over-close the powders, and hold [it] by the mouth open over the pipe's end so that the air may go into the sore tooth. That will slay the worms and do away with the ache.

For Nosebleeds

plantain: *Plantago lanceolata*, or ribwort plantain, is a medicinal herb, not the species of banana now called plantains

aeferthe: not identified, but possibly betony, an herbal weed used in a variety of medieval medicines

seethe: boil

water of agrimony: a concentrated solution made by boiling agrimony, an herbaceous plant, in water

Alexanders: a cultivated edible herb, also called horse parsley

Fornet's palm: unidentified, but Fornet refers to Fornjot, the Norse giant who was the mythical king of Gotland

dittander: common herbal plant, member of the mustard family

viper's bugloss: a common weed with tall blue flowers, *Echium vulgare*, part of the borage family

bilberry plants: common shrub that produces dark blue edible berries

cropleek: a form of common leek, member of allium family

corn cockle: a flowering weed commonly found in wheat fields; quite poisonous

cense: the use of incense in a device used during a mass

southernwood: aka southern wormwood, member of the sunflower family

puliol and *brodewort:* varieties of pennyroyal, a member of the mint family

latten: a kind of copper alloy

brooklime: a wild edible herb that grows abundantly in low-lying water; also known as cow cress and horse cress

smallage: wild celery, from Old English *smalache*

Herb-Robert: a variety of wild geranium

For bleeding at the nose, a good medicine. Take *brooklime, smallage, Herb-Robert* and have him to drink. Temper the draft with the white of an egg and put it in the nostrils. It shall certainly staunch. Also, drink the juice of plantain, and it shall staunch.

Source: *A Middle English Medical Remedy Book.* Edited by Francisco Alonso Almeida. Glasgow University Library MS Hunter 185 Heidelberg: Universitätsverlag, Winter, 2014. P. 85. Translated from the Middle English by Kimberly Fogarty Palmer.

AFTERMATH

The lack of understanding of the ways in which disease and illness are transmitted—as bacterial infections or viruses—meant that, until the development of germ theory in the nineteenth century, people throughout the world were at enormous risk of dying from epidemic diseases not well understood and almost completely uncontrolled. In addition, the most common response to disease was that it was a punishment or a test from God—or that a group of outsiders, such as the Jews or other marginalized people, had poisoned the air or the water supply. These kinds of explanations led to acts of violence against such people, or to uncontrolled epidemics—such as the Black Death of 1347–1350—that decimated populations throughout Europe.

ASK YOURSELF

1. In what ways could these medical cures be effective? In what ways would they be ineffective?
2. What do these medical recipes tell you about medieval notions of illness and health?
3. What do these recipes tell you about "typical" illnesses experienced by medieval people, and perhaps ones that are not so typical?

TOPICS TO CONSIDER

1. Compare the recipes from the early text to those from the later text. The early text clearly assumes the participation of a priest or other church member, while the later recipes are more pragmatic. Why do you think that might be?
2. Consider the role that literacy might have in the development of medieval medicine and its practical uses. Would the ability to read make it easier to be a medical practitioner? Women, although sometimes literate in their native language (not in Latin), were barred from gaining licenses as physicians after the late thirteenth century. Consider how this would affect the local medical practitioners, who were almost always women, and their ability to practice medicine.

Further Information

Getz, Faye. *Medicine in the English Middle Ages*. Princeton, NJ: Princeton University Press, 1998.

Rawcliffe, Carole. *Medicine and Society in Later Medieval England*. Stroud: Sutton Publishing, 1995.

Whiteman, Robin and Rob Talbot. *Brother Cadfael's Herb Garden: An Illustrated Companion to Medieval Plants and Their Uses*. Boston: Bullfinch Press, 1997.

7. Welsh Hospitality (Twelfth Century)

INTRODUCTION

Gerald de Barry, known as GERALD OF WALES, was a Cambro-Norman nobleman and cleric from the Pembrokeshire estate of Manorbier. His grandmother was the famous Nest, a Welsh princess who married Gerald's grandfather at the time of the conquests of south Wales by Norman knights in the mid-twelfth century, and was also a mistress of KING HENRY I (r. 1100–1135) after her husband's death. Gerald traveled throughout Wales and Ireland and wrote about his experiences in both lands. His descriptions are both flattering and critical—and at times also highly fictionalized, based on gossip and hearsay. His presentation of Welsh hospitality, however, is one of his more complimentary descriptions.

KEEP IN MIND AS YOU READ

Although Gerald was born and raised in Wales, he was more Norman than Welsh—he did not speak the vernacular, for example—and his sympathies lay with his paternal family, who were vassals of the Earl of Pembroke, RICHARD FITZGILBERT DE CLARE, called Strongbow, and who accompanied the earl to Ireland after his marriage to DIARMID MAC MURCHADA's daughter, AIOFE.

Document 1: **Description of Wales, Book I, Chapter 10**

In Wales no one begs. Everyone's home is open to all, for the Welsh generosity and hospitality are the greatest of all virtues. . . . When you travel there is no question of your asking for accommodation or of their offering it: you just march into a house and hand over your weapons to the person in charge. They give you water so that you may wash your feet and that means that you are a guest. . . . If you refuse the offer, it means that you have only dropped in for refreshment during the early part of the day and do not propose to stay the night. . . .

Guests who arrive early in the day are entertained until nightfall by girls who play to them on the harp. . . . When night falls and no more guests are expected, the evening meal is prepared, varying according to what the house has to offer, and to the number and importance of the men who have come. You must not expect a variety of dishes from a Welsh kitchen, and there are no highly seasoned tidbits to whet your appetite. In a Welsh house there are no tables, no tablecloths and no napkins. . . . You sit down in threes, not in pairs as elsewhere, and they put the food in front of you, all together, on a single large trencher containing enough for three, resting on rushes and green grass. Sometimes they serve the main dish on bread, rolled out large and thin, and baked fresh each day . . . Finally the time comes to retire to rest. Alongside one of the walls is placed a communal bed, stuffed with rushes, and not all that many of them. For sole covering there is a stiff harsh sheet, made locally and called in Welsh a "brychan." They all go to bed together.

Source: Gerald of Wales. *The Journey through Wales/The Description of Wales.* Translated by Lewis Thorpe. New York and London: Penguin Books, 1978. Pp. 236–237.

AFTERMATH

Gerald of Wales was enormously influential as a medieval ethnographer of the Welsh and Irish and his descriptions of both cultures and peoples shaped English attitudes about the Celtic neighbors they conquered for centuries. Even today, popular presentations of the Welsh as unusually hospitable appear in tourist guides and official tourist information pamphlets!

ASK YOURSELF

1. Gerald is presenting the Welsh as very hospitable. Why?
2. Is Gerald, whose alliances were almost all with his Norman paternal relations, being objective in his portrayal of the Welsh? Why might this portrayal be less than neutral?
3. Do you think that Gerald had personal experience of Welsh hospitality, and if so, did he enjoy it?

TOPICS TO CONSIDER

1. Consider comparing the domestic arrangements of the Welsh, at least according to Gerald, with those of English people. Take into consideration the issue that the Welsh were a subject people in conflict with their Anglo-Norman conquerors: their economic situation might have been more unstable than that of their English neighbors.
2. Consider the issue of Welsh "hospitality" from a longer historical perspective. Later presentations of the Welsh—and their own modern-day advertising—emphasize this idea of hospitality. The origins of this attitude might lie even deeper than the Middle Ages.

Further Information

Pounds, Norman J. G. *The Medieval Castle in England and Wales: A Social and Political History.* Cambridge: Cambridge University Press, 1993.
Walker, David. *Medieval Wales.* Cambridge: Cambridge University Press, 1990.

EDUCATION AND PROFESSIONAL TRAINING

8. The Education of an Anglo-Saxon Prince: Asser, *Life of Alfred* (ca. 890)

INTRODUCTION

Asser, a Welsh priest who acted as the confessor and biographer of King Alfred "the Great" (r. 871–899), was one among a group of scholars the king brought to his court at Winchester in order to reawaken learning and literary culture in Anglo-Saxon England in the midst of the Viking incursions—the English branch of the **Carolingian Renaissance**. Alfred's apparently sincere desire to become educated and to have an educated elite class capable of maintaining a sophisticated administrative machine is emphasized in Asser's biography, in particular in the passages in which he describes Alfred as a boy desiring, unlike his brothers, to own the book of poetry his mother offered as a prize to her sons.

KEEP IN MIND AS YOU READ

In the early Middle Ages, literacy and numeracy were not often considered valuable skills for boys who were not being trained for a profession in the church. Girls and women often had more "book learning" than elite men did at this time; peasants rarely had any access to formal education. In the centuries before the development of specific curricula and schools, education was conducted by using private tutors—often a member of the clergy. Moreover, literacy was considered to mean being able to read, but not necessarily to write, Latin as well as the vernacular language spoken.

Document 1: The Life of Alfred: Education of a Future King

21. I think I should return to that which particularly inspired me to this work: in other words, I consider that some small account . . . of the infancy and boyhood of my esteemed lord Alfred, king of the Anglo-Saxons, should briefly be inserted at this point.

22. Now, he was greatly loved, more than all his brothers, by his father and mother—indeed, by everybody—with a universal and profound love, and he was always brought up in the royal court and nowhere else. As he passed through infancy and boyhood he was seen to be more comely in appearance than his other brothers, and more pleasing in manner,

speech and behavior. From the cradle onwards, in spite of all the demands of his present life, it has been the desire for wisdom, more than anything else, together with the nobility of his birth, which have characterized the nature of his noble mind; but alas, by the shameful negligence of his parents and tutors he remained ignorant of letters until his twelfth year, or even longer. However, he was a careful listener, by day and night, to English poems, most frequently hearing them recited by others, and he readily retained them in his memory. . . .

23. One, day, therefore, when his mother was showing him and his brothers a book of English poetry which she held in her hand, she said: "I shall give this book to whichever one of you can learn it the fastest." Spurred on by these words, or rather by divine inspiration, and attracted by the beauty of the initial letter in the book, Alfred spoke as follows in reply to his mother, forestalling his brothers (ahead in years, though not in ability): "Will you really give this book to the one of us who can understand it the soonest and recite it to you?" Whereupon, smiling with pleasure she reassured him, saying: "Yes, I will." He immediately took the book from her hand, went to his teacher and learnt it. When it was learnt, he took it back to his mother and recited it.

24. After this he learnt the "daily round," that is, *the services of the hours*, and then certain psalms and many prayers; these he collected in a single book, which he kept by him day and night, as I have seen for myself; amid all the affairs of the present life he took it around with him everywhere for the sake of prayer, and was inseparable from it. But alas, he could not satisfy his craving for what he desired the most, namely the liberal arts; for, he used to say, there were no good scholars in the entire kingdom of the West Saxons at that time.

25. He used to affirm, with repeated complaints and sighing from the depths of his heart, that among all the difficulties and burdens of his present life this had become the greatest: namely, that at the time when he was of the right age and had the leisure and the capacity for learning, he did not have the teachers. . . . Nevertheless, just as he did not previously desist from the same insatiable desire, among the difficulties of the present life, from infancy right up to the present day . . . so too he does not yet cease to yearn for it.

> *the services of the hours:* the daily prayers of the medieval church, recited seven times a day

Source: Asser. *Life of King Alfred* in *Alfred the Great: Asser's Life of King Alfred and Other Contemporary Sources.* Translated by Simon Keynes and Michael Lapidge. New York: Penguin Books, 1983. Pp. 74–76.

AFTERMATH

Alfred's interest in education as a boy, according to Asser, led him to decide that an educated elite populace would be very helpful in establishing effective legal and administrative systems. Once he was king, he developed a unique curriculum of Latin texts translated into Anglo-Saxon—the vernacular in England—that he considered to be essential for a fundamental education. Not only did King Alfred collect a group of excellent scholars for his court that engaged in the process of translation of these texts, but he also translated some of them himself. He also made sure that all of his children—including his daughters—received a thorough education in both Latin and Anglo-Saxon.

ASK YOURSELF

1. Why would literacy be considered less important for an elite man engaged in secular activities (war, governing, etc.) than for a woman or a member of the clergy?

2. What motives do you think Alfred's mother had for trying to encourage her sons to learn to read their vernacular language?
3. In what ways would the experience Alfred had in acquiring the book from his mother influence his decisions later as king?

TOPICS TO CONSIDER

1. Consider the effect of education on an individual in the early Middle Ages. What opportunities would open for that person and how would education change the kinds of jobs an educated person would do?
2. Consider the influence of an educational program such as the kind King Alfred developed and how that could enhance the ability of kings to rule.

Further Information

Horspool, David. *King Alfred: Burnt Cakes and Other Legends.* Cambridge, MA: Harvard University Press, 2006.

Pollard, Justin. *Alfred the Great: The Man Who Made England.* London: John Murray, 2005.

9. The Education of a Scottish Monk:
The Life of St. Kentigern
(fl. Late Sixth Century)

INTRODUCTION

Like the histories of early medieval Ireland and Wales, the historical texts about early medieval Scotland were written down later, mostly after 1100, and often under the influence of the Anglo-Norman conquests of those Celtic lands, which brought a different focus on written texts to the Scots. Many of the stories of early Scottish history are little more than legends and myths, but they occupied an important place in the cultural consciousness of the Scots.

St. Kentigern, also known as St. Mungo, was of "royal" heritage—his mother is reputed to have been the daughter of a northern Scots king—but he was supposedly raised by St. Serf (whose own history is largely mythical) in the area known as Strathclyde. St. Kentigern is credited with building the first church in Glasgow (in the medieval district of Galloway) and is the patron saint of that city.

Jocelyn, the author of *The Life of Saint Kentigern*, was a monk of the Cistercian monastery of Furness (modern-day Barrow-in-Furness, Cumbria) who wrote hagiographies (saints' holy biographies) primarily of Celtic saints for an Anglo-Norman audience in Scotland in the late twelfth century.

KEEP IN MIND AS YOU READ

The lack of written sources and the persistence of oral traditions in Scotland, as well as Ireland and Wales, make it very difficult to assess the accuracy of any of the tales and "histories" of the early medieval Celtic world. Although later authors claimed to have based their own writings on written texts that were subsequently "lost," it is not possible to determine with any conclusiveness the accuracy of their accounts. The emotional connection of groups to their national, regional, or local saints was profound, however, leading to ever more elaborate stories about their favorite holy men and women.

Document 1: St. Kentigern's Education

However, when the age of discernment approached [Kentigern], and the time suitable and acceptable for learning, [Saint Serf, his guardian] handed him over to be instructed in letters. And he devoted much diligence and effort to him that in these things he might advance. And in this matter, [St. Serf] himself was not defrauded by his own desire, because the boy responded very well and fruitfully to his teaching by learning and retaining it *like a tree planted by the rivers of water, that bringeth forth his fruit in his season.* [Psalm 1:3] The boy made progress with the anointing of good hope and holy character instructing him in the discipline of letters, and not less in the practice of the holy virtues. For there were granted to him by the Father of light, from whom every good and perfect gift is given, an attentive heart, a keen nature for understanding, a firm memory to retain what had been learned, a persuasive tongue to produce what he desired, and a sublime voice: dripping with sweetness, harmonious, and as it were, never weary of singing the divine praises. Moreover all these gifts of grace gilded a life worthy of praise, and for that reason [Kentigern] was in the eyes of the holy old man more precious and loveable than all of his companions. And so it was his custom to call him in the language of his country Munghu which is spoken in Latin as "*Karissimus Amicus*" [Dearest Friend] and by this name up to this day the common people are accustomed to call him frequently, and to invoke him in their distress.

Source: Jocelyn of Furness [fl. 1175–1214], *The Life of Saint Kentigern.* © Translation by Cynthia Whiddon Green, as part of an MA thesis at the University of Houston, December 1998, with adaptations by the editor. Used here by permission. Available through the Internet Medieval Sourcebook, http://www.fordham.edu/Halsall/basis/Jocelyn-Lifeof Kentigern.asp

AFTERMATH

The importance of "native" saints such as Kentigern, especially after the Norman Conquest of England, was bounded up in the nationalist fervor of the Celtic regions that were being invaded or overrun by the Anglo-Norman conquerors. Whereas Normans, sometimes—as in the case of King Henry II's invasion of Ireland—with the blessing of the papacy, considered the Celtic peoples to be at best backward in their Christian observance, and at worst heretical and in need of "correction," the popularity and promotion of local saints in Scotland, Wales, and Ireland presented Celtic Christianity as both orthodox and sophisticated. In time, Anglo-Norman settlers in those regions also adopted local saints as their own, which produced a more multiethnic and diverse collection of British saints revered by all people living in the isles.

ASK YOURSELF

1. Why would it be important to emphasize the intellectual talents of a local saint such as Kentigern?
2. What kind of educational curriculum is implied in this text? What elements of human behavior are emphasized?

TOPICS TO CONSIDER

1. Compare the two early medieval texts concerning the education of a future king and a future priest-saint, respectively. In what ways would their educations differ? What would be similar? Why would these differences be important?

2. *The Life of Saint Kentigern* emphasizes Kentigern's sweetness and kindness. Consider how these characteristics differ from those emphasized for the elite man who was expected to go to war and whose martial qualities were considered most important. Consider also the potential conflicts that might arise between two competing notions of manhood—the secular warrior and the religious professional.

Further Information

Bradley, Thomas and John R. Walsh. *A History of the Irish Church, 400–700 A.D.* 2nd ed. Blackrock: Columba Press, 2003.

Charles-Edwards, T. M. *Early Christian Ireland.* Cambridge: Cambridge University Press, 2007.

10. The Education of a Knight: William Marshal (ca. 1144–1219)

INTRODUCTION

The anonymous *History of William Marshal* is a very long poem written at the behest of the Marshal's family after his death in 1219. In the *History*, William's life is narrated as a series of adventures and important events, from his birth during the volatile civil war between KING STEPHEN and EMPRESS MATILDA (1135–1155) to his early years as a landless and impoverished knight whose fortunes changed dramatically when QUEEN ELEANOR OF AQUITAINE and King Henry II (r. 1155–1189) attached him to their household and that of their eldest son, the Young King Henry. Once connected to the royal court, William Marshal advanced rapidly, ultimately winning the biggest prize a landless knight could desire: marriage to a wealthy and aristocratic heiress. William indeed married well: his wife was ISABELLA DE CLARE, heiress both to the earldom of Pembroke (as well as other properties) from her father, Earl Gilbert fitzRichard de Clare, and to the kingdom of Leinster in Ireland, from her mother, Aiofe, daughter of King Diarmid Mac Murchada. The *History* catalogues Marshal's career after marriage in detail, ending with a poignant scene of his death.

The poem itself survives in a single manuscript, discovered in a collection of manuscripts amassed by Sir Thomas Phillipps in the nineteenth century by French historian M. Paul Meyer. He published an edition in three volumes, with an abridged translation into modern French, between 1891 and 1901. The original manuscript was acquired by the J. Pierpont Morgan Library in New York City in 1958.

KEEP IN MIND AS YOU READ

As a very small boy, William Marshal was handed to King Stephen as a hostage in 1153 for the good behavior of his father, John Marshal. John Marshal reneged on his promises to the king and this marked William for abuse, at the very least, and possibly death. He was able, according to the poet, to disarm King Stephen with his intelligence and "courtesy" at such a young age: the product of the careful education of his father in the "rules" of chivalry. As a young man, William—landless and poor—was placed in the household of William of Tancarville, Lord Chamberlain of Normandy, in order to be educated as a knight. He was not treated with respect by the Chamberlain, in part because of the lowly status of being the youngest—and impoverished—son in a large family. Nevertheless, William Marshal persevered, and his experiences led him into an affiliation with the royal household.

Document 1: The History of William Marshal

The Marshal took stock:
he sent letters to the *King*,
asking him, if it so pleased him, to grant
a truce until such time as he had spoken
with his lady, the *Empress*.
The King would not have been at all willing to do this
on the strength of his word or an agreement,
for he did not trust him;
he would take no *pledges* or *surety* from him,
but, if he handed over to him hostages
such as he specified,
he would do as the Marshal asked.
Thereupon the matter was concluded,
with the result that the King
obtained one of the Marshal's sons as hostage,
which might well have turned out badly.
I am not speaking about the first son but the next,
William, about whom, from now on,
anyone willing to give his attention will hear many a fine tale.

. . .

The child's life was in danger,
for the King realized only too well
that he had been tricked.

. . .

Then deceivers stepped forward,
wicked and base men,
who advised him to hang the child.
Word came of this to his father,
but he said that he did not care
about the child, since he still had
the anvils and hammers
to produce even finer ones.
When the King heard of this reaction,
he was furious.
He ordered the child to be seized
and taken to the gallows for hanging;
he had him carried to the gallows,
but the King would not allow himself to go along with him
without the company of a great retinue,
since he had great fears of being ambushed.
And the child, as he was being carried off,
quite unsuspecting of the threat of death,
saw the earl of Arundel,

King: King Stephen
Empress: Empress Matilda
pledges/surety: formal oaths to behave loyally

who was holding a very fine javelin,
and he said in his simple childish way:
"My lord, give me that javelin."
When the King heard these innocent words,
not for all the gold in France
would he have allowed him to be hanged that day.
Instead, with great goodness and kindness,
for his heart was full of these qualities,
he took the child in his arms
and said: "I'll spare you this torture,
you can be sure you won't die here now."
They went back to join the army,
and a catapult was being set up
to aim at the keep
and the walls around it.
The advisers came back
to recommend to the King
that the child be taken forthwith,
placed in the sling
and fired at those within the walls
to strike fear in their hearts.
The child, too young to have much understanding of events,
was led away towards the catapult.
When he saw the catapult's sling,
he took a little step back,
and said: "Gracious me! What a swing!
It would be a good idea for me to have a swing on it."
He went right up to the sling,
but the King said: "Take him away! Take him away!
Anyone who could ever allow
him to die in such agony would certainly have a very cruel heart;
he comes out with such engaging childish remarks."
. . .

[The king's men continue to threaten young William with a painful death and insist that they will tie him to the catapult. In response, the castle's constable ties a millstone to the battlements, saying that the child will be squashed against it if they catapult him toward the castle.]

Seeing this, the child asked
what sort of new toy this could be
that they were hanging out of the window.
When the King heard him say this,
he burst out laughing
and said: "William, a toy like that
would be no good at all for you.
To do you any harm would be a great shame
because you haven't done anything wrong.
I shall spare you toys such as this,

you'll never die at my hands."
The King settled down to the siege.
One day he was sitting in his tent,
strewn with grasses and flowers
of a variety of colors.
William looked at the flowers,
examining them from top to bottom.
Happily and cheerfully
he went about gathering the "knights"
growing on the plantain,
with its broad pointed leaves.
When he had gathered enough
to make a good handful,
he said to the King: "my dear lord,
would you like to play knights?"
"Yes," he said, "my little friend."
The child immediately placed some
on the King's lap,
when he asked: "Who has the first go?"
"You, my dear little friend", replied the King.
So he then took one of the knights,
and the King placed his own against it.
But it turned out that in the contest
the King's knight lost its head,
which made William overjoyed.

. . .

These childish games and pranks
were not over in a day,
or even two or three,
but lasted more than two months.

. . . .

The Chamberlain and his retinue
returned to Tancarville,
and, in the peaceful conditions now prevailing,
it was possible to go **tourneying** throughout the land,
and any man seeking to win renown
would go to the tournaments, if he had the wherewithal.
The Marshal was much displeased
and greatly dismayed,
for all he had was his palfrey,
now that his fine horse had died
from the wounds it had received as he rode it.

. . .

The Chamberlain showed little kindness
towards the Marshal, and the latter was very ashamed;
he scarcely took any account of him.
In brief, it is well known
that poverty has brought dishonour
on many a nobleman and been the ruin of them;

such was the case with the Marshal,
for he had nothing to give and no source of wealth.

. . .

Everywhere the news spread
that between Sainte-Jamme and Valennes
there would be a tournament in a fortnight's time.

. . .

The news spread so far
that it reached Tancarville.
The Chamberlain made ready;
he was pleased to make the effort
to bear arms on that occasion.
The hall filled with knights
set to go to the tournament,
but the Marshal had not means of going
and was therefore downcast.
His lord the Chamberlain addressed him:
"What are you downcast about, Marshal?"
"My lord, I have no horse
and therefore I am very badly equipped."
"There is no need for you to be concerned on that score;
do not give it a further thought, Marshal,
for you will have horses aplenty."
The Marshal thanked him for this
and had great faith in the words he spoke.

. . .

The Chamberlain had seen to it that fine horses
were taken there as gifts for his knights.
But, in the sharing out of horses
the Marshal was forgotten.
He saw very well how they had been distributed,
but he said not a single word,
except: "The horses have been shared out,
but you have denied me a share."
At this the Chamberlain replied:
"Marshal, it makes no sense
that you were not one of the first to have one.
However, you are welcome to have
a fine, sturdy, horse, whatever the cost to me;
no expense will be spared."
Someone informed the Chamberlain
that there was still one left,
a strong, fine, and well-proportioned horse,
very lively, swift and powerful.
So the horse was brought out,
a horse fine and valuable,
had it not been for one flaw
that was a terrible drawback:
the horse was so wild

that it could not be tamed.
The Marshal mounted it.
Not once did he use his elbows;
instead he pricked it with his spurs,
and the horse, flying faster than a hawk,
bounded forwards.
At the point where it should have been reined in,
it turned out that it pulled incredibly hard.
Never had it had a master
able to make it pull less,
even if he had had fifteen reins to restrain it.
The Marshal gave the matter thought
and came up with a brilliant scheme:
he let out the bridle
at least three fingers' length from the bit
and so released the lock
of the bit that it
went down into its mouth
and so it had far less to bite on
than was usual.
For no amount of gold or other riches
could he have reined him in in any other way.
He considered that he had been very clever.
The horse was so improved by this new bridle
that he could have been ridden around
in half an acre of land
as if he were the tamest on earth.
When day broke, the knights arrived.
. . .
And I can tell you that in front of the lists
this was no formal joust;
there was not a single word of argument spoken
except of winning or losing all
Sir Philip de Valognes
was armed so elegantly
and so very finely,
and the handsomest knight of all of them;
he was also swifter than any bird.
For this many a knight observed him.
The Marshal observed him closely,
then immediately he left the ranks,
spurring on his horse Blancart;
he launched himself at great speed into their midst
and seized Philip's bridle.
Philip made every effort to defend himself,
but no effort was of any avail:
the Marshal by force dragged him towards himself
and took him away from the tournament.
Philip readily gave his pledge to the Marshal,

who so placed his trust in him
that, for that reason, he let him go.
And, after leaving Philip,
he rejoined the tournament
Immediately he knocked down a knight
with a lance he had managed to pick up;
it was only a stump, but he did so well with it
that the knight pledged his word
to become a prisoner.
So now he had two very valuable prisoners,
and that without doing injury or harm to them.
He stretched out his hand to take a third,
and, as a result of his great effort and application,
he had him soon pledging his word to be his prisoner.
. . .
My lords, in very truth, it is no lie
that God is wise and courtly:
he is swift to come to the help and assistance
of any man who puts his trust in him.
Only that day had the Marshal been a poor man as regards possessions and horses,
and now he had four and a half,
fine mounts and handsome, thanks to God.
He also had hacks and palfreys,
fine pack-horses and harnesses.
The tournament disbanded
and the Chamberlain left
with men in his company.
They paid the Marshal great honour
and treated him very courteously,
more so than they had done before.
Dough will rise according to the yeast you use.

Source: *History of William Marshal*. Volume I. Edited by A. J. Holden, translated by S. Gregory, notes by D. Crouch. London: Anglo-Norman Text Society, 2002. Pp. 23–35, 63–71. Edited by editor. Reprinted with permission.

AFTERMATH

William Marshal's education as a boy and a young man held him in good stead, as soon after the tournament described in the poem, William caught the attention of Queen Eleanor of Aquitaine in a dramatic way: he rescued her from capture during a skirmish with some vassals who were in revolt against the king and queen. She admired his intrepidness as well as his perfect manners and "courtesy" and brought him into the royal household. From there, William's career went from strength to strength. He became the perfect example of a "most perfect knight," and his life was used as a marker of excellence—in education, in training, in ability, and in unfailing courtesy—thereafter, even when the *History of William Marshal* itself was lost.

Tournaments were not the staid affairs that are presented as choreographed exhibitions in modern-day "Renaissance" festivals. They were enactments of battles with sharpened weapons—known as melees—as well as jousting, sword-fighting, and other activities. Knights frequently got hurt in tournaments and not a few were killed. This led kings to ban the presentation of tournaments in their kingdoms by the thirteenth century, although it was almost impossible to prevent them from occurring.

ASK YOURSELF

1. In what ways does the author of the poem present William Marshal as a very young boy as nobler and more worthy than the grown men who want to kill him in such gruesome ways?
2. How is King Stephen presented in the poem? In what ways does he perform the role of chivalrous king, in contrast to his soldiers?
3. In the tournament episode, what makes William Marshal more successful than the other knights? Is his ambition to succeed more important, or is it his "courtesy"?

TOPICS TO CONSIDER

1. Imagine the education of a young boy and young man in the twelfth century. Consider the kinds of professions an elite young man might be able to aspire to and what he would have to accomplish in order to achieve them.
2. Consider the notion of "courtesy" or "chivalry" and how this idea contributed to the socialization of young elite people in the Middle Ages. In particular, consider how artificial this idea could be in contrast to the realities of medieval life, which was often quite violent and unpoliced.

Further Information

Crouch, David. *William Marshal: Knighthood, War and Chivalry, 1147–1219*. 3rd ed. London: Longman, 2016.

Keen, Maurice. *Chivalry*. New Haven: Yale University Press, 1984.

11. Learning to Manage Estates and Manors: The "Rules of Saint Robert" (Thirteenth Century)

INTRODUCTION

A significant component to the education and training of children of the landed classes—the aristocracy and gentry—was how to oversee and manage their estates. This was true for girls and women as well as for boys and men. One of the most popular written works focusing on the education of the elites in estate management was a treatise written by ROBERT GROSSETESTE, bishop of Lincoln, for the newly widowed Countess of Lincoln, MARGARET DE LACY.

Robert Grosseteste (ca. 1168–1253) was one of the most important intellectuals of the Middle Ages in Britain. Highly educated, he contributed to the development of Oxford University, probably acting as its first chancellor and holding the title "Master of the Schools." His lectures and treatises on philosophy, theology, logic, and science were some of the most significant works produced in the Middle Ages, and he trained Roger Bacon, one of the most challenging intellectuals and theologians of the age. In 1236, following the death of Bishop Hugh of Lincoln, Robert was elected as his successor. He was innovative as a bishop as well and gained the patronage of the influential Countess of Lincoln, Margaret de Lacy, who had inherited the earldom from her mother, Hawise de Quency, and conveyed the title to her husband, John de Lacy, lord of Pontefract. When Countess Margaret was widowed in 1240, Bishop Robert wrote his treatise on estate management and dedicated it to her.

KEEP IN MIND AS YOU READ

This text is different from other treatises on estate management, such as the work attributed to Walter of Henley, in that it is directed to the lords and ladies of estates, not to their estate managers. Robert was quite aware that the control of manors and other kinds of feudal estates could be in the hands of women as well as men and deliberately wrote the treatise in an entirely gender neutral way.

Document 1: The Rules of Saint Robert
(Les Rules Seynt Roberd)

Here begin the rules that the good bishop of Lincoln, St Robert Grosseteste, made for the Countess of Lincoln to guard and govern her lands and residences: whoever will keep these rules well will be able to live on his means, and keep himself and those belonging to him.

The first rule teaches how a lord or lady shall know all their lands in each manor . . .

To begin with, buy the king's writ to make an inquest by the oath of twelve free men in each manor all the lands by their parcels, all the rents, customs, usages, services, **franchises**, **fees** and **tenements**, and let this be . . . distinctly **enrolled**, so that your chief **seneschal** may have one whole roll, and you another, and let each **bailiff** have what belongs to his **baillie**. And if petitioners come to you because of a wrong that anyone has done them first look yourself at the rolls or that manor to which the petitioner belongs, and according to them give answer and maintain justice.

The second rule teaches how you may know by common inquest what there is on each manor, moveable or not moveable

Next, cause to be made without delay a correct **inquest**, and enroll specifically in another roll every one of your manors in England, each by itself, how many ploughs you have in each place . . . ; how many acres of arable land, how many of meadow, how much pasture for sheep, and how much for cows, and so for all kind of beasts according to their number; . . . and keep this roll by you, and often look at the first roll, and this also that you may quickly know how to find what you ought to do. . . .

The third rule teaches the discourse that the lord or lady ought to have with their chief seneschal before some of their good friends

When the aforesaid rolls and inquests have been made, and as soon as you can, . . . call your chief seneschal before any of your people that you trust, and speak thusly to him: "Good sir, you see plainly that to have my rights set forth clearly, and to know more surely the state of my people, and of my lands, . . . I have caused these inquests and enrolments to be made; now I pray you, as one to whom I have committed trust, as many as I have under me guard and govern.

"And strictly I command you that you keep whole and without harm, all my rights, franchises and fixed possessions, . . . And my moveable goods and livestock increase in an honest and right way, and keep them faithfully. The returns from my lands, rents and moveables, without fraud, . . . bring to me and to my treasury to spend according as I shall direct, that God may be satisfied, and my honor and my profit preserved by the foresight of myself and you and my other friends.

"Further, I strictly command that neither you nor any of your bailiffs . . . in any way, by unlawful exactions of fear, or accusations, or receipt of presents or gifts, vex, hurt or ruin those who hold of me—rich or poor; and if in any of these said ways they are by anyone vexed, hurt or ruined, . . . quickly make amendment and redress."

The fourth rule teaches how a lord or lady can further examine into their estate, that is to say, how he or she can live yearly of their own

In two ways by calculation can you inquire your estate. First this, command strictly that each place . . . there be thrown in a measure at the entrance to the **grange** the eighth sheaf of every kind of **corn**, and let it be threshed and measured by itself. And by calculating that measure you can calculate all the rest in the grange. . . .

And if this does not please you, do it in this way. Command your seneschal that every year at **Michaelmas** he cause all the stacks of each kind of corn, within the grange and without, to be valued by prudent, faithful and capable men, . . . [and] set the sum in writing, and according to that assign the expenses of your household in bread and ale.

Also see how many quarters of corn you will spend in a week in dispensable bread, how much in alms. . . . And when you have subtracted this sum from the sum total of your corn, then you can subtract for the ale, according as weekly custom [of] brewing in your household. . . .

And with the money from your corn, from your rents, and from the **issues of pleas** in your courts, and from your stock, arrange the expenses of your kitchen and your wines and your wardrobe and the wages of servants, and subtract your stock. But on all manors take care of your corn, that it is not sold out of season without need; that is, if your rents and other returns will suffice for the expenses of your chamber and wines and kitchen, leave your store of corn whole until you have the advantage of the corn of another year, not more, or at the least, of half a year.

. . .

The seventh rule teaches you how you may know to compare the accounts with the estimate of the extent[s] . . . of [your] manors and lands

At the end of the year when all the accounts of the lands shall have been rendered, and [accounts of] the issues and all the expenses of all the manors, take to yourself all the rolls, and with one or two of the most intimate and faithful men that you have, make very careful comparison with the rolls of the accounts rendered, and of the rolls of the estimate of corn and stock that you made after the previous August, and according as they agree you shall see the industry or negligence of your servants and bailiffs, and according to that make [changes to the weekly routine].

. . .

The ninth rule teaches you what you ought to say often to the small and great of your household, that all do your commands

Say to all small and great, and that often, that fully, quickly and willingly, without grumbling and contradiction, they do all your commands that are not against God.

. . .

The eleventh rule teaches you who ought to be employed to be [a part] of your household . . .

Command that no one be received, or kept to be of your household indoors or outside, if one has not reasonable belief of them that they are faithful, discreet, and painstaking in the office for which they are received, and also honest and of good manners.

The twelfth rule teaches you what inquest ought often to be made in your household by your commandment

Command that often and carefully inquest be made if there be any[one who is] disloyal, unwise, filthy in person, gluttonous, quarrelsome, drunken, unprofitable; and those who shall be found so, or of whom such report is spread, let them be turned out of your household.

. . .

The fourteenth rule teaches you how your guests ought to be received

Command strictly that all your guests, secular and religious, be quickly, courteously, and with good cheer received by the seneschal from the **porters**, **ushers**, and **marshals**, and by all be courteously addressed and in the same way lodged and served.

. . .

The seventeenth rule teaches you how you ought to seat your people at meals in your house

Make your free men and guests sit as far as possible at tables on either side, not four here and three there. And all the crowd of grooms shall enter together when the freemen are seated, and shall sit together and rise together. And strictly forbid that any quarrelling be at your meals. And you yourself always be seated at the middle of the high table so that your presence as lord or lady may appear openly to all, and that you may plainly see on either side all the service and all the faults. . . .

The twenty-first rule teaches how your people ought to behave towards your friends, both in your presence and absence

Command that your knights, and chaplains, and servants in office, and your gentlemen, with a good humor and hearty cheer and ready service receive and honor, within your presence and outside it, everyone whom they perceive by your words or your manners to be especially dear to you, and to whom you would have special honor shown, for in doing so can they particularly show that they wish what you wish. And as far as possible except [in the case of] sickness or [excessive] fatigue, constrain yourself to eat in the hall before your people, for this shall bring great benefit and honor to you.

The twenty-second rule teaches you how you ought to behave towards your bailiffs and servants of your own lands and manors when they come before you

When your bailiffs and your servants of lands and manors come before you, address them fairly and speak pleasantly to them, and discreetly and gently ask if your people do well, and how your corn is growing, and how profitable your ploughs and stock are, and make these demands openly, and your knowledge shall be much respected.

. . .

The twenty-sixth rule teaches how at Michaelmas you may arrange your travel itinerary for all the year

Every year, at Michaelmas, when you know the measure of all your corn, then arrange your travel [from manor to manor] for the whole of that year, and for how many weeks in each place, according to the seasons of the year, and the advantages of the [region] in [abundance of] flesh and fish, and do not in any way burden by debt or long residence the places where you travel, but so arrange your itinerary that the place at your departure shall not remain in debt, but something may remain on the manor, whereby the manor can raise money from increase of stock, and especially cows and sheep, until your stock acquits your wines, robes, wax and all your **wardrobe**, and that will be in a short time if you hold and act after this treatise as you can see plainly in this way.

Source: *Walter of Henley's Husbandry, together with an Anonymous Husbandry, Seneschaucie, and Robert Grosseteste's Rules*, Edited and translated by Elizabeth Lamond, with an introduction by W. Cunningham. London: Longmans, 1890. Pp. 121–145. The Rules of "Saint Robert" [Rules Seynt Roberd]. Translated by Elizabeth Lamond, FRHS, 1890. Modernized and edited by editor.

AFTERMATH

Bishop Robert's work became one of the most popular texts on the subject of estate management in the Middle Ages, with numerous manuscript versions surviving, as well as early copies of printed versions after the invention of the printing press in 1450. Indeed, it was so popular that the canons of his own cathedral requested a Latin copy (the original was written in French, the language that the English nobility spoke most often) for their own use.

Elite households were very busy places, with many people engaged in different tasks, all overseen not only by estate officials but also by their employers, the lord and lady of the manor or castle. A significant amount, possibly even the majority, of the day-to-day maintenance and oversight of the household was performed by the lady of the household, who wore the symbols of her authority—a key ring known as a "chatelaine"—on her belt.

ASK YOURSELF

1. In what ways does this text encourage you to reconsider the typical presentation of relations between lords and peasants as entirely adversarial?
2. In what ways could this text suggest that the relationship between lords and peasants was profoundly adversarial?
3. Bishop Robert's stated motives for writing the treatise were to encourage noblemen and noblewomen to live within their means and to do this by being efficient managers of their estates. Why might this be an issue for many elites?

TOPICS TO CONSIDER

1. Consider the daily lives of medieval elites in terms of the varieties of work they were expected to accomplish.
2. Compare the daily account records presented in Section 1, Domestic Life and the Medieval Household, and the instructions in Bishop Robert's treatise. Consider how effectively elites were following "Saint Robert's Rules" and how becoming well-trained estate managers might affect their daily accounts.

Further Information

Archer, Rowena A. "'How ladies . . . who live on their manors ought to manage their households and estates': Women as Landholders and Administrators in the Later Middle Ages." In *Women in Medieval English Society*, edited by P. J. P. Goldberg, 149–181. Stroud: Sutton Publishing, 1997.

Mertes, Kate. *The English Noble Household, 1250–1600: Good Governance and Politic Rule.* Oxford: Basil Blackwell, 1988.

12. Educating the Gentry and the Urban Elites

INTRODUCTION

The education of the rural and urban "middle class" differed only slightly from that of the elites in medieval British society. Children of the **gentry** and the urban merchant classes were expected to be literate and were trained for managerial and administrative positions. Girls and women among the middle classes were trained in ways that were not so different from their elite neighbors: in estate and household management, in religious instruction, and in administration. The largest difference between the two social groups was that boys and men of the urban elite were not trained to be warriors and those of the gentry usually were trained to be archers and esquires, although those of the upper levels of the gentry could aspire to be knights.

By the fourteenth century, the training of children of the middle classes was becoming a profoundly literate process, with numerous "conduct manuals" produced, as well as poems and other kinds of literature designed to be taught and memorized. The two texts, "The Boy Standing at the Table" (*Stans puer ad mensam*) and "How the Goodwife Taught Her Daughter" are but two examples.

KEEP IN MIND AS YOU READ

Although both texts are designed to imply that the "speaker" is a parent, it is likely that the poem, "The Boy Standing at the Table," was written by a member of the clergy, perhaps a chaplain or tutor instructing his charges in good table manners, and "How the Goodwife Taught Her Daughter" was definitely written by a male member of the clergy who decided to produce a companion piece to the contemporary text, "How the Goodman Taught His Son."

Document 1: Educating Children

The Boy Standing at the Table

My dear son, first yourself enable
With all your heart to virtuous discipline;
Before your sovereign, standing at the table,
Dispose yourself, after my doctrine,

> *To all nurture thy courage to incline:* to all
> education your will should incline
> *let not your back abide:* stand straight
> *debate:* competition

To all nurture thy courage to incline.
First, let all recklessness in speaking cease,
And keep both hands and fingers still [and] at peace.
Be simple of cheer, do not look aside,
Gaze not about, nor turn your sight over all;
Against the post *let not your back abide,*

. . .

Pick not thy nose, and especially . . .
Before your sovereign do not scratch nor pick at anything.

. . .

Pare clean your nails, and wash your hands also,
Before sitting down to eat, and when you do arise [from the table],
Sit in that place you are assignéd to,

. . .

Grinning and making faces at the table eschew;
Cry not too loud; honestly keep silence.

. . .

With full mouth speak not, lest you make offence.
Drink not with a full mouth because of haste or negligence

. . .

Thy teeth at table pick not with no knife. . . .

. . .

Be well advised, and namely, from a young age,
To drink moderately, both wine and ale.

. . .

In children war is both mirth and now *debate*;
In their quarrel is no great violence;
Now play, now weeping, and seldom in one estate,
To their complaints give never any credénce.
A rod reformeth all their negligence.
In their hearts no rancor does abide.
Who that spares the rod all virtues set aside.

. . .

How the Goodwife Taught Her Daughter

The goodwife taught her daughter many times and often how to be a good woman. For she said, "Daughter come to me: something good now you must hear, if you will prosper."

Daughter, if you will be a wife, look wisely to your work; look lovingly and be good; love God and the Holy Church. Go to church whenever you may—even in the rain, for God might listen best on that day. . . .My dear child. . . .

Gladly give your **tithes** and offerings [to the church], to the poor and sick give your own goods and be generous, for seldom is the house poor where God is the steward: he is proved well whom the poor love, my dear child.

When you sit in church over your [rosary] beads, do not gossip or talk to friends. . . . Be generous of spirit and kind [because] through this your worship increases, my dear child.

If a man courts you and would marry you, do not scorn him no matter his station, but let your friends know [of his interest]. Do not sit near him, lest you should sin . . . my dear child.

The man who weds you before God with a ring, love him and honor him most of any earthly thing. Answer him meekly and not shrewishly, so that you may gentle his mood and be his dear darling. Fair and meek words slay anger, my dear child.

Be fair of speech, glad and mild of mood, true in word and deed and of good conscience. Keep from sin, villainy, and blame; and bear yourself so that no one can consider you shameful. For he who lives a good life has won his reward, my dear child.

Be seemly in your appearance, wise, and cheerful; do not respond to anything you hear. Don't be a giddy girl; don't laugh too loud or yawn too wide, but laugh softly and mildly and don't be too wild, my dear child.

When you walk, do not go too fast, don't move your head and shoulders [when you walk—that is, don't walk provocatively]. Don't talk too much and do not swear, because such manners lead to ill-fame . . . my dear child.

Do not go to town just to gawk; and do not go to the tavern after selling your homespun cloth at the market. For they who haunt taverns from thriftiness descend to want, my dear child.

And if you are in a place where good ale is sold, whether you are serving or being served, drink moderately so that no blame befalls you, for if you become drunk you will be shamed . . . my dear child.

Do not go to wrestling matches or cock-shoots like a strumpet or a giggling girl. Dwell at home and love your work, and so be rich sooner . . . my dear child.

Do not introduce yourself to men on the street or keep them talking, lest your heart be tempted. For not all men who speak fair words are true, my dear child.

Also, do not take gifts [from men] unless you know the reason [for the gift]; for men may with gifts overcome [faithful] women who are as true as steel or stone . . . my dear child.

And govern your house wisely, and do not be too harsh or liberal with your serving maids and men. But look to what most needs doing and set your people at it quickly and soon . . . my dear child.

And if your husband is away, do not let your servants behave badly; watch who does well and who does not; he that does well, reward, but he who does not, punish. . . . my dear child.

And if you are pressed for time and much to do, set to work . . . speedily; they will all do better [if they see you working]. For many hands make light work; and after your labor your reputation will rise, my dear child. . . .

[Be firm, but do not be tyrannical when dealing with servants; keep watch over the keys; pay everyone their fair wages promptly]

And if your neighbor's wife is richly attired, do not mock or be envious. But thank God for what you have from Him, and so you will live a good life . . . my dear child.

On working days act the housewife, but on Sunday clothe yourself well and honor the Holy Day, and God will cherish you . . . my dear child.

When you are a wife, you are also a neighbor, love your neighbors well, as God has commanded . . . and do to them what you would have done to you. If any discord occurs, make it no worse and mend it if you are able, my dear child.

If you are a rich wife, do not be stingy, but welcome your neighbors generously with food, drink, and honest cheer . . . my dear child.

[Do not make your husband poor by overspending. A man may spend only what he has . . . Do not borrow too much or put on ostentatious displays with borrowed money . . .]

And if your children become rebellious, do not curse or scold them; but take a rod and beat them until they cry mercy and admit their guilt. Dear child, through this lesson they will love you more.

And look to your daughters, that none are lovelorn [vulnerable to improper relationships]. Busy yourself in making good marriages and marry them off as soon as they are of age [thirteen]. [For] maidens are fair and amiable, but unstable in love, my dear child.

Now I have taught you, daughter, as my mother taught me; think about this night and day and do not forget. Be moderate as I have taught you, and whatever man weds you will not regret it. It would be better not to have been borne than ignorant of this lesson, my dear child. . . .

The blessing of God may you have, and of his mother, and all angels and archangels and every holy creature! And may you have grace to live rightly and go to the bliss of heaven, where God sits in His might!

Amen.

Source: Rickert, Edith. *The Babees' Book: Medieval Manners for the Young: Done into Modern English from Dr. Furnivall's Texts.* London/New York: Duffield & Co. 1908. Pp. 26–42. Modernized and edited by editor.

AFTERMATH

The popularity of conduct manuals and other pedagogic aids only grew in the later Middle Ages, especially with the invention of the printing press and the development of grammar schools and parish or municipal schools in the early modern period. Conduct manuals were among the most frequently reproduced books of the Middle Ages and form the model for etiquette manuals and conduct books even into the modern period.

ASK YOURSELF

1. What are the most important lessons that medieval middle-class children were expected to learn?
2. In what ways were the lessons to be learned different for boys and girls?
3. Why is there such an emphasis on good table manners and polite behavior?

TOPICS TO CONSIDER

1. Compare the kinds of training children of the middle classes experienced and the education of those of the elite class. In what ways were they similar? What are the differences?
2. In the *History of William Marshal*, the emphasis in William's young years was on courtesy and bravery. This is not emphasized in "The Boy Standing at the Table" although the idea of "courtesy" as a kind of etiquette is implied. Consider how the poem might have been used to instruct a young knight-in-training like William Marshal, whose social status—at least in his youth—was only slightly more elevated than the boy described as serving at the table.

3. Compare "The Rules of Saint Robert" and "How the Goodwife Taught Her Daughter." Consider the ways in which the two texts might be complementary and might be used to complete the training of a young woman destined to be married into a gentry or an elite family. Consider also how the two texts might not be compatible if the girl in question was from an urban elite family.

Further Information

Goldberg, P. J. P. "The Fashioning of Bourgeois Domesticity in Later Medieval England: A Material Culture Perspective." In *Medieval Domesticity: Home, Housing and Household in Medieval England*, edited by Maryanne Kowaleski and P. J. P. Goldberg, 124–144. Cambridge: Cambridge University Press, 2008.

Hanawalt, Barbara A. *Growing Up in Medieval London: The Experience of Childhood in History.* Oxford: Oxford University Press, 1993.

Orme, Nicholas. "Education and Recreation." In *Gentry Culture in Late Medieval England*, edited by Raluca Radulescu and Alison Truelove, 63–83. Manchester: Manchester University Press, 2006.

ECONOMIC LIFE

13. An Anglo-Saxon Marriage Contract

INTRODUCTION

Marriage in the early Middle Ages was not controlled by the church as it would be after the twelfth century. Germanic marriage practices, which were part of the culture of Anglo-Saxon England, included financial arrangements that often required extensive negotiation, especially among elite families. The marriage contract enumerated these arrangements, which included the most important gifts—the "**brideprice**," which was the property that the groom's family was willing to endow upon the bride and her family in exchange for her hand, and the "**morgengab**" or "**morning gift**," the property that the husband granted to his new wife and that she controlled independently if widowed. Although the Anglo-Saxons also included a small "**marriage gift**" or **dowry**—property the bride brought to the marriage—this was usually in the form of movable goods (such as her clothing and household furnishings) and not land or cash.

KEEP IN MIND AS YOU READ

Marriage was not an entirely financial arrangement, although the settlements and contracts of marriage might make it seem to be so. There were many reasons for couples to marry, including families' desire to form alliances and personal affection. Nevertheless, the financial arrangements, especially for the maintenance of the bride, were considered to be very important as a symbol of the partnership and formation of the new family and the preservation of the family in the future.

Document 1: Earl Godwine (1016–1020 CE)

This is the contract that [EARL] GODWINE made with Byrhtric [father of Godwine's second wife], when he [Godwine] wooed his daughter. First, Godwine, in order for her to consider his suit, should give her one pound weight of gold; and he should give her the land at Street and all that belongs with it; and 150 acres at Burwash with thirty oxen, twenty cows, ten horses, and ten serfs. This was agreed at Kingston, before King Cnut, [and witnessed by] Archbishop Lyfing and the monks at Christchurch; Abbot Ælfmær and the monks of St Augustine's; Æthelwine the **shire-reeve**; Sired the Old; Godwine son of Wulfeah; Ælfsige child; Eadmer at Burnham; Godwine son of Wulfstân; and Karl the king's page.

> *Brighting:* Brighton

And when they fetched the maiden from *Brighting*, there went for security, to accompany her, Ælfgar son of Syred, ad Frerth the priest at Folkestone; and from Dover Leofwine, priest, and Wulfsige, priest, and Eadred son of Eadelm, Leofwine son of Wærelm, and Cênwold Rust, Leofwine son of Godwine at Horton, Leofwine the Red, and Godwine son of Eadgifu and Leofsunu his brother. And let whichever of them [Godwine and his wife] live longer succeed to all the possessions, both in the land that I have given them, and in everything. Every good (doughty) man in Kent in Sussex, among the **thanes** and **churls** should be made cognizant of these terms. And there are three copies of this writing: one is at Christchurch, another at St Augustine's, and the third Byrhtric himself has.

Source: *Diplomatarium Anglicum Aevi Saxonici: A Collection of English Charters, from the Reign of King of Aethelberht of Kent to That of William the Conqueror.* Edited by Benjamin Thorpe. London: Macmillan & Co., 1865. Pp. 312–313. Modernized by editor.

AFTERMATH

Throughout the Middle Ages, similar kinds of financial contracts at marriage were made between families who were joining their children—or themselves—in marriage. Nevertheless, the insertion of the church into marriage arrangements, which began to affect the formation and stability of marriage, changed the nature of the institution and the ceremonies and rituals that validated it. At first, the church tried to control marriage by limiting the partners an individual could potentially have by forbidding marriage within seven degrees of kinship. This proved untenable and the number of proscribed "degrees" of kinship was reduced to four at the **Fourth Lateran Council of 1215**. In the twelfth century, the church emphasized the notion of marriage as one of the seven canonical sacraments and proclaimed that valid marriages should include a priest presiding over the ceremony, preferably in front of witnesses and "at the church door." This, too, proved more difficult to accomplish, so ultimately the church proclaimed that the only thing necessary to contract a valid sacramental marriage was the notion of consent of both parties. Nevertheless, families in the British Isles persisted in endowing the married couple with land and material goods at the time of marriage, and regulation of these endowments continued to be adjudicated in the secular courts.

ASK YOURSELF

1. Why might it be important for the prospective bride to be granted significant property at the time of marriage?
2. Anglo-Saxon and other Germanic law emphasized the payment of a "brideprice" and "morning gift" while Roman law emphasized payment of a "dowry" by the bride's family to the groom. Why do you think this is? How might the dynamic between husband and wife change depending on the system?
3. Why would it be important to have a written record of a marriage contract?

TOPICS TO CONSIDER

1. Consider the ways in which traditional marriage systems modeled the "ideal" relationship between husband and wife.

2. Consider the ways in which challenges to traditional marriage systems, such as the church's desire to gain control of marriage customs in the twelfth century, might destabilize marriage partnerships but also might open up opportunities for new kinds of marriage partnerships.
3. Consider the ways in which marriage could enhance political alliances in the early Middle Ages.

Further Information

Helmholz, R. H. "Marriage Contracts in Medieval England." In *To Have and To Hold: Marrying and Its Documentation in Western Christendom, 400–1600*, edited by Philip L. Reynolds and John Witte, Jr., 260–286. Cambridge: Cambridge University Press, 2007.

Reynolds, Philip L. "Dotal Charters in the Frankish Tradition." In *To Have and To Hold: Marrying and Its Documentation in Western Christendom, 400–1600*, edited by Philip L. Reynolds and John Witte, Jr., 114–164. Cambridge: Cambridge University Press, 2007.

14. Early Accounting Methods in the Twelfth Century: The Pipe Rolls

INTRODUCTION

The "Great Roll of the Pipe" was the earliest form of record-keeping in post-conquest England. Named for their shape—tightly wound rolls of parchment (sheepskin) that looked like clay water pipes found in the rudimentary water systems of the twelfth century—the pipe rolls recorded all monies taken in by the royal treasury at a time when it was not fully separated between the royal household and the **Exchequer**, which eventually became the main government office for dealing with national fiscal matters. Even after the two offices became separate, each with its own particular form of records (for the Exchequer, the pipe rolls; for the royal household, the Wardrobe Accounts and Memoranda), the terminology of the pipe rolls remained consistent, referring to the "treasury" and "treasurer" (in Latin, *thesauro* and *thesaurario*) rather than the now commonly used terms "Exchequer" and "Chancellor of the Exchequer."

The cash-based economy of medieval Britain was complex, even if the only coin minted for much of this period was the silver penny, with the halfpenny and the farthing (a quarter penny) being issued for the first time at the end of the thirteenth century, and the first gold coin, the noble, being introduced only in 1344. Even so, all accounting practices presumed the understanding—if not the actual existence of—the "pound sterling" and its division into shillings, and the alternative, the mark, which was two-thirds of a pound.

KEEP IN MIND AS YOU READ

The royal treasury was heavily dependent on revenue accumulated through the mechanisms described in the pipe rolls, including income from royal **demesne**, sheriffs' accounts, and the profits of the law. The importance of keeping track of royal income led to the invention of the pipe rolls, which in turn led to the development of many other instruments of royal administration. This has led historians to characterize the twelfth century in the British Isles as the beginning of a transition "from memory to written record."

Document 1: Great Roll of the Pipe, 10 Richard I (1197–1198)

[Roll No. 44. M 13, **dorse**]

Lancaster.

To Theobald Walter [the Chancellor of England], Nicholas the Butler presents his payment concerning £200 for the **farm** of the **Honor** of Lancaster. In the Treasury, £114 9s 8d.

And in his overage for the previous year, 14s 8d.

And in the lands given to William de Waleines, £10 in Cosho. And to William fitzWalkelin, £9 in Steinesby. And to Nigel de Greseleye, £4 16s in Drakelaw. And to Victor 18s in Wellingover. And to William Marshal, £32 in Cartmel. And to Hugh Janitor, £8 6s 8d in Crokeston for the exchange of his inheritance of Corsham and Culminton. And to Robert Russo, £13 in Newenby.

Robert Archdeacon of Chester owes 40 marks for his **default**.

Anna de Preston presents her payment concerning 4 marks 10d because she *withdrew her appeal*. In treasury 5s 3d. And she owes 49s 8d.

Henry de Rademan presents his payment concerning £11 3s 4d for the pardon of the King. In treasury £7 3s 4d. And he owes £4.

> *withdrew her appeal:* failed to prosecute a plea she introduced into the court of law
> *remit and quitclaim:* remove any claim to

Roger Ralph de St. George presents his payment concerning 40s for gaining his lands of Willingover. In treasury £1.

That same sheriff [i.e. Nicholas] presents his payment concerning the 100s of the remaining **scutage** for the Honor of Lancaster, which was assessed to be redeemed to the King. In treasury 20s. And he owes £4.

Orm Muschet presents his payment concerning half a mark because he withdrew. In treasury £1.

That same sheriff presents his payment concerning £4 for the farm of the woods and pasture of Mellings. Nothing in the treasury. And Roger de Munbegun [pays] £4 for the fine [agreement] he made by writ with the King.

That same sheriff presents his payment of 12d from Benedict Gernet for the farm of a certain house in Lancaster which had belonged to Jordan de Catton. In treasury £1.

Concerning the Second Scutage

The same sheriff presents his payment concerning £9 12s 8d of the scutage of the Honor of Lancaster. In treasury 40s. And he owes £7 12s 8d. The same concerning the same debt. In treasury £7 16s 8d. And he owes £4.

Concerning the Third Scutage

The same sheriff presents his payment concerning £13 16s 8d of the scutage of the aforementioned Honor. In treasury 40s. And he owes £11 16s 8d. . . .

Hugh Putrel owes 5 marks for having his right in a quarter part of two knights' fees in Barton, as is contained in Roll 8.

Henry son of Gilbert presents payment concerning 20s for having the **serjeanty** of Berkshire, as contained in Roll 8. In treasury 11s 2d. And he owes 8s 10d.

Adam de Lancaster presents payment concerning £10 in order to have custody of the lands and heir of Richard son of Waldief, as per the pledge of Benedict Gernet. In treasury £1.

Andrew de Belchamp owes 1 mark for the agreement made between himself and Peter de Wingeham and William de Boseville, to be written in the Great Roll, as it was made in the King's Court and recorded. Namely, that Peter and William *remit and quitclaim* all their right in the inheritance of Robert Basset to Andrew and Eve his wife, for them and their heirs in perpetuity.

Source: *The Lancashire Pipe Rolls of 31 Henry I, A. D. 1130, and of the Reigns of Henry II, A. D. 1155–1189; Richard I, A. D. 1189–1199; and King John, A. D. 1199–1216.* Transcribed and annotated by W. Farber. Liverpool: Henry Young and Sons, 1902. Pp. 100–102. Translated by editor.

AFTERMATH

Although of supreme importance in the twelfth century, the pipe rolls were eventually superseded by other forms of record-keeping as the royal administration grew in sophistication and complexity. By the end of the thirteenth century, a highly efficient system of bookkeeping and preservation of records with multiple departments that maintained elaborate archives had supplanted the pipe rolls. This could be considered the true origin of government and administration and marked the complete separation of the private household of the king and the public "household" of the Crown.

> The Royal Exchequer was the first accounting and treasury department in medieval Europe to be separated from the royal household's "wardrobe." It got its name from the system used to add up the daily tallies of debts paid, profits deposited, and expenses remunerated. The "exchequer" itself was a giant cloth woven in a checkerboard pattern, with different denominations (pounds, shillings, pence, and marks) identified in one direction, and numerical amounts identified in the other direction. Wooden counters were used to keep track of all the numbers being added or subtracted.

ASK YOURSELF

1. Why would royal administrations find it important to begin to maintain records of economic transactions in the twelfth century when it had not been as important before?
2. Why would financial record-keeping precede the maintenance of other kinds of records, such as the records of litigation or of royal letters?
3. What do the pipe rolls tell us about the fiscal relationship between the king and his officials, or between the king and his subjects?

TOPICS TO CONSIDER

1. Consider using the pipe rolls to investigate the use of mercenary soldiers—paid through the scutage dues that were required in lieu of military service—in the armies of King Richard I.
2. Consider the motivations behind individuals paying for the privilege of enrolling agreements in the royal chancery, as evidenced by the pipe rolls.
3. Compare, using different kinds of fiscal records such as the pipe rolls, the kinds of financial transactions that typically took place between the Crown and individuals in the twelfth and thirteenth centuries.

Further Information

Clanchy, M. T. *From Memory to Written Record: England 1066–1307*. 3rd ed. Chichester: Wiley-Blackwell, 2012.

Keefe, Thomas K. "King Henry and the Earls: The Pipe Roll Evidence." *Albion* 13, no. 3 (1981): 191–222.

15. Finances and the Jews of England

INTRODUCTION

William the Conqueror brought the first Jewish communities to England from Normandy after 1066. Jews were restricted from owning land in most European kingdoms and were also often forced into certain kinds of jobs that Christians were not supposed to engage in. One such job was moneylending, which was forbidden officially by the church on the grounds that no one should make money from money. This prohibition, however, made it impossible to conduct business, so Jewish bankers and merchants were welcomed into medieval kingdoms in order to facilitate the flow of capital. Jewish families were international in scope, and their businesses were similarly international. As a result, they could operate as bankers for Christians in need of such services—and Christians were perpetually in need of money to borrow.

In England, by the late twelfth century, Jews were considered to be servants of the king—in other kingdoms they were legally considered to be serfs whose labor was owned by the king—and so all debts owed to the Jews were technically owed to the king. This made it possible for kings to exploit Jewish banking businesses mercilessly. At the same time, kings beginning with KING RICHARD I found it necessary to regulate interactions between Christian borrowers and Jewish lenders, as disputes between the two populations could not be adjudicated in the standard courts of assize or the King's Bench. Hence, a series of statutes were drawn up, known collectively as "The Ordinances of the Jews," in 1194, and a separate office of the treasury, the Exchequer of the Jews, was established. The court was designed to moderate disputes between Jews and Christians over debt. It was very active in the thirteenth century, in the reigns of HENRY III and Edward I, but was disbanded when King Edward expelled the Jews from England in 1290 and banned their return.

KEEP IN MIND AS YOU READ

Because of the intense levels of hostility against Jewish communities throughout Europe by the twelfth century, Jewish families lived under extremely insecure conditions and were often subjected to violence as well as exploitation on the part of the king, the local administration, and local elites. Although the laws and regulations regarding Jewish–Christian interactions (especially financial ones) were seemingly designed to protect both parties, in fact they were easy mechanisms for the king to use to gain revenue and assume control over debts of his vassals.

Document 1: The Ordinances of the Jews, 1194

All the debts, pledges, mortgages, lands, houses, rents, and possessions of the Jews shall be registered. Any Jew who hides any of these shall forfeit his body and the thing concealed to the King, and likewise all his possessions and chattels. It shall not be lawful for the Jew to recover the thing he hid.

> *registrars:* recorders of the agreements

Likewise six or seven places to which they will take all their contracts shall be provided, and two lawyers that are Christians and two lawyers that are Jews, will be appointed, [along with] two legal *registrars*, and before them and the clerks of William of the Church of St. Mary's and William of Chimilli, they will make their contracts.

And charters in the form of **indentures** will be made from the contracts. One part of the indenture shall remain with the Jew, sealed with the seal of him, to whom the money is lent, and the other part shall remain in the common chest: wherein there shall be three locks and keys, whereof the two Christians shall keep one key, and the two Jews another, and the [two] clerks[: one clerk] of William of the Church of St. Mary and [one clerk] of William of Chimilli shall keep the third. And moreover, there shall be three seals to it, and those who keep the seals shall put the seals thereto.

Moreover the clerks of the said William and William shall keep a roll of the transcripts of all the charters, and as the charters shall be altered so let the roll be likewise. . . . From this point forward no contract can be made [between Jews and Christians] or any alteration to the charters [already made] without the presence of [the keepers of the rolls] . . .

Moreover every Jew shall swear on his Roll that he has enrolled all his debts and pledges and rents, and all his goods and his possessions, and that he shall conceal nothing as is aforesaid.

Source: *Chronica Magistri Rogeri de Houdene.* Edited by William Stubbs. Vol. III. Rolls Series. London, 1870. P. 266. Translated in *The Jews of Angevin England: Documents and Records.* Edited and translated by Joseph Jacobs. London, 1893. Pp. 156–159. Modernized and edited by editor.

Alternate translation: *The Annals of Roger de Hoveden.* Translated by Henry T. Riley. Vol. II. London: H. G. Bohn, 1853. Pp. 338–339.

Document 2: Extracts from the Court of the Exchequer of the Jews, Easter Term, 1244

Martin, prior of Bentley, causes Moses Crespin and his brother Isaac to be summoned to the court to answer him concerning his plea that Moses and Isaac unlawfully **distrained** him for a debt that Martin claims not to owe them; this distraint damaged him to the sum of ten **marks**. The Jews come and defend the distraint as being lawful, and they produce two **chirographs**. The first was made between the Prior of Bentley and Moses, son of Jacob Crespin on 8 December 1239, in which the Prior promises to repay his debt of 2 ½ marks on Michaelmas, 24 Henry III. The second, dated 8 February 1241, was between the Prior and Isaac Crespin, in which the Prior acknowledges a debt of 60 shilling, 10s of which will be paid on 1 November 1242 and the remaining 50s at Easter 1243.

The Prior answers that he is not required to acknowledge the 60s debt because he never received a loan from Isaac and claims he never received his copy of the chirograph, and he petitions the maintainers of the London Chirograph-Chest. Isaac also makes a petition and so the Chest is to be searched for the potentially missing chirograph.

Concerning the debt of 2 ½ marks, the Prior says that he was distrained unlawfully, because the two parties agreed to a date of payment in a month after Easter [that is, about two months after the court session]. Moses denies that any such agreement had been made, except the one concerning the 60s debt. The parties are summoned to court for the session heard a month after Easter, in order to hear the judgment; in the meantime the Prior's goods are **replevied**.

Afterwards [before the court date], the two parties make an agreement, with the approval of the Justices, and the Prior gives half a mark for the agreement.

Robert Cristfinesse complains that he had gone to the house of Diaia, son of Soleil, on the Sunday before the celebration of the Exaltation of the Holy Cross, in order to borrow 2s, presenting a bowl of mazer-wood with a silver foot and two silver buckles [as collateral for the loan, known as **gages**], and that Bona, wife of Diaia, at the command of her husband, gave Robert 3s in **clipped coin** in exchange for the bowl and buckles. After he had left Diaia's house, he encountered Robert, bailiff of Chichester, who inquired about the clipped coins; Robert Cristfinesse told him that he had borrowed them from the Jewess Bona.

Diaia answered for himself and his wife that he never gave Robert those coins, or lent him any coins for the gages [the bowl and buckles], and that he had not clipped the coins. He and Robert both put themselves [in the hands of the jury] Henry Ketelbern, Geoffrey of West Street, and Ralph of La Sende. Diaia goes on to say that Jacob of Coutances, a Jew, by malicious contrivance, clipped the coins, and he pays the king half a mark for the verdict of the jury. The jurors say that they fully believe that Robert borrowed the coins from Bona, but not in the presence of Diaia, who was not in town at the time. They also say that Robert entered his suit by the advice of Jacob of Coutances.

Because Jacob is suspected of coin clipping, he must present pledges, if anyone has anything to say against him; they are Jacob son of Sluria, Deulecresse son of Genta, Manasser of Bedford, and Aaron of Colchester.

Afterwards, Diaia made an agreement [a **fine**] with Robert and paid 10s for the gages and damages; he must pay on the day after the feast of the Ascension.

Source: *Select Pleas, Starrs, and Other Records from the Rolls of the Exchequer of the Jews A. D. 1220–1284.* Edited and translated by J. M. Rigg. Selden Society, v. 15. London: Bernard Quaritch, 1902. Pp. 7–9.

AFTERMATH

The entire conflicted relationship between Jews and Christians in the British Isles culminated in the Edict of Expulsion of 1290. The edict related specifically to England and Wales; Jews might have fled to Scotland, which had no history of Jewish settlement, and to Ireland, which does not seem to have enforced the expulsion and where small Jewish settlements seem to have been established in areas where English rule was nonexistent. One reason why Jews were expelled from England, as well as from France, in the years around 1300 is that the church's attitude about banking and moneylending had changed.

In the wake of the rapid rise of merchant activity and the development of banking and investment instruments in Italy, Spain, and Portugal, the church changed its stance on banking, as well as its definition of "usury," and these changes were first expressed in the Fourth Lateran Council of 1215. By the middle of the thirteenth century, Italian bankers—called in England the "merchants of Lucca"—began to establish branches in major cities and also became the preferred lenders to the crowned heads of Europe, English kings included. With Jewish bankers no longer so vitally necessary to the financial support of the Crown and the nobility, it became possible to justify their exploitation and eventual expulsion on religious grounds without adversely affecting the fisc. As a result, Jews had no supporters willing to advocate for them. And they were not permitted by law to return until the reign of the Lord Protector Oliver Cromwell in 1656.

ASK YOURSELF

1. In what ways did the Jewish community make the best of a difficult situation and establish a viable series of businesses even as they were restricted in their independence?
2. Was the king being genuine in establishing laws that regulated relations between Christian and Jews, or was this simply another cynical ploy for further exploitation?
3. Do you think that Jews were more successful than Christians in protecting their business interests or less successful when they went to court? Do the sources you have read suggest that they were fundamentally disadvantaged, or do they suggest a more egalitarian stance in the court?

TOPICS TO CONSIDER

1. Consider the conflicted relationship between Christians and Jews and how this could have been exacerbated by the financial relationships in which they engaged.
2. Compare the accusations of "blood libel" as demonstrated in the "Life" of St. William of Norwich (in Section 4, Religious Life and Religious Conflict) and the documents regulating financial arrangements between Christians and Jews. In what ways would the mistrust of the Christian population be heightened by stories of ritual murder, and how would this affect their business relationships?
3. Consider Bishop Robert Grosseteste's admonition (in Section 2, Education and Professional Training) that the nobility should learn to manage their estates so that they would not have to rely on loans to get by in light of these financial documents. What does this juxtaposition suggest as to the financial efficiency of the nobility?

Further Information

Brand, Paul. "The Jewish Community of England in the Records of English Royal Government." In *Jews in Medieval Britain: Historical, Literary and Archaeological Perspectives*. Edited by Patricia Skinner, 73–84. Woodbridge: Boydell Press, 2003.

Elman, P. "The Economic Causes of the Expulsion of the Jews in 1290." *The Economic History Review* 7, no. 2 (1937): 145–154.

Stacey, Robert C. "The Jews under Henry III." In *Jews in Medieval Britain: Historical, Literary and Archaeological Perspectives*. Edited by Patricia Skinner, 41–54. Woodbridge: Boydell Press, 2003.

16. Doing Business and Regulating Trade in the City of London

INTRODUCTION

The City of London was an independent municipality, technically free from the intervention of the royal administration, but it nonetheless operated its own administrative, judicial, and fiscal institutions in ways that paralleled those systems throughout the realm—including Ireland and Wales. In particular, the operation of businesses in London required extensive regulation, including overseeing contracts between masters and apprentices, adjudicating disputes, and overseeing financial transactions. One very common system was known as "the **assize** of bread and ale." This was designed to regulate both quality and price of two fundamental foodstuffs of medieval Britain. Regulated locally, in urban as well as in rural milieus, the assize oversaw the production and sale of bread and ale, established standard weights for loaves and vessels in which ale was sold, and regulated prices for both commodities. This was one of the most important jurisdictional activities in which local governments engaged and they took it very seriously.

The law courts in the City of London did not differ significantly from courts held at Westminster before the royal justices, or courts held in other municipalities in England, Wales, and Ireland (we do not have extant sources from Scottish cities, except for Aberdeen, which seems to have operated very similar institutions). One of the main duties of local government was regulation of the populace, either with the assistance of the Crown, in the form of the sheriff and his local officials, or independently, depending on the jurisdiction of the region. In London, the Guildhall, headed by the Lord Mayor, was the official regulatory body, and the sheriffs and other officials were appointed by it, not by the king. In areas outside the City (the square mile of London surrounded by walls and gates), royal jurisdiction prevailed. When conflicts arose between residents within and outside the city, the location of the disturbance determined the jurisdiction of the case. Most of the cases found in the records of the City of London concern financial disputes.

KEEP IN MIND AS YOU READ

Courts of law in the medieval British Isles were concerned not only with specifically criminal or disruptive behavior, but also—and on a very large scale—with regulating commercial and economic transactions. As a result, the kinds of information the reader can derive from records of courts of law provide vital information on both the ways in which such regulations were managed and also the ways in which individuals tried to bypass or overcome them. This offers the reader another dimension of understanding of the economics of the medieval world.

Document 1: The Assizes of Bread, Ale, and Foodstuffs, London, 5–6 Edward I (1277–1278)

These are the Assizes of the City of London read by the Mayor and reputable men, the second year of the Mayoralty of Gregory [de Rokesle], Robert de Arraz and Ralph le Fevere being Sheriffs and the third year of the same Mayoralty, Walter le Cornewaleys and John, son of John Adrian, Sheriffs.

First, that the peace of the lord the King be well kept between Christians.

Also that two loaves be made for 1*d.* and four loaves for 1*d.*, and that none be coated with bran or made of bran [or inferior wheat or grain].

Also that no baker sell his bread before his oven, but in the market of the lord the King, and if he be found selling it in his own house he shall be **in mercy** to the Sheriff; nor shall any one buy such bread, under pain of losing the said bread if it be found; and that no one make bread beyond the assize.

Also every baker shall have his seal on his bread, both brown bread and white, that it may the better be known whose the bread is.

. . .

tourte bread: round loaf made of sour rye
brewster: a female brewer of ale
pottle: half gallon
corn: a generic term for grain of any kind

Also that no baker of white bread make *tourte bread* nor maker of tourte bread make white bread, for sale under the same penalty, nor any baker buy corn to sell again.

A gallon of [best] ale [is to be sold] for three **farthings** and [second-best ale] for one penny and no dearer.

And that no *brewster* henceforth sell except by true measures, viz., the gallon, the *pottle*, and the quart. And that they be marked with the seal of the Alderman, and that the tun be of 150 gallons and sealed by the Alderman.

. . .

Also that no retail dealer of *corn*, fish, poultry, or victuals shall buy victuals before the hour of **Prime**, nor before the reputable men of the City have bought, under penalty of forfeiting the goods bought.

Also that no cart serving the City by bringing water, wood, stones, &c., be shod with iron [i.e. use iron-clad wheels]

. . .

Also that no **regratress** go beyond London Bridge to buy bread and to carry it into the City, because the bakers of Southwark are not of the Justice of the City nor are [their goods] allowed to be brought back from outside the City.

. . .

And that no foreign butcher sell meat in the City except in the manner accustomed, nor cause meat to be harbored or permit it to be again carried out of the City; nor buy meat from the Jews to sell again to Christians, or meat slaughtered for Jews and by them rejected.

. . .

And that a porter of corn shall not sell nor measure corn, nor presume to enter a church-yard, house, or ship to remove corn, nor lay his hand upon corn, until he be called by those who have bought the corn.

Also that no cartman shall for the future enter the City with wood or charcoal for sale, but shall remain outside the gate at Smithfield or elsewhere as provided, except only at Cornhill, under forfeiture.

. . .

Also that no market be held on London Bridge, nor elsewhere except in places appointed.

Also that no one of the City go to Southwark to buy corn, cattle, or other merchandise there, so as to create a market there, under penalty of forfeiture of the thing bought.

. . .

Also that no one shall carry on merchandise in the City, nor make bread nor ale for sale, unless he be willing to be of the Justice of the City.

. . .

Also vendors of fish shall not throw their water into the highway, but cause it to be carried to the Thames.

Source: *Calendar of Letter-Books of the City of London*: A, 1275–1298. Edited by Reginald R. Sharpe. London, 1899. Pp. 215–219.

Document 2: The Assize of Bread and Ale in London, November 1, 1377

Wednesday after the Feast of All Saints [1 Nov.], 11 Edward III. [A.D. 1337], came all the brewers and brewsters of the City and suburbs before Henry Darcy, the Mayor, John de Grantham, Gregory de Nortone, John Hamond, Andrew Aubrey, Ralph de Uptone, Simon Fraunceys, Nicholas Crane [Aldermen], and others of the Commonalty, and it was forbidden them by the said Mayor and Aldermen to sell by any other measure than the gallon, the pottle, and quart, or by any measure not sealed with the seal of the Alderman of the Ward they were further forbidden to sell a gallon of the best ale for more than $1\frac{1}{2}d.$, a gallon of medium ale for more than $1d.$, and of the cheaper ale for more than $\frac{3}{4}d.$, the penalty for the first conviction being imprisonment for three days and a fine of $4d.$; for the second offence, imprisonment for six days and a fine of half a mark; and for the third, abjuration of the City.

Source: *Calendar of Letter-Books of the City of London*: F, 1337–1352. Edited by Reginald R. Sharpe. London, 1904. P. 189.

Document 3: Extracts from Pleas before the Mayor and Aldermen of London

1276

The Ward of Anketin d'Auverne within the Gate

On Wednesday the Feast of St. Vincent [22 January 1276], . . . it was agreed between Walter de la Ford, *corder*, and Richard Maunsel, formerly his apprentice, that the said Walter released the said Richard from his term [of service] for the sum of 17 marks, whereof 1 mark is paid in hand and the rest is to be paid by installments of 2 marks, commencing at Easter.

> *corder:* someone who twists cord for making shoes

On Monday the **octave of St. Hillary** [13 Jan.], 4 Edward I [1276], John Arnold, "garlic-monger," came [into court] and made himself indebted to Henry the Seal-maker (*Sigillarius*) for the sum of 40*s*. John is to repay Henry in two payments: 20*s*. at Shrove Tuesday (*Carniprivium*) and 20*s*. at Michaelmas. Because of this pledge, Henry has granted and released William Elys, his apprentice, to the aforesaid John [in exchange] for the above sum . . .

1300

Peter de Monmouth was **attached** to answer William Delisle's plea that Peter render him an account for the time that the said Peter was receiver of [William's] moneys in London. William complains that Peter was his apprentice and had in his custody goods and chattels of the said William to the value of £200, [which he held] from Easter, 27 Edward I [1299] until the following Christmas; the said Peter had refused to render account of the goods and chattels and William claims he has incurred a loss to the amount of 100 marks.

Peter came to court and argued his defense. He acknowledged freely that he was William's apprentice and that he had certain goods and chattels of the said William in his custody, but he says he already rendered a full account to William. . . . William says that no account had been rendered, and this he is prepared to prove in any way the Court desires. And Peter says, as before, that he had rendered an account. However, when he was asked if he had any evidence of having rendered his account, he says he has not, but he says it was sufficiently known to all of his craft if he had dared put himself upon them. Being asked if he could find security for rendering an account, he says that he is unwilling to render another account. And the aforesaid William demands judgment, etc. And because the said Peter refused to render an account of what he had here acknowledged he had received, and had produced no proof that he had already rendered an account, but refused to produce the evidence demanded by the said William and to find security for his rendering a reasonable account, it is adjudged by the Mayor and Aldermen that he be committed to prison, etc.

1335

On Thursday before the Feast of Pentecost [4 June], 9 Edward III [1335], Alice de Warlee, wife of John Ingelard and widow of Philip de Graschurch, and Isabella, daughter of the said Philip, came before [the Mayor and his Court] and requested that a sum of 10½ marks, which was bequeathed to the said Isabella by her father, and is now in the custody of the said Alice, might be used to pay for Isabella's maintenance and for teaching her a trade as an apprentice. The petition is granted.

1346

Deed whereby Margery, widow of John Deumars, binds her daughter Hawysia as an apprentice to Richard de Herpesfeld, corder, for a term of fifteen years from Easter, 20 Edward III [1346].

Agreed by Richard Lacer, Mayor, and Edmund de Hemenhale and John de Gloucestre, Sheriffs. Witnesses: John de la Rokele, Bartholomew Deumars, Thomas de Ispania, John Brutyn, Richard de Wycoumbe, and others [not named]. Dated Easter Sunday [16 April], the above year.

Acknowledged before Thomas de Maryns, the Chamberlain, on Saturday before the Feast of St. Margaret [20 July].

1351

Deed of covenant is entered into, between Thomas Levelyf, executor of John de Totenhale, late **fripperer** and John Robynet, fripperer, concerning the placing of John, son of the aforesaid John de Totenhale, as an apprentice with the said John Robynet for a term of twelve years.

Agreed to by Richard de Kyslyngbury, Mayor; John Nott and William de Wyrcestre, Sheriffs. Witnesses: Ralph de Cauntebregge, Richard de Claverynge, Hugh de la March, and others [not named]. Dated 12 July, 25 Edward III [1351].

Sureties for the payment of a sum of £8 12*s*. 9*d*. to the apprentice at the end of his term are Walter le Forester and Richard de Claverynge, skinners, and William Laurence, fishmonger.

Deed of covenant is entered into between the above Thomas Levelyf and Hugh de la Marche, fripperer, concerning the placing of John, the younger son of the above John de Totenhale, as apprentice with the said Hugh for a like term. Witnesses: Ralph de Cauntebrugge, Richard de Claverynge, William Credil, and others [not named]. Dated 15 July, 25 Edward III. [1351].

Sureties for similar payment as above are William Lawrence, fishmonger, and Thomas atte Noket, **draper.**

Sources: *Calendar of Letter-Books of the City of London*: A, 1275–1298. Edited by Reginald R. Sharpe. London, 1899. Pp. 226–227; *Calendar of Letter-Books of the City of London*: C, 1291–1309. Edited by Reginald R. Sharpe. London, 1901. Pp. 184–185; *Calendar of Letter-Books of the City of London*: E, 1314–1337. Edited by Reginald R. Sharpe. London, 1903. P. 200; *Calendar of Letter-Books of the City of London*: F, 1337–1352. Edited by Reginald R. Sharpe. London, 1904. Pp. 142, 234.

AFTERMATH

The city of London was one of the most vibrant urban centers in medieval Europe and one reason for its success was the effectiveness of the Guildhall as administrator of the city. Even so, the city experienced high levels of disorder and stress, which was expressed as time went on by conflict between masters and apprentices during the Great Rising of 1381 (also known inaccurately as the English Peasants' Revolt) as well as altercations between the city and its adjoining municipalities of Westminster and Southwark. London was also vulnerable as a financial and commercial center during times of war, especially when King Edward I went to war with France in the 1290s and during the Hundred Years' War (1330–1453) because of restraints on trade and the deporting of foreign merchants from the city. Nevertheless, the kinds of interactions taking place in the sources were the daily business of the mayor's administration and his court, and they only expanded in number and complexity as time went on. London remained the model for other British cities—

including Dublin in Ireland and Edinburgh in Scotland—in managing their economic systems and institutions.

ASK YOURSELF

1. Why would it be so important to regulate the production of bread and ale?
2. Why would standardizing of weights and measures be considered essential in maintaining effective governance of the medieval economy?
3. What kinds of relationships between masters and apprentices are demonstrated in these sources? What conflicts could arise between them? How could families protect their children who had been taken on as apprentices?

TOPICS TO CONSIDER

1. Consider the fact that the usual wage for an unskilled laborer was about a penny a day—in the fourteenth century, that rose to two to three pennies a day—but that the transactions demonstrated in these sources suggest that far larger sums were being exchanged by individuals. What does this say about the value of apprenticeship to young people?
2. Consider the kinds of jobs mentioned in these sources. Many of them are gender-specific; for instance, the term "brewster" was used only for women who brewed ale and "regrators" or "regratesses" were also female-only jobs. This suggests that gender significantly affected the kinds of jobs open to different people as well as their earning potential.

Further Information

Bennett, Judith. *Ale, Beer, and Brewsters in Medieval England: Women's Work in a Changing World, 1300–1600.* Oxford: Oxford University Press, 1999.

Davis, James. "Baking for the Common Good: A Reassessment of the Assize of Bread in Medieval England." *The Economic History Review* 57, no. 3 (2004): 465–502.

Thrupp, Sylvia. *The Merchant Class of Medieval London, 1300–1500.* Ann Arbor: University of Michigan Press, 1948.

RELIGIOUS LIFE AND RELIGIOUS CONFLICT

17. Tithing in Early Medieval Ireland (ca. 750)

INTRODUCTION

All Christians were expected to give a "tithe" amounting to 10 percent of their income to the church every year. In economies that were not based on capital, these tithes took the form of goods or services. Early medieval Ireland was one such economy. Indeed, the "monetary" value of items was based on a mode of exchange that was somewhat unusual in comparison to the use of the silver penny in England: the standard of wealth in Ireland was linked to the number of cows a kinship unit owned. Therefore, the tithe was in the form of cattle, or other agricultural products.

In addition to the tithe, another traditional grant to the church was known as "first fruits": the first product of the harvest was donated to the church, for the use of the local priest and parish church or abbot and monastery—in early medieval Ireland, this was often one and the same person and institution.

KEEP IN MIND AS YOU READ

Early medieval Ireland was a very rural society with no urban centers until after the Viking invasions of the ninth century. Land was owned by entire kin groups, rather than by individuals, and the economy was based heavily on pastoral activities: the raising of cattle and sheep. The financial demands of the church on the Christian population could be quite burdensome, which is one reason why the canons might have been written down: to enforce the requirements of the church.

Document 1: The Irish Canons: Collection of the Tithe and First Fruits

1. The jurists say that tithes of cattle should be offered once [in a person's life]. . . . But others of the true faith affirm that we should give tithes of living and mortal things to God every year, since every year we enjoy His gifts.

2. Also, [from] all fruits of the soil a tithe ought to be offered once a year to the Lord, for as it is said: "Whatever has been once consecrated to God, will be most holy in the sight of the Lord." For the tithe should not be offered repeatedly from those things, as the learned

COLUMBANUS has taught us. But of the fruits of the soil a tenth part ought to be offered every year, because they are produced every year.

3. Also, tithes are from all living things. So the first fruits of everything, and the animal that is born first in the year should be given. For the first born of animals are like first fruits; and the first born of men and of animals may be offered. [the eldest children should be consecrated to the church]

4. Also, concerning tithes in herds and first fruits. First born are those that are born before any others are born in that year. It should be known how great is the weight of the first fruits, *i.e.*, nine or twelve measures. Hence, the measure of the offering should be sufficient material for nine or twelve loaves. But of vegetables it should be as much as can be carried in the hand. It ought to be paid at the beginning of the summer, just as it was offered once a year to the priests of Jerusalem. But in the New Testament each would offer it to the monastery to which he belongs. And toward this would be especially charitable; of the first-born let males, never females, be offered.

5. Also, if any have less substance than the tithe [own less in value than the standard offering] they shall not pay the tithe.

6. Also, in order that all might find it convenient to offer tithes in some way to God, if they have only one cow or ox, let them divide the price of the cow into ten parts and give a tenth part to God.

Source: Migne, J. P., ed. *Patrologiae Cursus Completus*, Vol. XCVI. Paris, 1862. Pp. 1319–1320. Reprinted in Roy C. Cave and Herbert H. Coulson, eds. *A Source Book for Medieval Economic History.* Milwaukee: Bruce Publishing Co., 1936; Reprint ed., New York: Biblo & Tannen, 1965. Pp. 378–379. The text has been modernized by Prof. Jerome S. Arkenberg, California State University, Fullerton. Available through the Internet Medieval Sourcebook, http://www.fordham.edu/Halsall/source/750Eiretith.asp

AFTERMATH

The church's income is derived largely from tithes and fees for services such as masses for the dead, the blessing of marriages, and the performance of sacraments such as baptism and last rites (extreme unction). In Ireland, these profits remained very much localized, especially as the monastic and episcopal structures were often intertwined. After the conquest of Ireland by King Henry II in 1173, the Irish church was reorganized along more conventionally orthodox lines, with a diocesan structure based on that of England and Wales and a separation of monastic houses from local parish work. This radically changed the financial relationship between the native Irish people and the church, as the Irish were subject, after the conquest, to the kinds of payments owed by English people, such as Peter's Pence and the fees due for a far more sophisticated and expanded administrative structure.

ASK YOURSELF

1. Even though there is the stipulation that those who are too poor to be able to pay the tithe should not have to, could the payment of the tithes, especially the "first fruits," be perceived as burdensome to the populace in Ireland? What effects could the reduction of family income by 10 percent have on the family?

2. Why was it considered more honorable to give male animals rather than female animals as part of the tithe? Wouldn't female cows and sheep be more useful, in that they could provide milk and give birth to young?
3. What did the church do with all of the income it received as tithes?

TOPICS TO CONSIDER

1. Consider how popular reaction to the tithing requirements could change depending on the level of prosperity or poverty in a given group.
2. Consider how tithing would create a level of wealth in the church that could not be matched by the secular leaders in early medieval Ireland. How would the political and social dynamics be influenced by a wealthy institution operating in the midst of a relatively impoverished region?

Further Information

Charles-Edwards, T. M. *Early Christian Ireland.* Cambridge: Cambridge University Press, 2000.

Hughes, Kathleen. "The Church in Irish Society, 400–800." In *A New History of Ireland, volume 1: Prehistoric and Early Ireland,* edited by Dáibhí Ó Cróinín, 301–330. Oxford: Oxford University Press, 2005.

18. Monastic Grant of King Cnut (before 1035)

INTRODUCTION

CNUT (r. 1017–1035), the king of Denmark and Norway who conquered England after killing King Ethelred II in 1017 and marrying his widow, QUEEN EMMA OF NORMANDY, technically converted to Christianity upon his marriage (he was really a part-time Christian because he did not practice the religion outside England), and he and Queen Emma became enthusiastic patrons of the church. Cnut also was a very effective administrator, adopting many of the administrative systems of the kingdom of Wessex for use in other parts of his collection of kingdoms.

The "Old Monastery" of Winchester was reputed to have been founded during the Roman occupation of Britain, thus predating the Saxon conquests. In the early Middle Ages, it formed part of the complex of Winchester Cathedral. It received a significant level of patronage from the royal house of Wessex and several prominent kings and queens were buried there, including, in 1118, Queen Matilda, the wife of King Henry I.

KEEP IN MIND AS YOU READ

Charters, as documents that operated both as contracts and as letters, did not have a standard formalized style in the early decades of their development. As a result, one charter could be quite different from another written at the same time. Not all charters, for example, contained a "curse clause" such as the one included in this document. Indeed, such curse clauses disappeared from most charter formats by the thirteenth century.

Document 1: Charter of King Cnut to the Old Monastery of Winchester

I, Cnut, king through God's grace of all England and of all the Danes, make known to my bishops and my earls and all of my thanes, both Danish and English, what I grant to the Old Monastery in Winchester, to the praise of God, and St Peter and St Paul, and of the saints that there within rest. That is, I command that that monastery be free of all secular services, except that which is common to all the folk; that is: military service—either on board ships

> *hâmsocn:* breaking and entering/burglary
> *forestalls:* preventing a market from taking place
> *mundbræcs:* assaults—literally "man-breaking"

or as foot soldiers—and building bridges, and building walls, and whatever may be the common need of all people. Thus with regard to the monastery, [the services] remain as they were in the days of the kings who were before us. Now I here declare, in this writing, what I am adding [to the grant] I previously gave, for the redemption of my soul and those of all my predecessors and successors. That is, [I grant the income from charges of] *hâmsocn,* and *forestalls,* and *mundbræcs,* and every penalty, small and great, over all the men who have to obey the abbot who has [received the] charge of that monastery from the hand of God. I now grant these liberties, for the honor of my Lord, who has given men all the good which has in this world awaited me, and of the blessed St Peter, who has the power in heaven and on earth to bind and to loosen the fast knots of nefarious sins. If therefore anyone, audaciously, or at the devil's instigation, will [try to] break [or invade] this liberty, or dare to inhibit this settlement, may he be accursed with all the curses that are written in all the holy books, and may he be severed from the communion of our Lord and all his saints; and may he be bound, while he lives in this life, with the same bonds that God Almighty through himself has delivered to his holy apostles, Peter and Paul; and, after his accursed departure hence, may he lie forever in the groundless pit of hell, and burn in the eternal fire, with the devil and with the accursed spirits that dwell with him forever without end; unless, ere his departure hence [before he dies], he make amends.

Source: *Diplomatarium Anglicum Aevi Saxonici: A Collection of English Charters, from the Reign of King of Aethelberht of Kent to That of William the Conqueror.* Edited by Benjamin Thorpe. London: Macmillan & Co., 1865. Pp. 333–334. Modernized by editor.

AFTERMATH

King Cnut was able to secure the support of the clergy in part because of his generosity to the church in Anglo-Saxon England. Nevertheless, even though his reign coincided with an era of significant reform and renewal in the Roman church, the reforms do not appear to have been considered in England until the reign of Edward the Confessor and, more energetically, after the Norman Conquest. As a result, English kings retained far more power over the appointment of bishops and abbots than their continental peers; this is something Cnut and his wife Queen Emma exploited in rewarding their allies.

ASK YOURSELF

1. What benefits would a layperson—even a king—gain by donating land or liberties to the church?
2. In what ways does the charter express a religious perspective for King Cnut and Queen Emma?
3. Why would Anglo-Saxon people consider curse clauses important or necessary in creating charters?

TOPICS TO CONSIDER

1. Think about the ways in which a nominally Christian king like Cnut could make use of his alliance with the church in England while retaining aspects of pagan belief in his other realms.

2. Consider the motivations of churchmen in soliciting grants from laypeople: what benefits could the church derive from such grants?

Further Information

Blair, John. *The Church in Anglo-Saxon Society.* Oxford: Oxford University Press, 2005.

Smith, Mary Frances, Robin Fleming, and Patricia Halpin. "Court and Piety in Late Anglo-Saxon England." *The Catholic Historical Review* 87, no. 4 (2001): 569–602.

19. Lay Patronage: Founding Monastic Houses (1204)

INTRODUCTION

The founding of monasteries and nunneries was one of the most common and most visible expressions of piety among the elites of medieval Europe. Such foundations, and the support of new monastic orders as they grew in popularity, symbolized both Christian notions of charity and secular notions of power and authority. Founding monasteries was a very expensive business that benefited not only the donor's soul but also the souls of all his or her family members and provided significant benefits to local communities. Founding a monastic house also meant that the patron or donor dominated the political and economic landscape in a particular region and felt comfortable about giving up a substantial portion of that power in order to attain the prestige inherent in monastic patronage.

The Cistercians were one of the most wealthy and influential monastic orders of the Middle Ages. Founded in 1098 in the town of Cîteaux (hence the name "Cistercian" after the first monastic house) by a group of reforming Benedictine monks under the leadership of Abbot Robert of Molesme, the Cistercians were not subject to the discipline of the local bishop, and were answerable only to the pope and the General Chapter of the Cistercian Order. ST. BERNARD OF CLAIRVAUX was one of the early leaders of the movement. Lay elites founded dozens of Cistercian houses throughout Europe, especially in areas that were considered "wilderness" or lay outside the usual parish/village/town/urban boundaries.

The founding of the abbey of Duiske in 1204, also known as Graiguenamanagh (in Irish, the Grange of the Monks), by Earl William Marshal and his wife, Countess Isabella de Clare, on land in Ireland which Isabella had inherited from her mother, Aiofe daughter of Diarmid Mac Murchada, former king of Leinster, represents only one of many acts of religious patronage effected by the couple. It was also designed to provide a foothold of Anglo-Norman Cistercian authority in an area of Ireland that was dominated by houses founded by Irish princes and chiefs, among them the Cistercian abbeys of Mellifont and Jerpoint.

KEEP IN MIND AS YOU READ

This charter of foundation is both typical of Cistercian foundation charters, in that it directs that the abbey should be independent of local control and exempt from local obligations, customs, and dues, and unique to Irish foundations, in that the obligations mentioned form a clear hybrid of custom between Irish, Norse/Danish, and Anglo-Norman practices.

Document 1: Foundation Charter of the Cistercian Abbey of Duiske [Graiguenamanagh], 1204

Charter of Foundation, by William Marshal, earl of Pembroke, of the monastery of St. Saviour, in honour of God and of the Blessed Virgin Mary, for Cistercian monks and Duiske:

Granting them, for the good of his soul and that of his wife Isabella, [and others] the land of Duiske, eleven **carucates** at Annamult, ten carucates held by Stephen de Valle near Kilkenny, a **burgage** in Kilkenny, one in Wexford, and one in the Island; and confirming to the abbey all that it may hereafter acquire by donation or purchase. All the foregoing [are] to be held with the churches and chapels and all liberties and free customs, . . . with freedom in land and water. The monks [are to be] exempt, themselves, their men and servants, from **geld**, Danegeld, fines, payment of cows for heads of outlaws, and various specified exactions, aids and contributions.

The Abbey and its tenants [are] not to be subject to forest regulations, and the monks are to have all forfeitures of their own men, with jurisdiction of life and limb to be retained by the Founder [William Marshal] and his heirs, although throughout all the forests in the region they are to have free pasture for their hogs, and materials for building and firing.

Those who molest or aggrieve the monks to incur a fine of 10 marks, and the malediction of God and the Founder.

Witnesses: Lord Albinus, bishop of Ferns, and Hugh [de Rous] bishop of Ossory, John Marshal, John de Erley, William de Londres, Ralph de Bendeville, Milo son of the bishop, Philip Prendergast, Thomas fitzAnthony, Walter Procell, William de St Léger, Thomas de Dummer, Maurice de Londres, Andrew Avenel, William de Cantington, John de Penriz, Eustace de Bertrimont, Terry de Niver, Thomas Russel, and many others.

Source: *Proceedings of the Royal Irish Academy: The Charters of the Abbey of Duiske.* Vol. XXXV, Sect C, No. 1. Edited by Constance Mary Butler and John Henry Bernard. Dublin, 1918. Pp. 18–19. Translated by editor.

AFTERMATH

The foundation of Duiske, which was quite close to a number of Irish-founded Cistercian houses, was controversial on the island and caused a great deal of conflict between it and the "native" houses in central Ireland, especially Mellifont, Baltinglass, Killenny, and Jerpoint. That Duiske was the wealthiest of all of the mid-Ireland Cistercian houses was yet another sore point for the Irish monks, who were not permitted to join houses that had been founded by Anglo-Norman donors. When Killenny, an Irish house that struggled with its economic viability, was joined to Duiske because of its impoverishment, Jerpoint protested, and conducted a 70-year suit against Duiske before the General Chapter. Other conflicts between Cistercian houses in the thirteenth century are outlined in the next reading.

ASK YOURSELF

1. Why would a nobleman found a monastery?
2. Why would donors to monasteries prefer Cistercians over other monastic orders?
3. How would the founding of a monastery change the local culture in the surrounding area?

TOPICS TO CONSIDER

1. Compare the grant made by King Cnut and that made by William Marshal.
2. Consider the impact of Cistercian monasticism in Ireland, where native monastic systems were very different.

Further Information

Flanagan, Marie Therese. "Saint Malachy and the Introduction of Cistercian Monasticism to the Irish Church: Some Suggestive Evidence from Newry Abbey." *Journal of the Armagh Diocesan Historical Society* 22, no. 2 (2009): 8–24.

Watt, John. *The Church in Medieval Ireland*, 2nd ed. Dublin: University College Press, 1998.

20. Conflict in Medieval Ireland: The Cistercians in the Thirteenth Century

INTRODUCTION

The establishment of Cistercian monastic houses, especially in remote parts of the British Isles, was wildly popular in the late twelfth and early thirteenth centuries. Some of the most magnificent and wealthy houses in England were Cistercian abbeys in Yorkshire; these also oversaw many of the foundations built in even more remote parts of the isles, such as in Wales and Ireland. Competition among the Cistercian houses was, however, fierce, especially when they were located too close to each other and they were founded and patronized by elites of different ethnic groups. This was particularly the case in Ireland, where the Cistercian houses of Mellifont (Louth), founded in 1142 by St. Malachy, Archbishop of Armagh; Baltinglass (Wicklow)—a sister house of Mellifont—founded in 1148 by Diarmid Mac Murchada, king of Leinster; and Duiske (aka Graiguenamanagh, Kilkenny), founded by William and Isabella Marshal in 1204, were at constant loggerheads over jurisdiction, the advancement of monks, and conflicts with both the General Chapter and each other. Stephen of Lexington, the abbot of Stanley, a prominent Cistercian house in England, was sent to investigate, and his letters to the General Chapter are an extraordinary testament to the bellicosity of monks when confronted with unwanted competition.

KEEP IN MIND AS YOU READ

Monastic houses in medieval Europe were centers of learning, dominated the local economies of the regions in which they were located, and represented, ideally, the highest level of Christian piety and commitment to Christian practice. Like all institutions, however, monastic orders and the houses of monks and nuns could also be rife with corruption, competition for power and resources, and jealous of wealthier and more influential neighbors—both lay and ecclesiastical. The Cistercians were the most powerful and most widely respected order in the Middle Ages, but they were also frequently open to charges of economic manipulation and exploitation of their peasant tenants.

Document 1: Documents Relating to the Conflict of the Cistercians in Ireland (1228–1229)

[Letter 1] To the Abbot of Citeaux and to the community of abbots in General Chapter, greetings.

It is unbecoming for us to detail Your Paternity for long with our letter, for we know how occupied and burdened you are in many ways with unavoidable and demanding concerns of the Order. However, we have decided to bring to the attention of Your Holiness as briefly as we can this particular matter in Ireland . . .

[W]e came to Ireland where we heard of enormous crimes and horrible and notorious conspiracies which they were shameless enough to add this year to the former offences against those representing our Order . . .

The appeal of modesty and the tediousness of verbosity compel us to say nothing more about the number and the abominable gravity of their crimes, and to keep the knowledge of them away from the hearing of such holy men. But we will conclude with a summation: . . . we have with us the seal of a certain abbot which was pawned in a tavern for eighteen pence, and we saw the seal of another abbot in the same manner in the possession of a secular; consequently, on account of this the monasteries are reduced almost to nothing . . . Consequently, compelled by need almost all those in charge of the land wander away from the cloister as they please under the pretext of begging; there is no silence, no monastic discipline in the chapter-house, few are living in community, but they live in miserable huts outside the cloister in groups of threes and fours; they take up a collection and send to the village traders to purchase what they need instead of making use of the provisions of their properties. . . . Internally all the spiritualties are dissolved, externally the temporalities are almost completely wasted, so that for the most part we can say in truth: there is nothing of the Order there apart from the wearing of the habit.

And so, having exchanged counsel everywhere with worthy and God-fearing men, religious and secular, of high rank and low, we succeeding in discovering one solitary path of recovery and restoration, which we send to Your Holy Paternity under our seal and that of the abbots of Ireland; kindly act in accordance with what is stated there, and confirm it with your authority and insert into the statutes of the present year, lest the Enemy . . . will entrench himself forever against us and the visitors send after us, and we, who were sent to this region with your authority, will be exposed through negligence to mortal danger or perpetual confusion in this regard, to the shame and scandal of our religious life. Farewell. . . .

[Letter 2] From the Council of Abbots. (June, 1228, from Dublin)

When the venerable man, the abbot of Stanley came to the region of Ireland with the authority of the General Chapter, he undertook to summon us together and very firmly to engage us there under oath on the authority of the same Chapter and the Order to determine carefully how the Order there could recover and be restored to its proper state. . . . [W]e have been unable to discover any means of bringing an end to the horrible conspiracies and inveterate disorders, and of reviving religious life, except that some monasteries be taken away from obedience to undisciplined houses and be subjected by perpetual law to monasteries in other realms than their mother-houses, which are ready and able quickly to restore the ruin of the Order in spiritualties and temporalities . . .

Therefore, all the council came to one and only one decision as to what was most necessary for the restoration of Order and the preservation of the same in its proper state, and it was this: that the monastery of Clairvaux should have as daughter-houses the houses of

Boyle, Bective, and Kockmoy, together with Mellifont; the monastery of Fountains the houses of Baltinglass, Jerpoint, and Monasterevin; the monastery of Margam the houses of Maigue, Holy Cross, Chore, and Odorney; the monastery of Furness the houses of Owney, Suir, Fermoy, and Corcomroe; the monastery of Buildwas the house of Kilbeggan together with Dublin. Further, because the small monastery of Glanewydan is extremely poor and completely lacking in movable and immovable possessions, . . . it is to be joined in perpetuity . . . to the monastery of Dunbrody . . .

> The Cistercians built numerous small "daughter" houses in areas near the major foundations. When the disruptions between the Irish and English Cistercian houses began and the entire monastic system in Ireland was investigated by the General Chapter, it was decided to remove the jurisdiction over the smaller daughter-houses from the mother-houses in Ireland and to redistribute them to more reliable overseers in France, England, and Wales. Clairvaux in France was second only to Cîteaux in importance; Fountains was the primary Cistercian foundation in England; Margam was one of the major foundations in Wales; Buildwas was an important house in the Welsh March, and Furness was the primary Cistercian house in Cumbria, on the border of Scotland.

[Letter 3] To the Abbot of Trois Fontaines, greetings. (August, 1228 relating events that had occurred in 1227—the abbot had accompanied the abbot of Froidmont in the initial visitation)

. . . Venerable Father, immediately after the departure of the abbot of Froidmont the aforesaid sinful race and worthless seed rose up on all sides against his orders. . . . Consequently, many monasteries claimed to be under no obligation to receive a visitation through him, but united in evil, they completely rejected the visitor sent to them. . . . Indeed, . . . they also inflicted the greatest injuries on the abbot of Owney, whom the aforesaid lord abbot of Froidmont had appointed as his representative in these parts. His horses were secretly stolen, his cattle plundered, and some of his servants were killed. . . .

Furthermore, when the abbot of Baltinglass . . . returned to the monastery, . . . he was thrown from his horse in a disgraceful manner by his own monks and lay-brothers in front of the gates of the monastery, and his seal was violently snatched from his belt and he was shamefully expelled in the midst of a great commotion . . .

[Letter 4] To the King of Cenel Eoghain [the king of the southern Ui Neill], greetings.

At your insistence we have freed the bearers of this letter from the chain of excommunication with which they were bound and have reconciled them to the Order; accordingly, they will be allowed back into the monastery of Mellifont on condition that they bring back the cross, chalices and charters which they took away with them, together with certain books. In addition, as you requested, we have kindly and through dispensation provided, with all the honor we can and dare, according to the rules of our Order, for all who went out from or were expelled from Mellifont, that they never again be fugitives, no matter what they claim to Your Excellency, unless they spurn our counsel and refuse to obey the Order in future. . . .

Therefore, we kindly beseech Your Reverence with all the devotion we are capable of, for your perpetual honor and safety of soul, to protect and defend the aforesaid house of Mellifont, together with the abbot and the persons there assembled, in the way which is proper for so great a prince, never allowing anyone under your power and dominion to harm the aforesaid house or persons or to molest it in any way. . . .

Farewell.

[Letter 5] Report of Abbot Stephen, Sent from Stanley Abbey to General Chapter (November–December, 1228)

The visitations of Ireland being duly carried out according to the rules of the Order with authority of the General Chapter by Brother Stephen, Abbot of Stanley and his companions at great expense in repeated danger, some monks and lay-brothers of Maigue heard that they were on the point of departure to their own country, and they planned an unheard-of conspiracy and attempted to carry out some horrible deeds. For they violently expelled and completely drove away from the monastery their abbot and the monks and lay-brothers who had been sent there with the authority of the Order to teach the rule, . . . and to reform discipline. In addition, turning the monastery, the **cloister** as well as the church, into a fortress against God, they stored thirty head of cattle, slaughtered and salted down, under the dormitory; they strongly fortified the dormitories of the monks and lay-brothers with great stones, stakes, *palings*, and weapons according to the custom of their people. They stored large amounts of grain, hay, flour and other necessities in the church and they placed vessels and containers adequate to hold water in the cloister; in addition, they strongly fortified the shelter above the altar with provisions and weapons so that they could live in it as if it were their keep. Finally, the brought thirty head of cattle on the hoof into the cloister, grazing them on the grass there and on hay stored in the church.

> *palings:* stakes used in making wooden fences

In addition, and we say this with shame and horror, each one of the monks and lay-brothers equipped himself as best he could with weapons prepared especially for him . . . They joined with themselves under arms about two-hundred house-servants and lay-abouts of the district, partly by money, partly by other means. . . .

Finally, . . . the sentences of lesser excommunication and then of greater excommunication of such unheard-of, obdurate rebellion were gradually and successive brought against them, and at last they were threatened that, unless they withdrew themselves very deliberately and quickly from such a crime, the secular power would be invoked against them to seize and imprison them. . . . But they considered everything . . . to be of no account, and they rang the bells and rashly presumed to celebrate a solemn mass; they stripped the clothes from all the altars to the northern section [of the church] and, we speak the truth, they piled up heaps of stones; in addition, they ate flesh-meat publically with their followers and accomplices in the cloister and the lay-brothers' dormitory. Finally, the visitor [Stephen of Lexington] . . . wrote to the lord bishop of Limerick [Hubert de Burgh], . . . asking him to bring the . . . excommunicates to a spirit of saner council, or otherwise . . . to seize them and bind them with chains until through contrition and penance induced by punishment they deserved to be freed by the decree of the Order.

The aforesaid bishop kindly consented to do this . . . and he sent warnings with all diligence in person and through men of religion, . . . but in vain. [A]ll that was left now to do was to seize the aforesaid rebels following the customary procedure of the Church. . . .

Therefore, a large number of people broke in, and others from the opposing side battled fiercely, striking with the above-mentioned weapons, and two of the evil accomplices perished in the course of battle and of their wickedness, as was reported by the bishop's official and many others. The aforesaid excommunicates were brought before the bishop, but they were not prepared to give their consent to the judgment of the Order on any condition and they were sent away as fugitives on the decision of the bishop. . . . When the disturbance had been quelled and the observance of religious life had been commenced there to the honor of God and the Order, the . . . visitor together with his companions set out on his journey to [England] and he committed representation of the General Chapter to the abbot of Owney so that he might absolve and reconcile to the Order the above-mentioned excommunicates, excepting the four ring-leaders whose reconciliation he reserved to the General Chapter . . .

In witness of which matter the abbots of Mellifont, Bective, Grey Abbey and Tracton, together with the abbot of Stanley, place their seals.

[Letter 6] To the abbot of Duiske, greetings. (May 1229)

. . . We have learnt, if the reports are correct, that a man called Charles, in name a Cistercian monk though in reality an angel of Satan, stirs up the inexperienced, arouses conspiracies, seduces the crows and leads them in error against the rules of the Order and the obedience to General Chapter, and is plotting to destroy in Ireland that which the Lord in his great compassion has planted and raised up. Wherefore, we require Your Holiness with a very strict injunction to summon the aforesaid monk to you . . . and sternly admonish him with careful and considered words to restrain himself in future from such evil acts in deeds, gestures, and words . . . But if after he has been first suspended from divine services he still proves obdurate, . . . then on our behalf by the authority of the General Chapter and the Order bind him with a chain of anathema for his rebellion . . .

[Letter 7] Articles to be observed throughout the whole of Ireland. May, 1229

1. No one shall be received as a monk, no matter what his nation, unless he knows how to confess his faults in French or Latin, so that when the visitors and correctors of the Order come they may understand [the monks] and be understood by them.

2. The charters and legal documents of the houses shall be carefully gathered together in safe keeping under lock and key . . .

3. The Rule shall only be expounded in French and the chapter of the monks conducted in French or Latin in future, so that in this way those who want to be received in future may attend school in some place where they may learn some gentle manners.

4. In punishment for the conspiracies having arisen throughout the Irish houses generally, it is strictly forbidden for anyone of that language to be appointed abbot for a period of three years, so that their obedience to the Order may be fully tested and they may first learn to be students that in due time and place they may become more capable masters without danger to their souls and to the Order.

5. It is forbidden under threat of anathema for lands or tenancies to be alienated without the consent and confirmation of the father-abbot having been obtained beforehand. . . .

6. Property shall not be leased beyond a term of seven years so that in this way there may be recent memory of the transaction. . . .

7. In order that the property of the house be not uselessly squandered or the crime of simony committed imprudently in future, it is strict decreed under the penalties mentioned that in future monks shall not buy lands or accept the patronage of churches unless it has been established through a thorough inquiry carefully conducted beforehand that they can have clear right of entry and secure title.

8. It is strictly decreed for all officials in the monasteries and in the granges who are in charge of the possessions of the monasteries that they render a true and accurate account to the abbot and council of the house or to those whom the abbot specially appoints for this. . . .

9. It is decreed under the same penalty that lay-brothers are not to sell anything without the consent or permission of the abbot or the cellarer.

10. Monks or lay-brothers who have been sent away are not to be recalled without the special permission of the lord abbot of Clairvaux . . .

11. Under threat of anathema and penalty of deposition or officials and discharge of members of the council, it is strictly forbidden for any woman ever to be received as a nun the aforesaid houses of Ireland in future, on account of the shameful disorders and scandals arisen from such practices.

12. By authority of the Order and the General Chapter, the abbots of St Mary's Abbey, Dublin, and Duiske are strictly commanded by virtue of obedience to promulgate throughout all the houses of Ireland all the above-mentioned articles, copied down word for word on separate leaves with their seals affixed.

13. Each house shall have its own copy of these for itself. The aforesaid abbots shall order this to be read once each month through the whole year under sure and serious sentence of law and it is to be kept very carefully.

Source: Stephen of Lexington. *Letters from Ireland: 1228–1229.* Translated by Barry W. O'Dywer. Cistercian Fathers Series: Number Twenty-Eight. Kalamazoo, MI: Cistercian Publications, 1982. Pp. 43–50, 70–71, 105, 188–191, 197–199, 210–212. Modified by editor. Copyright 1982 by Cistercian Publications, Inc. © 2008 by Order of Saint Benedict, Collegeville, Minnesota. Used with permission.

AFTERMATH

The Cistercian Order in the British Isles was not unfazed by the problems such as those that occurred in Ireland in the early part of the thirteenth century, but it did not stop the order from gaining in power and influence—and in wealth—throughout the century. In particular, the Cistercians took advantage of the remote locations of their monasteries to develop advanced methods of breeding sheep that dominated the wool and parchment markets in the latter half of the century. Even so, the General Chapter of the Order was compelled to investigate charges of intra-order conflict in both Ireland and England among Cistercian houses.

ASK YOURSELF

1. Why would monastic communities sometimes descend to such a level of competition and violence as described in this reading?
2. In what ways did competition between the Irish and the Anglo-Norman settlers contribute to the conflict among the Cistercian communities in Ireland?
3. What did the laypeople who supported these monasteries think of what was going on?

TOPICS TO CONSIDER

1. Consider the ways in which founding monasteries close together could contribute to competition and conflict between them.
2. Discuss the ways in which donations by laypeople to monastic houses might make competition among them worse.
3. Consider the impact of ethnic bias on the ways in which conflicts such as these might be adjudicated by the superiors of the monastic order.

Further Information

Lynch, Breda. *A Monastic Landscape: The Cistercians in Medieval Ireland.* Dartford: Xlibris, 2010.

21. CHRISTIANS AND JEWS IN MEDIEVAL ENGLAND: GROWING CONFLICT

INTRODUCTION

The first Jews to arrive in the British Isles came with William the Conqueror; before that time, although there might have been Jewish traders, no communities of Jews were permanently established. After 1066, Jews from Normandy and other areas of France under Norman and Angevin control settled in major commercial centers in England, especially London, Norwich, and Lincoln. It did not take long for accusations of "blood libel" to surface, but the first canonization of a murdered child on the basis that he had been ritually sacrificed by Jews appears only after about a hundred years of Jewish settlement in England.

The growing conflicts between Jewish communities and their Christian neighbors, especially in England, were problematized by the economic exploitation of Jewish bankers by the king, which had an adverse impact not just on Jewish businesses but also on their relations with Christian clients, who saw them as preying on impoverished members of the community for their own gain. Anti-Jewish feeling and violent attacks on Jewish communities began to grow in the thirteenth century, leading to the expulsion of Jews from England in 1290.

KEEP IN MIND AS YOU READ

Paranoia in England about Jews practicing secret ceremonies in which they were alleged to kidnap and ritually murder Christian children stemmed not from actual verifiable evidence of this occurring but instead from rumor and claims of witnessing the gruesome effects of such rituals. Some scholars have suggested that a psychopathic killer might have engaged in acts of murder that involved torture of the victim, but it is difficult to verify that these killings even occurred at all. The claim of "eyewitness" accounts is never reliable in medieval texts. Moreover, the kinds of crimes of which the Jews were accused by Christians were also alleged to have occurred in areas of crusading activity—especially the Middle East and the Iberian Peninsula—perpetrated by Muslims against Christians, by Jews against Christians and Muslims, and by Christians against Muslims and Jews. Claims of ritual slaughter are always effective propaganda tools designed to demonize one group by another.

Document 1: Thomas of Monmouth: The Life and Miracles of St. William of Norwich, 1173

HOW WILLIAM WAS WONT TO RESORT TO THE JEWS, AND HAVING BEEN CHID BY HIS OWN PEOPLE FOR SO DOING, HOW HE WITHDREW HIMSELF FROM THEM

When therefore he was flourishing in this blessed boyhood of his, and had attained to his eighth year [about 1140], he was entrusted to the skinners [furriers] to be taught their craft. Gifted with a teachable disposition and bringing industry to bear upon it, in a short time he far surpassed lads of his own age in the craft aforesaid, and he equaled some who had been his teachers. So . . . he betook himself to the city and lodged with a very famous master of that craft, and some time passed away. He was seldom in the country, but was occupied in the city and sedulously gave himself to the practice of his craft, and thus reached his twelfth year [1144].

Now, while he was staying in Norwich, the Jews who were settled there and required their cloaks or their robes or other garments . . . to be repaired, preferred him before all other skinners. For they esteemed him to be especially fit for their work, either because they had learnt that he was guileless and skillful, or, because attracted to him by their avarice, they thought they could bargain with him for a lower price, or, as I rather believe, because by the ordering of divine providence he had been predestined to martyrdom from the beginning of time, and gradually step by step was drawn on, and chosen to be made a mock of and to be put to death by the Jews, in scorn of the Lord's Passion, as one of little foresight, and so the more fit for them. [William is to be put to death to mock the crucifixion.]

For I have learnt from certain Jews, who were afterwards converted to the Christian faith, how that at that time they had planned to do this very thing with some Christian, and in order to carry out their malignant purpose, at the beginning of Lent they had [chosen] the boy William, being twelve years of age and a boy of unusual innocence.

So it came to pass that when the holy boy, ignorant of the treachery that had been planned, had frequent dealings with the Jews, he was taken to task by Godwin the priest, who had the boy's aunt as his wife, and by a certain Wulward with whom he lodged and he was prohibited from going in and out among them any more. But the Jews, annoyed at the thwarting of their designs, tried with all their might to patch up a new scheme of wickedness, and all the more vehemently as the day for carrying out the crime they had determined upon drew near; and the victim, which they had thought they had already secured, had slipped out of their wicked hands.

Accordingly, collecting all the cunning of their crafty plots, they found—I am not sure whether he was a Christian or a Jew—a man who was a most treacherous fellow and just the fitting person for carrying out their execrable crime, and with all haste—for their Passover was coming on in three days—they sent him to find out and bring back with him the victim which, as I said before, had slipped out of their hands.

HOW HE WAS SEDUCED BY THE JEWS' MESSENGER

At the dawn of day, on the Monday [March 20, 1144] after Palm Sunday, that detestable messenger of the Jews set out to execute the business that was committed to him, and at last the boy William, after being searched for with very great care, was found. When he was found, he got round him with cunning wordy tricks, and so deceived him with his lying promises . . .

HOW ON HIS GOING TO THE JEWS HE WAS TAKEN, MOCKED, AND SLAIN . . .

Then the boy, like an innocent lamb, was led to the slaughter. He was treated kindly by the Jews at first, and, ignorant of what was being prepared for him, he was kept till the morrow. But on the next day [Tuesday, March 21], which in that year was the Passover for them, after the singing of the hymns appointed for the day in the synagogue, the chiefs of the Jews . . . suddenly seized hold of the boy William as he was having his dinner and in no fear of any treachery, and ill-treated him in various horrible ways. For while some of them held him behind, others opened his mouth and introduced an instrument of torture which is called a *teazle* and, fixing it by straps through both jaws to the back of the neck, they fastened it with a knot as tightly as it could be drawn.

> *teazle:* wooden gag

After that, taking a short piece of rope of about the thickness of one's little finger and tying three knots in it at certain distances marked out, they bound round that innocent head with it from the forehead to the back, forcing the middle knot into his forehead and the two others into his temples, the two ends of the rope being most tightly stretched at the back of his head and fastened in a very tight knot. The ends of the rope were then passed round his neck and carried round his throat under his chin, and there they finished off this dreadful engine of torture in a fifth knot.

But not even yet could the cruelty of the torturers be satisfied without adding even more severe pains. Having shaved his head, they stabbed it with countless thornpoints, and made the blood come horribly from the wounds they made. [Jesus had worn a crown of thorns before his death.] And so cruel were they and so eager to inflict pain that it was difficult to say whether they were more cruel or more ingenious in their tortures. . . .

And thus, while these enemies of the Christian name were rioting in the spirit of malignity around the boy, some of those present adjudged him to be fixed to a cross in mockery of the Lord's Passion . . .

Conspiring, therefore, to accomplish the crime of this great and detestable malice, they next laid their bloodstained hands upon the innocent victim, and having lifted him from the ground and fastened him upon the cross, they vied with one another in their efforts to make an end of him.

And we, after enquiring into the matter very diligently, did both find the house, and discovered some most certain marks in it of what had been done there. [This was supposed to be the house of a rich Jew, Eleazar, who was later murdered by order of his debtor, Sir Simon de Novers]. For report goes that there was there instead of a cross a post set up between two other posts, and a beam stretched across the midmost post and attached to the other on either side. And as we afterwards discovered, from the marks of the wounds and of the bands, the right hand and foot had been tightly bound and fastened with cords, but the left hand and foot were pierced with two nails. Now the deed was done in this way, lest it should be discovered from the presence of nail-marks in both hands and both feet, that the murderers were Jews and not Christians, if eventually the body were found. [Both hands and feet were not nailed lest it look like a crucifixion.]

But while in doing these things they were adding pang to pang and wound to wound, and yet were not able to satisfy their heartless cruelty and their inborn hatred of the Christian name, lo! after all these many and great tortures, they inflicted a frightful wound in his left side, reaching even to his inmost heart, and, as though to make an end of all, they extinguished his mortal life so far as it was in their power. [Jesus was similarly pierced by a lance while nailed to the cross. The chronicler here imitates the Apostle John's narrative.] And since many streams of blood were running down from all parts of his body, then, to stop the blood and to wash and close the wounds, they poured boiling water over him.

Thus then the glorious boy and martyr of Christ, William, dying the death of time in reproach of the Lord's death, but crowned with the blood of a glorious martyrdom, entered into the kingdom of glory on high to live forever. Whose soul rejoiceth blissfully in heaven among the bright hosts of saints, and whose body by the Omnipotence of the divine mercy worketh miracles upon earth . . . [St. William after his death worked many miracles that brought streams of people to his shrine.]

Source: Marcus, Jacob Rader, ed. *The Jew in the Medieval World: A Sourcebook, 315–1791.* New York: JPS, 1938. Pp. 121–127. Reprint: Marcus, Jacob Rader, ed. *The Jew in the Medieval World: A Source Book: 315–1791.* Introduction by Marc Saperstein. Revised Edition. Cincinnati: Hebrew Union College Press, 1999. Pp. 135–140. Text is taken from Internet Medieval Sourcebook: http://legacy.fordham.edu/halsall/source/1173williamnorwich .asp, and modified by editor.

AFTERMATH

The ability to demonize a group on scant evidence leads to a willingness to enhance further any sanctions against the group that might already be in place. This is very much the case in England in the thirteenth century. As kings Henry III and Edward I systematically extorted the wealth of the Jewish community—often in the form of Christian debts, as discussed in Section 3—they also encouraged the growing anti-Semitism that presented Jews as perpetrators of "blood libel" against Christians. It is perhaps ironic that when the expulsion occurred, Jews fled not only to the continent, where they settled in eastern Europe as well as in Spain, but also to Ireland, which, although under the relative control of the English Crown and chancery, did not engage in such extreme levels of intolerance.

ASK YOURSELF

1. Why would Christians become convinced that Jews in their community were engaging in such awful acts?
2. How did the circulation of these kinds of stories, and their promotion by church leaders, affect Jews in those communities?

TOPICS TO CONSIDER

1. Consider the ways in which these kinds of stories contributed to the growth of anti-Semitism throughout Europe in the Middle Ages and beyond.
2. Consider the political uses of accusations of "blood libel" on the part of both kings and the church.

Further Information

Edwards, John. "The Church and the Jews in Medieval England." In *Jews in Medieval Britain and Europe,* edited by Patricia Skinner, 85–96. Woodbridge: Boydell Press, 2003.
Felsenstein, Frank. "Jews and Devils: Antisemitic Stereotypes of Late Medieval and Renaissance England." *Literature and Theology* 4, no. 1 (1990): 15–28.
Menache, Sophia. "Faith, Myth and Politics: The Stereotype of the Jews and Their Expulsion from England and France." *The Jewish Quarterly Review* 75, no. 4 (1985): 351–374.

22. Christian Orthodoxy, Christian Heresy: Responses to "Lollardy" in the Fifteenth Century

INTRODUCTION

Although the church of Rome in the Middle Ages presented itself as "catholic"—that is, universal—in fact there were many and diverse forms of "officially approved" Christian expression in the medieval world, from the western Roman form of orthodoxy to eastern orthodox forms in the Byzantine Empire, eastern Europe, and western Asia, and in the southern Mediterranean and Middle East. In addition to these dominant forms, multiple alternative versions of Christianity appeared, which were labeled as "heretical" by the leaders of institutionalized Christianity.

In England, one such alternative developed in the fourteenth century under the intellectual leadership of JOHN WYCLIF (ca. 1331–1384), a theologian and Master of Law at Oxford University. Wyclif, whose ideas would form a significant component to the doctrines espoused in the Protestant Reformation, objected to the dominance of church precepts that did not originate in the Bible. For example, he rejected the doctrine of Purgatory, the theology of transubstantiation, the Catholic Church's sacramental system, and the idea that the Bible could not be translated into vernacular languages. Although he was protected by the highly influential Duke of Lancaster, JOHN OF GAUNT (son of Edward III and father of the future king HENRY IV), Wyclif's teachings were condemned at the Council of Constance (1414–1418) and his followers, who were derogatively called "**Lollards**" (that is, ignorant and uneducated persons), were labeled heretics. By the later fifteenth century, all homegrown dissenters of orthodoxy were referred to as Lollards.

The Lollard movement, especially in the later fourteenth and fifteenth centuries, had a significant political component, one borrowed from the precepts of the Great Rising of 1381. The Lollards claimed that a "priesthood of all believers" should also render all men equal not just in the eyes of God but also in society. They rejected the institution of villeinage and the notion of the "natural" superiority of the aristocracy and the clergy. As can be imagined, this led to significant suppression of Lollards on the part of both the Crown and the Church.

Although Lollardy had been strenuously attacked during the brief reign of Henry V (1413–1422), it resurfaced during the long minority of his son, HENRY VI (1422–1462, 1470–1471), who succeeded to the throne as an infant and did not achieve his majority until 1437. The two documents that follow trace a trajectory of increasing radicalism in the Lollard community, one which was never completely eradicated, leading to sympathy for King Henry VIII's rejection of the authority of Rome and the establishment of the Church of England in the following century.

KEEP IN MIND AS YOU READ

In the Middle Ages the Roman Church forbade the translation of the Bible into any vernacular language and discouraged laypeople from reading it, even if they were educated in Latin. The Catholic mass was conducted in Latin and sermons were not preached routinely in English and other vernaculars until the beginning of the fourteenth century. Therefore, the typical Christian experience of churchgoing was ritualized and performative, with little understanding of the subtleties of the Catholic mass. Nevertheless, the communities of Europe longed for a more personal relationship with religion, and this is what drew many to Lollardy and similar movements on the Continent.

Document 1: Letters of King Henry VI to the Abbot of Bury St. Edmunds and to the Aldermen and Bailiffs of the Town of St. Edmunds, Concerning the Suppression of the Lollards (1431)

Letter 1: King to The Abbot of Bury St. Edmunds

Right trusty [faithful] and well-beloved [abbot], for as much as that, in this holy time of Whitsun week, the misgoverned men of diverse Shires of this our land, and especially the Shire of Kent—Lollards as well as other robbers and pillagers of our people—were, in great number and in riotous ways, gathering in the said Shire of Kent, to do whatever harm they might, and to have subverted all the politic rule of this our land. Among the misgoverned men, Sir Nicholas Coneway, knight, who is now taken and set fast in prison, should have been a Captain; a great number of other men have been imprisoned as well. We have been informed that there is likely to be an assembly gathering in Cambridgeshire, around Cambridge town. We command, therefore, that anyone, after the sight of these our letters, with all diligence . . . prevent the gathering of such misgoverned men, and at all times to be ready, with all the might and power that they can and may get in order to resist their malicious intent and purpose. . . . And moreover We command you to report to us in this behalf, from time to time, as the case shall happen and require. Given under our privy seal, at Westminster, the 5th day of June.

Letter 2: From the King to our trusty [faithful] and well beloved Alderman and Bailiffs of our town of Bury [St. Edmunds].

Trusty and well-beloved men: the malicious intent and purpose of the traitors against God and ourselves, heretics in this our Realm, commonly called Lollards, who have lately been posting seditious bills, and in addition, have traitorously exhorted, stirred, and moved the people of our land, to assemble, gather, and arise against God's peace and ours, is not unknown to you: nay to no man endowed with reason, foresight, or discretion. You know how subtle, fraudulent, and treacherous they are: they feign, pretend, and write such things as they know will blind the innocent, and [which will] draw them by their hearts and emotions to them and their intent, intending . . . without any doubt, the subversion of the Christian faith, . . . and would destroy all politic rule and governance, spiritual and temporal. And consider that they, against God's law and man's, stir our people, without our commandment or authority, to assemble and arise, and therewith propose and would take upon them and usurp as well our royal power and authority in the churches, . . . [which] by the law of this our land, is treason . . . [The Lollards are interested only in robbing, despoiling, murdering, and destroying] all men of [high] estate, thrift, and [orthodox] worship, . . . and would make lords of lads and low-born men . . . [And even though "our beloved uncle of Gloucester"—Thomas of Woodstock, duke of Gloucester—and other judges and commissioners have arrested and] lawfully executed [many of] the said traitors of God and ourselves, . . . nevertheless it is credibly reported to our said lieutenant and counsel here, . . . that the wicked and malicious purposes of the said traitors do not cease but continue. [We wrote to you before about this issue but do not know if the letters arrived.] We write again . . . charging you on the faith, truth, and allegiance that you owe to God and to us, that with all diligence, and without delay or tarrying, you ordain and array you and yours, and stir others as will accompany you, to be ready to assemble, with other of our true liege men to do the same, and withstand, mightily chastise, and subdue the damnable malice and enterprise of these traitors. . . . And especially, we will and charge you, that you [investigate] which of the inhabitants in [your region] have absented themselves, or absent themselves hereafter, for reasons other than what is required of their work; and also [inquire about and investigate] strangers and [people unknown to the community], of whom ill suspicion may reasonably fall, and that you arrest, search, and examine them in the straightest ways: whence they come, and where they have been, and of all the days, times, and places of their absence, and also of sowers of seditions, slanders, or violent language, or tales. In addition, do not permit private assembling of people or illicit meetings to be had or made, by night or by day . . . [and, if needed, request help from] our said lieutenant and council, whom you will find ever well disposed to provide [assistance]; and faileth not in due and diligent execution of these things, as they [are necessary for the maintenance of] our prosperity and yours and welfare. Given under our privy Seal at Westminster the 6th day of July.

Source: *Archaeologia: or Miscellaneous Tracts Relating to Antiquity.* The Society of Antiquaries of London. Volume XXIII (1830). Pp. 339–343. Translated by Kimberly Fogarty Palmer. Modernized and modified by editor.

Document 2: Lollardy in Lincolnshire: The Beliefs of William and Richard Sparke (1457)

List of heretical tenets publicly maintained by William Sparke and his brother Richard Sparke, of Somersham, in the diocese of Lincoln, and afterwards publicly acknowledged by them before John, lord bishop of Lincoln. [1457]

1. Crosses and Images set up in Churches ought not to be worshipped; and offerings ought not to be made at them, since they are only stocks and stones. A human being [would be better off to] worship a man with arms stretched out cross-wise, since that is a true cross and image of God.

2. Pilgrimages ought not to be made to places where the bodies of saints rest. The expenditure incurred in such pilgrimages is wasted, and the toil undergone is profitless.

3. A child whose parents have been baptized has no need of baptism, and ought not to be baptized, since its parents' baptism is sufficient for it.

4. Laymen who are married or who are engaged in manual labor are not [required] to fast. Christ is nowhere found to have instituted fastings of this sort. The Canonical Rule of the Church put forward in this respect is binding only on clerics and on inmates of convents.

5. To bury a corpse in consecrated ground does the soul of the dead person no more good than if the corpse had been thrust into a bog. The solemnities of funerals were invented to provide fees for money-loving priests. It would be better if funeral expenses went in alms to the poor than to enrich priests.

6. A priest has no more power to make "the body of Christ" than the wheat-stalk has. After the words of consecration the bread remains only bread as before; and, in fact, is debased by having had such spell-words pronounced over it.

7. Thirty breads [i.e. the communion wafer] of this sort are sold for one halfpenny, but Christ was sold for thirty pence. The sacrament after this fashion is therefore a figment devised to enrich priests.

8. Confession made to a believer of the Lollard sect is more soul-healing than confession made to a priest.

9. Inasmuch as God is searcher of all hearts and the knowers of all secrets, an unspoken prayer is just as good as a spoken prayer, and a prayer made in a field or other unconsecrated place is just as efficacious as if it were made in a church.

10. The sole requisite for a valid marriage is mutual consent between the man and the woman, and no other solemnity is needed to justify their living together as man and wife. The marriage-service was brought in solely to provide fees for priests.

11. Extreme unction does not benefit the soul of any man. The only result of this anointing ("greasing," we call it in English) is to dirty and make vile the person's body.

12. The Pope is Antichrist; priests are the disciples of Antichrist. All persons in Holy Orders are incarnate devils.

13. Every human being is called "the church of God." Therefore, if any Lollard is brought before the judge of an ecclesiastical court and required to answer the question "Dost thou believe in the Church?" he may answer without scruple "I do"; since by his belief in the Church he states only that he believes in man, who is "the temple of God."

14. Each of the accused publicly admitted that, in a large meeting of Lollards, he had solemnly taken oath upon the Bible (i) that he would use his utmost diligence to bring into the Lollard sect as many as ever he could prevail upon, and (ii) that he would reveal to no outsider the existence of the sect or names of its adherents until they were strong enough in numbers to destroy Antichrist and all Antichrist's disciples; and this (he at that time asserted) would soon be.

Source: *Lincoln Diocese Documents, 1450–1544.* Edited by Andrew Clark, London: Early English Text Society, 1914. Pp. 92–93.

AFTERMATH

The teachings of John Wyclif were absorbed by the Bohemian theologian JAN HUS, who started a Wyclifite movement in Prague in the late fourteenth century; his followers were known as Hussites. Although he also was condemned at Constance and indeed executed as a heretic, Hus's followers persisted and would eventually influence the ideas of Martin

Luther. Lollardy, in large part because of its political overtones, was widely and viciously suppressed in the aftermath to the rebellion of Jack Cade (1450). It nevertheless survived to some extent, to form the center of belief of English followers of Martin Luther in the sixteenth century. The ideas of religious equality and one's personal relationship with God spread rapidly through Europe, assisted by the invention of the printing press, and the Protestant Reformation was one result.

ASK YOURSELF

1. Why would the king and his council equate Lollardy with political insurrection?
2. In what ways did the expression of Lollard beliefs challenge not just religious hierarchies but also social and political ones?
3. What elements of Christian ritual and practice were challenged by Lollards and why?

TOPICS TO CONSIDER

1. Compare the beliefs of followers of Wyclif with those of Catholic orthodoxy and consider their significance to social and political systems in medieval England.
2. Consider the possible reasons why people who followed Lollard beliefs might also be political dissidents.

Further Information

Ozment, Stephen. *The Age of Reform, 1250–1550: An Intellectual and Religious History of Late Medieval and Reformation Europe*. New Haven: Yale University Press, 1981.

Somerset, Fiona, Jill C. Havens, and Derrick G. Pitard, eds. *Lollards and Their Influence in Late Medieval England*. Rochester: Boydell Press, 2003.

POLITICS, LAW, AND ADMINISTRATION

23. Adjudication of Disputes and Other Aspects of Anglo-Saxon Law (Eleventh Century)

INTRODUCTION

Although we have law codes from the Anglo-Saxon period, which survived in large part because of King Alfred's compilation of the laws of Kent, Wessex, and Mercia in the ninth century, it is difficult to determine exactly how the law might have been utilized. For example, were disputes resolved in front of the king or his representative in a formal setting, such as a court, or were they resolved on a more ad hoc basis? Two examples of legal procedures follow, both of which are known to us through the survival of written charters. In the first, King Cnut's **shire-moot** adjudges a family dispute over land. In the second, a slave owner, possibly on her deathbed, frees a number of her slaves. Slave-owning was regulated by secular law, yet the charter of manumission is couched in terms similar to grants made to religious institutions, thus demonstrating how connected the two systems—royal and church administration—were.

KEEP IN MIND AS YOU READ

Similar to modern-day court procedures, the process of dispute adjudication in early medieval England required some kind of formal petition or charge. Unlike modern-day Anglo-American law, however, disputes were not resolved in front of a "jury of one's peers" but rather by a council of male elites who acted as royal representatives, since justice ultimately flowed from the king. Although individuals could distribute their "movable" wealth—which included ownership of slaves—at their own discretion, these transfers of property could be challenged and therefore come under the auspices of the royal law court.

Document 1: Legal Disputes

A Dispute Over Land (before 1036)

Fânwen.

This writing makes known that a shire-moot sat at Ægelnoth's stone, in the day of King Cnut, presided over by Bishop Æthelstân, Ranig the **aldorman**, Eadwine the aldorman's son, Leofiwine son of Wulfsige, and Thurkil White; and Tofig Prud [Earl Tostig "the Proud"] came there on the king's behalf; and also there were Bryning the **shire-reeve**, Ægelweard at Frome, Leofwine at Frome, Godric at Stoke, and all the thanes in Herefordshire.

Then Eadwine, Eanwen's son, came to the moot and raised a claim against his own mother to a portion of land, namely at Wellington and Cradley. The bishop asked, who would answer for [represent] his mother? Then answered Thurkil White that he would, if the claim was made known to him. Since he did not know the specifics of the claim, three thanes were selected from the moot, [who were instructed to ride] to where she was: that is, to Fawley. The [thanes chosen] were Leofwine at Frome, Ægelsige the Red, and Winsige scægthman.

And when they came to her, they asked what claim she had to the lands for which her son was suing. She replied that she had no land that in any way belonged to him, and was very bitterly incensed against her son; and then called Leoflæd her kinswoman to her, Thurkil's wife, and, before them all, thus spoke to her: "Here sits Leoflæd my kinswoman, to whom I give not only my land, but my gold, and my garments, and robes, and all that I own, after [I have died]." And she then said to the thanes, "Do nobly and well: announce my decision to the moot before all the good men, and declare to them to whom I have given my land and all my property; and to my own son never anything; and of this bid them be witness." And they then so did, rode to the moot, and declared to all the good men what she had commanded them to do. Then Thurkil White stood up in the moot, and prayed all the thanes to grant to his wife claim the lands which her kinswoman had given her; and they did so. And Thurkil then rode to StÆthelberht's monastery, with the leave and witness of all the folk, and caused it to be set in a Christ's book.

Manumission of Slaves (no date)

Geatflæd has given freedom, for love of God and for her soul's need, to Ecceard the smith, and Ælstan and his wife, and all their offspring, born and unborn, and to Arkil, and Cole, and Ecferd Aldhun's daughter, and all the men whose persons she took for their food in the evil days. Whoso shall alter this and bereave her soul thereof, may God Almighty bereave him of this life and of the kingdom of heaven; and be he accursed, dead and quick, ever to eternity. And she has also freed the men whom she solicited from Cwæspatric, that is: Ælfwald and Colbrand, Ælsie, and Gamal his son, Eðred, Tredewude and Uhtred his stepson, Aculf, and Thurkyl, and Æsige. Who shall bereave them of this, may God Almighty and St Cuthbert be wroth to them.

Source: *Diplomatarium Anglicum Aevi Saxonici: A Collection of English Charters, from the Reign of King of Aethelberht of Kent to That of William the Conqueror (1865).* Edited by Benjamin Thorpe. London: Macmillan & Co., 1865. Pp. 336–338, 621.

AFTERMATH

Disputes over land were probably common in the Anglo-Saxon period, especially since the most common form of inheritance was "partible"—all the children in a given family inherited. Although the outlines of land ownership changed dramatically after the Norman Conquest, conflicts over land persisted and were heard in increasing numbers in the formal court systems devised by King Henry II (r. 1155–1189) and his sons. In addition, slavery after the conquest largely disappeared from England, although it did persist in areas of the British Isles, notably in Ireland. Slavery was replaced by villeinage, which rendered a peasant personally free but tied to the land she or he was charged to work.

ASK YOURSELF

1. How would early medieval people gain access to royal justice? Was it only the provenance of elites?
2. How do you think peasants gained access to justice and who would preside?
3. How did people become slaves in early medieval England, and what did slaves do after they were freed?

TOPICS TO CONSIDER

1. Compare the description of dispute resolution in the reign of King Cnut to the records of later medieval litigation as exemplified in this section.
2. Consider the relative differences in status between slavery and serfdom (or villeinage) in the Middle Ages.
3. Consider the ways in which sociopolitical status and gender could affect an individual's access to justice in the Anglo-Saxon period.

Further Information

The Laws of the Earliest English Kings. Edited and translated by F. L. Attenborough. Cambridge: Cambridge University Press, 2015 [1922].

Oliver, Lisi. *The Body Legal in Barbarian Law.* Toronto: University of Toronto Press, 2011.

24. Two Royal Images: King William II "Rufus" of England and King Malcolm III "Canmore" of Scotland

INTRODUCTION

If relations between the kingdoms of England and Scotland were contentious before the Norman Conquest—as exhibited in the description of the battle of Brunanburh in Section 6, Warfare, Conquest, and Diplomacy—they became even more so after the conquest and establishment of the Norman kings. At the same time, the conflict over the border between England and Scotland led to a greater political cohesion in the northern kingdom, as well as a more unified identity as Scots, even though the western edge, the Irish Channel and Northern Isles, and the northernmost reaches of Britain were still ruled by Scandinavian or Gaelic-Scandinavian kings. KING MALCOLM III (r. 1058–1093), known as Malcolm Canmore, is credited with bringing together Scotland's diverse populations into a more unified identity, especially in the heart of the Scottish kingdom, the borderlands, and the regions of Fife and Perth. He did this largely through squabbles with the kings of England, William I and WILLIAM II (r. 1087–1100), over the borders between the two regions that secured a new sense of identity and purpose among the Scottish military elites.

King William II "Rufus" (because of his red face and fair hair) was designated as heir to England by his father, while Normandy was granted to his older brother, Robert "Curthose." This did not deter Rufus from seizing control of Normandy by purchasing its **wardship** from Robert, who was in need of funds in order to go on the First Crusade. He was seen as an effective if ruthless monarch of indefatigable energy and no little scorn for the trappings of religion and social niceties.

KEEP IN MIND AS YOU READ

Chronicler writers frequently presented the personalities of kings and queens in deliberately oppositional ways. The bias of Henry of Huntingdon against King William II came not from a dislike of the king's overall competence but because of King William's exactions on the church and a suspicion common among churchmen that he was skeptical about religion in general and Christianity in particular. In contrast, Malcolm III Canmore, married to the saintly MARGARET OF WESSEX (the last direct descendent of the kings of Wessex), might have been somewhat neglectful of what the churchmen considered he "owed" the community—he founded only one abbey, that of Dunfermline—but his piety was conventional and unremarkable.

Document 1: Relations between British Kings: William Rufus and Malcolm Canmore

[1090] In the meantime, Malcolm, king of Scots, ravaged England and carried off much booty; wherefore the king and his brother Robert [Duke of Normandy] came to England, and led an army into Scotland, and Malcolm, in alarm, did **homage** and swore fidelity to the king of England.

****

Of the prudence of the Scottish king Malcolm.

[1090] As I have mentioned Malcolm, king of Scots, I will briefly relate his disposition and modesty of character. It was once told him, that one of his chief nobles had made an agreement with his enemies to kill him: the king ordered the accuser to be silent, and said nothing himself until the arrival of the traitor . . . The nobleman soon after came to court with a large retinue . . . [and] the king commanded his hunters with their dogs to attend him early the next morning. . . . The king . . . retained the traitor with himself alone, whilst the others followed the dogs and the chase. When they were all out of sight, the king said to him, "You and I are now here alone, armed alike, and mounted on equally good horses . . . If, then, you have the courage, do what you intend . . . If you wish to kill me, where will you have so good, so secret, and so fair a chance? If, however, you meant to poison me, you should have left that for the women to do. If you meant to murder me in my bed, a girl from the streets might do that as well as you. If, however, you meant to stab me with a concealed weapon, this is the act of an assassin and not of a knight . . . [F]ight me on equal terms, and . . . your conduct will be only disloyal, but not cowardly and disgraceful." The knight . . . fell from his horse to the ground and . . . fell on his knees before the king. "Be not afraid," continued the king, "I shall do you no harm."

****

Of the faults of king William.

[1100] It was right that king William was cut off by death in the midst of his injustice; for he was beyond all other men, and always did whatever evil was in his power, following the advice of his evil counselors. He was a tyrant to his own people, worse to strangers, but worst of all to himself, and annoyed his subjects by continual gelds and **tallages,** whilst he provoked his neighbors by wars and exactions, and England could not take breath under the burdens which he laid upon it. . . . This wicked king, hateful to both God and to his people, on the day of his death held to his own use the archbishopric of Canterbury, the bishoprics of Winchester and Salisbury, besides twelve abbacies, which he either sold, or let out to farm, or kept in his own hands; neither did he practice his crimes of debauchery in secret, but openly in the light of day [William Rufus was rumored to be homosexual]. . . . He was buried the day after his death at Winchester; but his tomb was watered by no one's tears, so great was the joy which the people felt at his departure.

Source: Roger of Wendover. *Flowers of History.* Translated by J. A. Giles. 2 vols. London: Henry G. Bohn, 1849. Volume 1. Pp. 360–361, 445–446.

The great tradition of history writing established by the Anglo-Saxon Chronicle was enhanced by the energies of monastic chroniclers after the Norman Conquest. Roger of Wendover (d. ca. 1235) was a monk at the abbey of St. Albans, which was the center of chronicle and history writing well into the fifteenth century. The St. Albans chroniclers, beginning with Wendover, maintained a consistent history of political doings in the British Isles as well as of major events on the Continent and the Holy Land. Although two other St. Albans historians, Matthew Paris and Thomas Walsingham, are more famous than their fellow authors Roger of Wendover and William Rishanger, the consistency of purpose surrounding the chroniclers and the maintenance of their history continued from beginning to end. Roger derived a great deal of his material from earlier chroniclers, especially Henry of Huntingdon, whose description of the battle of Hastings is in Section 6.

AFTERMATH

King Malcolm III Canmore was succeeded by four of his sons—Duncan II was son of his first wife (or, perhaps, concubine), Ingibiorg of Orkney, while Edgar, Alexander I, and DAVID I were all products of his second marriage to Margaret of Wessex. His and Margaret's daughter, Edith (aka Matilda of Scotland), married Rufus's brother and successor, King Henry I. Over the course of the twelfth century, the kings of Scotland and England both pushed against their borders—invading Wales and Ireland on the part of the English monarchs, and solidifying Scots' control of the entire region north of the River Tee on the part of the rulers of the Scots. In addition, in part because of the intermarriage of the two royal families, relations between the kings of England and Scotland grew more intimate and significant as the twelfth century progressed.

ASK YOURSELF

1. What did the kings of Scotland think about the Norman Conquest?
2. Why would relations between the kings of England and Scotland be contentious?
3. What would be the purpose of invading northern England, aside from the possible territorial gains, when the king of England had more resources and men?

TOPICS TO CONSIDER

1. Consider the role of piety and allegiance to the church in the presentation of kings as "good" or "bad."
2. Consider reasons why church officials were opposed to paying "taxes" to the king.
3. Consider the strategies kings of the Scots must have had to employ in order to unify such a diverse region.

Further Information

Barlow, Frank. *William Rufus.* 2nd ed. New Haven, CT: Yale University Press, 2008.
Hudson, Benjamin T. "Kings and Church in Early Scotland." *The Scottish Historical Review* 73, no. 196, pt. 2 (1994): 145–170.

25. CHARTERS OF LIBERTIES BEFORE MAGNA CARTA: KING JOHN AND THE JEWS (1201)

INTRODUCTION

The idea of documentation of the "liberties" granted to a particular group or organization was not original to the Great Charter of 1215. Kings in England had routinely, if not consistently, included such stipulations in coronation oaths since the ninth century, with particular standouts being those of King Henry I in 1100 and King Henry II in 1155. Kings also stipulated such liberties when incorporating cities and towns with royal charters: the city of London received such guarantees in writing as early as 1067, when King William I confirmed the city's "ancient" liberties.

Written stipulations of liberties and the legal guarantees accompanying them operated as a form of protection for both the grantor and the receivers of the grant. The grantor outlines the rights and privileges he or she is presenting to the receiver, while the receiver acknowledges the obligations such rights and privileges carry with them. This is particularly the case with King John's charter of "liberties" which he granted in 1201 to the Jews living in England. Although they were granted the privilege of living under the protection of the king, the Jewish communities were under no illusions that the king—especially one like John—would not use the opportunity of lordship to exploit them at will. Nevertheless, the provisions in this charter, which states that these are merely reiterations and clarifications of earlier charters of liberties enjoyed by the Jewish community in England, clarify the relationship between the king and the Jews as subjects, as well as between Jews and Christians coexisting in the kingdom. Moreover, the prestige of the witnesses—which include some of the most prominent men of the kingdom—attests to the importance of the charter.

KEEP IN MIND AS YOU READ

Although the charter of liberties outlines specific protections of Jews in England, there were few opportunities for Jews to defend themselves on the basis of the charter. In part, the dilemma faced by Jews had to do with their status vis-à-vis the Crown: Jews were considered to be, if not villeins (as in some kingdoms where they were considered royal serfs), then persons of not quite free status whose actions were limited by royal fiat. The establishment, during the reign of King John, of the Court of Exchequer of the Jews was designed to expand upon the jurisdictional issues raised in the charter that no Jew was permitted to engage in a suit except before the king or his justices.

Document 1: Charter of Liberties Confirmed to the Jews of England in the Second Year of the Reign of King John (10 April 1201)

John, by the grace of God etc. Know that We have granted to all Jews of England and Normandy that they reside in freedom and honor in our land, and hold of Us all that they held of King Henry [I], our father's grandfather, and all that they now rightfully hold in lands, fees, gages and purchases, and that they have all their franchises and customs, as they had them in the time of the said King Henry, our father's grandfather, in better and more peaceful and honorable enjoyment. . . .

And when a Jew be dead, let not his body be detained above ground [the body should not be prevented from being buried within the Judaic legal 24 hour limit], but let his heir have his money and his debts; so that thereof he may have peace if he have an heir to answer for him and to do right touching his debts and his forfeiture.

And be it lawful for Jews . . . to receive and buy all things brought to them, except those which pertain to the Church and bloodstained cloth.

And if a Jew be **appealed** by any without witness, he shall be quit [acquitted] of that appeal by his bare oath upon his Book [the Torah]. And in like manner he shall be quit of an appeal touching those things that pertain unto our Crown by his bare oath upon his Roll [a Torah scroll].

And as often as there shall be dispute between Christian and Jew touching a loan of money, the Jew shall prove his principal and the Christian the interest.

And be it lawful for the Jew quietly to sell his gage when it shall be certain that he has held it for a full year and a day.

And Jews shall not enter into pleas save before Us, or before those who have ward of our castles, in whose **bailiwicks** Jews dwell.

And wherever Jews be, be it lawful for them to go wheresoever they will with all their chattels, as our proper goods, and be it unlawful for any to delay or forbid them.

And We ordain, that throughout the whole of England and Normandy they be quit of all customs and tolls and **prisage** of wine as our proper chattel. And We command you and ordain, that you have them in ward and guard and countenance.

And we forbid any to implead them of the said matters against this Charter, on pain of forfeiture, as to the Charter of our father, King Henry, rightfully witnesses.

Witness: Geoffrey FitzPeter, Earl of Essex; William Marshal, Earl of Pembroke; Henry de Bohun, Earl of Hereford; Robert de Turnham; William Briwere, etc. Given by the hand of Simon, Archdeacon of Wells, at Marlborough, on the tenth day of April in the second year of our reign.

Source: *Select Pleas, Starrs, and Other Records from the Rolls of the Exchequer of the Jews A. D. 1220–1284.* Edited by J. M. Rigg. London: Selden Society, 1902. Pp. 1–2.

AFTERMATH

It is unclear whether the charter of liberties presented to the Jews by King John was able to be enforced in any systematic way. There is evidence, however, that baronial resentment of the protection of the Jews—as well as the appropriation of Christian debts to the Jews by the king—grew over the course of King John's reign. In the 1215 Great Charter, chapters specifying problems concerning debts owed to Jewish bankers stipulate that heirs and widows of deceased people who owed debts to Jewish bankers were not to be charged interest on the debt after the debtor had died, and the debt had to be paid only out of the cash and movable property assets of the deceased. The purpose behind those statements in Magna Carta had to do with protecting landed estates from exploitation by the king: Jews who acquired land as collateral for unpaid debts were not permitted to retain it but instead had to hand it over to their "lord"—the king. This was perceived as a form of exploitation not only of Jews, who lost the value of the collateral to the king, but also of Christian debtors, whose lands were in the hands of someone who was aversive about returning it. As discussed in Section 3, Economic Life, the royal exploitation of the Jewish communities did not abate but rather grew more demanding. By the reign of King Edward I, the ability of Jews to protect themselves through providing windfalls for the continuously cash-strapped Crown had ceased. This situation was one of the reasons why the Jews were expelled from England in 1290.

ASK YOURSELF

1. In what ways did the charter of Jewish liberties protect Jews living in England? In what ways did the charter privilege the Christian majority?
2. Why would the baronage have resented the protections afforded the Jews by this charter?
3. Why would the king decide to produce a charter protecting a minority population such as the Jews?

TOPICS TO CONSIDER

1. Imagine yourself a Jew in early thirteenth-century England. Consider some of the ways in which your life would be affected by both friendships and professional associations and the exploitative practices of the Crown and Church.
2. Consider the connections between political and economic attitudes toward and policies concerning the Jewish population in the medieval British Isles.

Further Information

Brand, Paul. "Jews and the Law in England, 1275–90." *The English Historical Review* 115, no. 464 (2000): 1138–1158.

Dobson, R. B. "The Jews of Medieval Cambridge." *Jewish Historical Studies* 32 (1990–1992): 1–24.

Lipman, Vivian D. "Jews and Castles in Medieval England." *Transactions & Miscellanies (Jewish Historical Society of England)* 28 (1981–1982): 1–19.

26. REFORMING THE KINGDOM IN THE THIRTEENTH CENTURY: THE PARLIAMENT OF OXFORD (1258)

INTRODUCTION

King Henry III (r. 1216–1272) might have been the longest reigning monarch in England before Queen Victoria, but his rule was not particularly trouble-free or secure. The son of King John, Henry was only nine years old when he succeeded to the throne, thus necessitating a long minority period in which the kingdom was governed by regents, including the prestigious Earl of Pembroke, William Marshal; the Earl of Kent, Hubert de Burgh; the Earl of Chester, Ranulph de Bundeville; and two papal legates, Guala Biccieri (legate 1216–1218) and Pandulf Masca (legate 1213–1216 and 1218–1221). By the time Henry had reached his majority (partially by 1225 and fully by 1230), the machinery of royal administration had been expanded by the guardians of the realm into a far more bureaucratized system that was also becoming less dependent on the personal attentions of the king himself.

Henry's attempts to regain the French territories lost by his father, King John, as well as a failed scheme to gain the throne of Sicily for his younger son Edmund, dangerously overextended the finances of the Crown. When Henry attempted to recoup his losses through higher levels of taxation, his barons—especially the younger generation—rebelled. Led by the French nobleman—and King Henry's brother-in-law—Earl of Leicester SIMON DE MONTFORT, the barons met at Oxford to draw up a list of demands they required of the king in order to vote in favor of any additional taxation. Many of the demands were personally directed at Henry and the barons' perceptions that he was unduly influenced by people they dubbed "foreigners." Perhaps the most pointed demand was one that required that the king's half-siblings, the sons of his mother Isabelle and her second husband, Hugh de Lusignan, be exiled, in particular Henry's youngest brother, William de Valence, who was married to Joan de Munchensy, one of the heirs to the earldom of Pembroke and lordship of Leinster in Ireland.

KEEP IN MIND AS YOU READ

The identification of King Henry's siblings as "foreigners" is not as clear-cut as it is claimed in the reading that follows. Many members of the baronial party, including Earl Simon himself, as well as Savoyard and Poitevan members of the queen's family, were just as "foreign" as the Lusignans. The issues were largely political, in that Henry consulted and listened to his Lusignan kin; he rewarded William de Valence with marriage to the wealthiest heiress of the time; and he had been somewhat dismissive of Earl Simon's efforts to consolidate royal power in Gascony. Moreover, there was little love lost between Earl Simon de Montfort and William de Valence because of the latter's control of Pembrokeshire, in Wales, which Simon claimed should have been part of the dower of his wife, Eleanor, sister of King Henry III and widow of William Marshal the Younger (d. 1231). Thus, family disputes within and among the heirs to the Marshal earldom significantly influenced the political stances of the baronial leaders, many of whom were coheirs, along with Joan de Valence, of those estates.

Another aspect of the narrative concerning the Oxford Parliament has to do with the chroniclers who reported it. The hostility of contemporary historians, especially of the St. Albans chronicler, MATTHEW PARIS, whose *Chronica Majora* (Great Chronicle) continues to wield influence among modern-day historians, colors the entire narrative. Matthew claimed to receive his news from eyewitnesses. Nevertheless, the insertion of speeches should suggest a great deal of authorial editing.

Document 1: The Parliament Held at Oxford, June 1258

As the feast of St. Barnabas [June 11, 1258] drew near, the magnates and nobles of the country hastened to the parliament that was to be held at Oxford, and gave orders to all those who owed them knightly service, to accompany them, equipped and prepared as if to defend their persons against the attacks of enemies. This they accordingly carried into effect, concealing their real reasons for so doing under the pretense that their coming in such a way was to show themselves ready to set out with their united forces against the king's enemies in Wales. . . . Moreover, the nobles took the further precautions of carefully guarding the seaports. At the commencement of the parliament, the proposed plan of the nobles was unalterably decided on; and they most expressly demanded that the king should faithfully keep and observe the conditions of the charter of the liberties of England, which his father, King John, had made and granted to his English subjects, and which he, the said John, had sworn to observe . . . They moreover demanded that a **justiciary** should be appointed to render justice to those who suffered injuries, with equal impartiality toward the rich and the poor . . . and they moreover insisted that the king should frequently consult them and listen to their advice in making all necessary provisions; and they made oath, giving their right hands to one another as a pledge of faith, that they would prosecute their design, at the risk of losing their money, their lands, and even their lives, as well as those of their people. The king acknowledged the reasonableness of the remonstrances, and solemnly swore that he would give heed to their counsels; and his son Edward was bound down by a similar oath. This oath, however, was refused by John, earl of Warenne, and the uterine brothers of the king, William de Valence, and others. . . .

After they had prolonged their stay at Oxford for some days, they met together at a house of the *Preacher brethren*, to deliberate as to what was to be done in the difficult matter of ameliorating the condition of the disturbed kingdom. There they renewed afresh their alliance, and reiterated their oath, and confirmed their determination that they would not allow themselves, for life for death, or for their possessions, for hatred or love, or for any reason whatever, to be bent from, or weakened in, their

Preacher brethren: the Dominican Order

design of purifying from ignoble foreigners the kingdom which gave birth to themselves and their ancestors, who were men of noble race, and of regaining proper and commendable laws; and they resolved that if any one, whosoever he might be, should oppose this determination, he should be compelled, even though against his will, to join them. Although the king and his eldest son, Edward, had taken the oath, the latter began as far as he could, to draw back from it, as did also John, Earl Warenne. HENRY [of Almain], THE SON OF RICHARD, KING OF GERMANY [*sic*; technically, Richard, Earl of Cornwall and King Henry III's brother, was titled "King of the Romans"], wavered, and said that he would on no account take such an oath without the advice and permission of his father; whereupon he was told plainly and publicly, that even if his father himself would not acquiesce in the plan of the barons, they should not keep possession of one furrow of land in England. The aforesaid brothers of the king had, moreover, sworn positively, by the death and wounds of Christ, that they would never, as long as they lived, give up the castles, revenues, or guardianships which their brother, the king, had freely given them, although Simon, earl of Leicester, had given up gratis to the king of his castles of Kenilwithe and Odiham, which he had repaired and fortified a few days previously. When they made this declaration, affirming it by unmentionable oaths, Simon, earl of Leicester, addressing himself to William de Valence, who was blustering more than the others replied: "You may rest assured that you will either give up the castles which you hold from the king, or you will undoubtedly lose your head;" and the other earls and barons said the same, and swore to it in a most determined manner. The **Poitevins** were, in consequence, in great alarm, and knew not what to do; for if they betook themselves for concealment to any castle, being destitute of all stores and means of defense, they would be besieged, and would perish of hunger; for even if the nobles did not do so, the whole community of the people at large would besiege them, and destroy their castles to the very foundations. They therefore suddenly and secretly took to flight, whilst dinner was being prepared; and that their design might not be found out, they pretended that they wished to sit down to dinner. As they fled, they frequently looked behind them, and made some of the retainers ascend high towers to watch if the barons followed in pursuit of them; nor did they spare their horses' sides till they reached Winchester, where, in their fear, they placed themselves, as it were, under the protecting wings of the bishop elect of Winchester, on whom all their hopes depended; and moreover, they had hopes of finding a safe place of refuge in the castles belonging to him, the said bishop elect. The nobles in the mean time became more firmly leagued together, and appointed as their justiciary, HUGH BIGOD, brother of the earl marshal, an illustrious and high-born knight, of pure English blood, and well skilled in the laws of the country; and he fulfilled the duties of justiciary with vigour, and would not allow the rights of the kingdom to totter on any account. When the nobles were made aware of the certain flight of the Poitevins, as aforesaid, they feared that the fugitives might get near to the sea-coast and summon foreigners, Poitevins and others, from the continent, to their aid. Seeing, then, that delay brought on danger, they gave strict orders to their vassals, and to all their partisans, to fly to arms, and to mount their horses with all haste; and thus ended the parliament at Oxford, without any fixed and definite result.

Source: Paris, Matthew. *English History.* Translated by J. A. Giles. London: Henry G. Bohn, 1854. 3: 285–288.

AFTERMATH

King Henry was forced to agree to the Provisions of Oxford, but the pope—still technically the overlord of the kingdom since King John had made England a papal fief—nullified

Henry's oaths and threatened the barons with excommunication. This did not quell the uprising: civil war ensued, with the king and the barons exchanging the upper hand. In 1264, Earl Simon and his baronial supporters won a victory against the royal army at Lewes, in Sussex. They captured King Henry and his family, forcing William de Valence and other royal supporters to flee. The royalists returned, freed Henry's son Lord Edward (future Edward I) from captivity, and won a stunning victory at the battle of Evesham on August 4, 1265. Earl Simon was killed in the battle and his body mutilated—his severed head and genitals were sent to Lady Maud de Mortimer, who had aided in the liberation of Lord Edward and had housed the royalists at Wigmore Castle. The royal forces also—in a rare show of vengeance not typical in medieval battles—killed many members of the baronial army and command. Peace was restored only with difficulty, but this process was aided by a combination of reasonable negotiations between the now-dispossessed rebels and the Crown, codified in the Dictum of Kenilworth, and the use of crusade vows to reconnect royalists and rebels: many of the barons on both sides accompanied Edward on crusade in 1270.

ASK YOURSELF

1. Why did the barons—who themselves were of French heritage—consider King Henry's "foreign" advisors so dangerous?
2. Matthew Paris suggests that the response of King Henry's brothers—to flee the country—was an act of cowardice. Do you think that staying and fighting would have been beneficial?
3. Why were the barons so intent on controlling the actions of King Henry?

TOPICS TO CONSIDER

1. Some historians consider the Oxford Parliament and the "Provisions" of Oxford to be the origins of parliamentary democracy; others reject this claim. Consider and debate both sides.
2. Baronial anxieties about the power of the king did not really die down after the death of King John and the reissue of Magna Carta. Consider how this anxiety might have led to the rebellion against King Henry III and the influence that memories of his father might have had on baronial decision making.

Further Information

Carpenter, D. A. "King, Magnates, and Society: The Personal Rule of King Henry III, 1234–1258." *Speculum* 60, no. 1 (1985): 39–70.
Ridgeway, H. W. "Foreign Favourites and Henry III's Problems of Patronage, 1247–1258." *The English Historical Review* 104, no. 412 (1989): 590–610.
Stewart, Susan. "Simon de Montfort and His Followers, June 1263." *The English Historical Review* 119, no. 483 (2004): 965–969.

27. Anglo-Irish Relations in the Fourteenth Century: The *Remonstrance of the Irish Chiefs against English Rule to Pope John XXII* (1317)

INTRODUCTION

This lengthy letter, written to Pope John XXII, was spearheaded by the Irish chieftain Domhnall [Donal] Ó Néill [O'Neil] at a time when, after the invasion of Ireland in 1315 by ROBERT BRUCE's brother EDWARD, the papacy in Avignon was trying to negotiate between King Robert I and King Edward II [r. 1307–1327] concerning rule in Scotland, and the English were violently repelling the Bruce invasion of Ireland. The document's focus, like the later Scottish *Declaration of Arbroath*, was on the mythic heroic past of Ireland, the need for independence from a foreign occupying power, and the right of the Celtic lands to autonomy because of their long-standing loyalty to the Church. The format, however, owes a debt to Magna Carta, in that it outlines the specific grievances of the Irish chieftains against the English Crown and demands redress. The pope, who was heavily dependent on the support of the English for the maintenance of his authority in exile from Rome and whose twelfth-century predecessor Hadrian IV had presented King Henry II with a papal bull in 1155 inviting him to invade Ireland, does not seem to have replied. The invasion of Edward Bruce failed when he was killed at the battle of Faughart, County Louth, in 1318.

KEEP IN MIND AS YOU READ

Petitions to the pope for redress of wrongs done by kings to their subjects had a checkered history, as kings tended to view papal interference in political interactions with considerable hostility. Moreover, the fourteenth-century papacy struggled with its credibility because of the popes' removal from Rome and their settlement in Avignon, a papal fiefdom on the border of France. The ongoing hostilities between the kings of England and France meant that competition for papal support formed a part of their political activity.

Document 1: The Remonstrance of the Irish Chiefs

Lest the sharp-toothed and viperous calumny of the English and their untrue representations should to any degree excite your mind against us and the defenders of our right, which God forbid, and so that there may be no ground for what is not well known and is falsely presented to kindle your displeasure, for our defense we pour into yours ears with mighty out-cry by means of this letter an entirely true account of our origin and our form of government, if government it can be called, and also of the cruel wrongs that have been wrought inhumanly on us and our forefathers by some kings of England, their evil ministers and English barons born in Ireland, wrongs that are continued still; and this we do in order that you may be able to approach the subject and see in which party's loud assertion the truth bears company. And thus being carefully and sufficiently informed so far as the nature of the case demands, your judgment, like a naked blade, may smite or correct the fault of the party that is in the wrong.

Know then, most Holy Father, that since the time when our early ancestors, the three sons of Milesius or Micelius of Spain, by God's will came into Ireland (then destitute of all inhabitants) with a fleet of thirty ships from Cantabria, a city of Spain standing on the bank of the river Ebro or Hiberus (from which we take the name we bear), 3,500 years and more have passed, and of those descended from these men 136 kings without admixture of alien blood assumed the monarchical rule over all Ireland down to king Legarius, from whom I, Donald, have derived my descent in a straight line. It was in [the] days that our chief apostle and patron St. Patrick, sent [to] us [by Pope Celestine] in the year 432 taught the truths of the Catholic faith with the fullest success to our fathers.

And after the faith had been preached and received, 61 kings of the same blood, without intervention of alien blood, kings admirably in the faith of Christ and filled with works of charity, kings that in temporal things acknowledged no superior, ruled here uninterruptedly in humble obedience to the Church of Rome until the year 1170.

And it was they, not the English nor others of any nation who eminently endowed the Irish Church with lands, ample liberties and many possessions, although at the present time she is, for the most part, sadly despoiled of those lands and liberties by the English.

And although for so long a time those kings with their own power had stoutly defended against tyrants and kings of divers countries the inheritance that God had given them and had always kept their birthright of freedom unimpaired, yet at last, in the year of the Lord 1155 [corrected], at the false and wicked representation of King Henry of England . . . Pope Adrian [aka Hadrian IV], your predecessor, an Englishman not so much by birth as by feeling and character, did in fact, but unfairly, confer upon that same Henry . . . this lordship of ours by a certain form of words, the course of justice entirely disregarded and the moral vision of that great pontiff blinded, alas! by his English proclivities. And thus, without fault of ours and without reasonable cause, he stripped us of our royal honor and gave us over to be rent by teeth more cruel than any beast's; and those of us that escaped half-alive and woefully from the deadly teeth of crafty foxes and greedy wolves were thrown by violence into a gulf of doleful slavery.

For, from the time when in consequence of that grant the English iniquitously but with some show of religion entered within the limits of our kingdom, they have striven with all their might and with every treacherous artifice in their power, to wipe our nation out entirely and utterly to extirpate it. . . . [T]hey have compelled us to seek mountains, woods, bogs, barren tracts and even caverns in the rocks to save our lives, and for a long time back to make our dwellings there like beasts. Yet even in such places as these they harass us continually and endeavor all they can to expel us from them and seek unduly to usurp to themselves every place we occupy, mendaciously asserting in their blind madness that there is to be no free abode for us in Ireland but that all the land is entirely theirs by right.

Whence, by reason of all this and much more of the same kind, relentless hatred and incessant wars have arisen between us and them, from which have resulted mutual slaughter, continual plundering, endless rapine, detestable and too frequent deceits and perfidies.... For we hold it as an established truth that more than 50,000 human beings of each nation, ... have fallen by the sword in consequence of that false representation and the grant resulting from it, since the time when it was made. Let these few general particulars of the origin of our ancestors and the wretched position in which a Roman Pontiff placed us suffice on this occasion.

Know, most holy Father, that King Henry of England ... and also the four kings his successors have clearly gone beyond the limits of the grant made them by the Pope's bull in certain definite articles, as appears plainly from the very text of the bull.... [The English have not supported and protected the Church in Ireland. They have corrupted the Irish people and deprived them of their native laws, replacing them with unjust and wicked ones.]

In the King of England's court in Ireland these laws are rigidly observed, viz. that any person that is not an Irishman may bring any Irishman into court on any cause of action without restriction; but every Irishman, cleric or lay, excepting only prelates, is refused all recourse to law by the very fact of being Irish.

Also, as usually happens for the most part when by perfidy and guile some Englishman kills an Irishman, however noble and inoffensive, whether cleric or lay, regular or secular, even if an Irish prelate should be killed, no punishment or correction is inflicted by the said court on such a nefarious murderer; nay more, the better the murdered man was and the greater the place be held among his people, the more his murderer is honored and rewarded by the English ...

Also, every Irishwoman, whether noble or otherwise, who marries any Englishman, is entirely deprived, after her husband's death, of the third part of his lands and possessions, her rightful dower, precisely because she is Irish. [Under English Common Law, a widow has right of use of one-third of her late husband's lands; the claim is that this English law was ignored when the widow was of Irish nationality]

...

[The English enslave the Irish and refuse to allow them to make wills.]

[The archbishop of Armagh has forbidden any Irish from entering monastic houses founded by English lords.]

[The English, exemplified by Peter de Bermingham, Thomas de Clare, Geoffrey de Pencoyt, and John fitzThomas, murder their Irish dinner guests with impunity and sell their heads.]

Let these few cases, notorious to everyone, out of the countless misdeeds of that nation suffice as instances, on this occasion.

And though acts of this kind appear horrible and detestable to all Christians, yet to those of that oft-mentioned nation ... they seem honorable and praiseworthy, since those that do them reap not at all the punishment of which they are deserving ... For not only their laymen and secular clergy but some also of their regular clergy dogmatically assert the heresy that it is no more sin to kill an Irishman than a dog or any other brute....

[The author relates a number of cases of conflict between monastic houses and Irish neighbors and religious foundations.]

And ... all of them indifferently, secular and regular, assert with obstinacy that it is lawful for them to take away from us by force of arms whatever they can of our lands and possessions of every kind, making no conscientious scruple about it even when they are at the point of death. And all the land they hold in Ireland they hold by usurpation in this way.

And of whatever condition or station he may be that should withstand this error or preach in opposition to them, for that alone he is proclaimed an enemy to the king and kingdom of England, as guilty of death and outlawed by the King's council. For, lusting eagerly for our lands, they . . ., by sowing perpetual dissensions between them and us, have craftily and deceitfully kept us apart from them, lest of our own free will we should hold from the King directly the lands that are rightfully our due. . . .

And as in way of life and speech they are more dissimilar from us and in their actions from many other nations than can be described by us in writing or in words, there is no hope whatever of our having peace with them. For such is their arrogance and excessive lust to lord it over us and so great is our due and natural desire to throw off the unbearable yoke of their slavery and to recover our inheritance wickedly seized upon by them, that as there has not been hitherto, there cannot now be or ever henceforward be established, sincere good will between them and us in this life. For we have a natural hostility to each other arising from the mutual, malignant and incessant slaying of fathers, brothers, nephews and other near relatives and friends so that we can have no inclination to reciprocal friendship in our time or in that of our sons. . . .

Let no one wonder then that we are striving to save our lives and defending as we can the rights of our law and liberty against cruel tyrants and usurpers, especially since the said King, who calls himself lord of Ireland, and also the said kings his predecessors have wholly failed in this respect to do and exhibit orderly government to us and several of us.

Wherefore, if for this reason we are forced to attack that King and our said enemies that dwell in Ireland, we do nothing unlawful but rather our action is meritorious and we neither can nor should be held guilty of perjury or disloyalty on this account, since neither we nor our fathers have ever done homage or taken any other oath of fealty to him or his fathers. . . .

Furthermore, we are ready and prepared to maintain by the testimony of twelve bishops at least and of many other prelates the articles here set forth and to prove the wrongs herein recited, lawfully in due time and place and by way of law which is due to us of right; not like the English, who in the time of their prosperity and power will never stand to any due course of proceedings or process of law . . .

Therefore, on account of the aforesaid wrongs and infinite other wrongs which cannot easily be comprehended by the wit of man . . .; and in order to shake off the hard and intolerable yoke of their slavery and to recover our native liberty, which for a time through them we lost, we are compelled to wage deadly war with them, preferring under stress of necessity to put ourselves like men to the trial of war in defense of our right, rather than to bear like women their atrocious outrages.

And that we may be able to attain our purpose more speedily and fitly in this respect, we call to our help and assistance Edward de Bruce, illustrious earl of Carrick, brother of Robert by the grace of God most illustrious king of the Scots, who is sprung from our noblest ancestors. [The Irish chieftains have declared him their High King.]

May it please you therefore, most Holy Father, for the sake of justice and general peace mercifully to approve what we have done as regards our said lord and king, forbidding the King of England and our aforesaid adversaries henceforward to molest us, or at least be pleased to render us with fitting favor our due complement of justice in respect of them.

For know, our revered Father, that besides the kings of lesser Scotia who all drew the source of their blood from our greater Scotia, retaining to some extent our language and habits, a hundred and ninety seven kings of our blood have reigned over the whole island of Ireland.

Here ends the process set on foot by the Irish against the king of England.

Source: Ó Néill, Domhnall. *Remonstrance of the Irish Chiefs to Pope John XXII.* Edited by Edmund Curtis. Corpus of Electronic Texts Edition. Accessed online http://www.ucc.ie/celt/published/T310000-001/index.html. Original publication: Curtis, Edmund, ed. *Irish Historical Documents, 1172–1922.* New York: Barnes and Noble, 1968 [1943]. Pp. 38–46. Modernized and edited by editor. Reprinted with permission from CELT.

AFTERMATH

The Irish chiefs were not successful in gaining papal authority for their ongoing struggle against English rule. Indeed, King Edward III (r. 1327–1377), whose son LIONEL OF ANTWERP, duke of Clarence, married ELIZABETH DE BURGH the heiress to the earldom of Ulster, sent him to Ireland to rule as governor of the lordship. While there, Duke Lionel promulgated the *Statutes of Kilkenny* (1366), which gave teeth to the radical separation of the Irish and the English under law. The Irish—and their "Old English" allies and neighbors—resented the interference of the English king and ignored the statutes. Clarence, in disgust, returned to England. With the exception of KING RICHARD II in 1394 and 1399, no English royal set foot in Ireland again in the Middle Ages.

The purpose behind the Scots and the Irish presenting themselves as having an ancient classical lineage has a great deal to do with their notions of cultural independence and sovereignty. Just as the Romans claimed descent from Aeneas, the prince of Troy who escaped with the help of his mother, Venus, to found a Trojan colony in Italy, the Welsh claimed descent from another Trojan, Brutus, and the Irish and Scots from a Greek-Scythian king in Spain, Milesius. These lineages—with their claims to unbroken passage from the ancient past to the present day—were designed to compete successfully with the shorter and less civilized lineages of the English, descended traditionally from the Saxons Hengist and Horsa, and the Normans, descended from Vikings.

ASK YOURSELF

1. What were the specific grievances of the Irish chiefs against the kings of England?
2. Why would the Irish chiefs write to the pope instead of addressing their grievances to the king, as was done in Magna Carta and the Provisions of Oxford?
3. Why was the petition unsuccessful in the long run, and how would that have affected Irish attitudes about the English in the years after?

TOPICS TO CONSIDER

1. Compare this document and the Declaration of Arbroath.
2. Compare this document and the principles behind the Provisions of Oxford. How are they similar, and how different?
3. The Irish chiefs did not break out in a widespread organized rebellion, such as the baronial rebellions that occurred in England in the thirteenth century. Speculate as to why they did not.

Further Information

Phillips, J. R. S. "The Irish Remonstrance of 1317: An International Perspective." *Irish Historical Studies* 27, no. 106 (1990): 112–129.

Scully, Diarmuid. "The Remonstrance of Irish Princes, 1317." *History Ireland* 21, no. 6 (2013): 16–19.

28. Anglo-Irish Diplomacy in Aid of Irish Tenants (1319)

INTRODUCTION

When the *Remonstrance* failed to lead the papacy to check English royal predations against the Irish, and the invasion of Edward Bruce ended with his death, Anglo-Irish magnates whose families had settled more than a hundred years before on the island took matters into their own hands. As peers of the realm, John fitzThomas, Earl of Kildare, and Baron John de Bermingham might have felt that they had better access to the ear of the king—in this instance King Edward II (r. 1307–1327)—and therefore took it upon themselves to petition the Crown for Irish subjects to gain access to English law. John fitzThomas had just been elevated to the earldom by the king, so he must have felt that he had an advantage in the negotiations. The petition seems to have done the trick, at least for the Irish tenants of Earl John fitzThomas and Lord John de Bermingham.

KEEP IN MIND AS YOU READ

The Anglo-Norman settlers who followed the conquest of Ireland in the 1170s had intimate ties of marriage and family not only to each other but also to noble families in Wales and England. The ones who chose to remain in Ireland—many who held land in Ireland did so as absentees, which created its own set of problems—considered themselves a unique group; they came to be referred to as "Old English" in comparison to the "New English" settlers sent by fourteenth- and fifteenth-century kings to expand English influence on the island.

Document 1: Ancient Petitions, no. 5944

Petition of Earl Thomas fitzJohn of Kildare and John of Bermingham that all the Irish who so desire may embrace English law and custom [1319].

To our lord king and his council, the gentlemen Thomas fitzJohn Earl of Kildare and John de Bermingham, in order to maintain the good estate of the king and expand his power in Ireland, pray that the lord king grant and give the power by commission to his justiciar of Ireland to receive all the Irish into the law and custom of England who desires it, and who pray to be at peace and faith with our lord king; and that they and their heirs be able to enjoy and maintain themselves under English law in the land [of Ireland] for all their days. And they additionally pray that the lord king, for the profit of this said land, grant the aforementioned Thomas and John power by his commission to receive the Irish in their lands and on the marches to the law aforementioned in the form written below so that they have the power to certify for the king concerning those who are thusly received into the peace and who pray to have the aforementioned law, and that they are able to have charters of the king.

Dorse
The king concedes this petition by fiat.

Source: *Documents on the Affairs of Ireland before the King's Council.* Edited by G. O. Sayles. Dublin, 1979. P. 90. Translated by editor.

AFTERMATH

Although some Irish tenants took advantage of gaining access to English law, most of the native population, especially those living outside the area of English rule known as "The Pale," had little if any interest in becoming more anglicized. It is not clear that the English kings much cared either, as the *Statutes of Kilkenny* of 1366 demonstrates. English political control of the lordship of Ireland dwindled during the course of the fourteenth century, as did royal revenues.

ASK YOURSELF

1. Why would Irish people want to have access to English legal institutions?
2. What benefits would the English lords derive from having their Irish tenants have access to English law?
3. What role does ethnic identity have in deciding whether or not to live under a different system of law?

TOPICS TO CONSIDER

1. Consider the relationship between the *Remonstrance* and the request to place Irish people under the rule of English law.
2. Consider the role of the Anglo-Irish baronage in the competition between Irish and English law and customs in Ireland.

Further Information

Duffy, Patrick. "The Nature of the Medieval Frontier in Ireland." *Studia Hibernica* 22/23 (1982/1983): 21–38.

Gwynn, Aubrey. "Edward I and the Proposed Purchase of English Law for the Irish, c. 1276–80." *Transactions of the Royal Historical Society* 10 (1960): 111–127.

Mitchell, Linda E. "Gender(ed) Identities? Anglo-Norman Settlement, Irish-ness, and the Statutes of Kilkenny of 1367." *Historical Reflections/Réflexions Historiques* 37, no. 2 (2011): 8–23.

Sheehy, Maurice. "English Law in Medieval Ireland." *Archivium Hibernicum* 23 (1960): 167–175.

29. Anglo-Scottish Relations in the Fourteenth Century: The Declaration of Arbroath (1320)

INTRODUCTION

Perhaps inspired by the *Remonstrance of the Irish Chiefs*, the peers of the realm of Scotland took it upon themselves to write their own (much shorter) letter to Pope John XXII petitioning his intervention in the ongoing war between England and Scotland. The document was probably drafted by Abbot Bernard of Arbroath Abbey and written in the abbey's scriptorium. It outlines the "historical" reasons for Scotland's independence from England at a time when the independence of Scotland—and the legitimacy of its king, Robert I—was contested. The papacy had sided with King Edward I of England in declaring Scotland subordinate to the English Crown and had also excommunicated Robert Bruce in 1306 for the murder of JOHN III COMYN OF BADENOCH. In this, as in other documents identifying nationalist reasons for independence of the same era, such as the *Remonstrance* of a few years before, the focus is on both a heroic mythic past that validates the claim to independence and on the injustices of rule by a foreign power.

KEEP IN MIND AS YOU READ

The presentation of a long history of independence and of origins from a mythic Roman, Trojan, or Greek past for the contemporary population and its culture were common tropes in petitions against an invading power. This can be seen in the protests of the Welsh princes against English encroachment, as well as in the Irish and Scottish examples seen here. This "Declaration" is also touted by modern-day Scots as the foundation of their independence and sovereignty: a kind of medieval declaration of independence. Indeed, there is some evidence that Thomas Jefferson was familiar with this document and that it influenced his drafting of the Declaration of Independence of the American colonies in 1776.

Document 1: The Declaration of Arbroath, April 6, 1320 (15 Robert I)

To the most Holy Father and Lord in Christ, the Lord John, by divine providence Supreme Pontiff of the Holy Roman and Universal Church, his humble and devout sons Duncan, Earl of Fife, Thomas Randolph, Earl of Moray, Lord of Man and of Annandale, Patrick Dunbar, Earl of March, Malise, Earl of Strathearn, Malcolm, Earl of Lennox, William, Earl of Ross, Magnus, Earl of Caithness and Orkney, and William, Earl of Sutherland; Walter, Steward of Scotland, William Soules, Butler of Scotland, James, Lord of Douglas, Roger Mowbray, David, Lord of Brechin, David Graham, Ingram Umfraville, John Menteith, guardian of the earldom of Menteith, Alexander Fraser, Gilbert Hay, Constable of Scotland, Robert Keith, Marshal of Scotland, Henry St Clair, John Graham, David Lindsay, William Oliphant, Patrick Graham, John Fenton, William Abernethy, David Wemyss, William Mushet, Fergus of Ardossan, Eustace Maxwell, William Ramsay, William Mowat, Alan Murray, Donald Campbell, John Cameron, Reginald Cheyne, Alexander Seton, Andrew Leslie, and Alexander Staiton, and the other barons and freeholders and the whole community of the realm of Scotland send all manner of filial reverence, with devout kisses of his blessed feet.

Most Holy Father and Lord, we know from the chronicles and books of the ancients we find that among other famous nations our own, the Scots, has been graced with widespread renown. They journeyed from *Greater Scythia* by way of the Tyrrhenian Sea and the *Pillars of Hercules* and dwelt for a long course of time in Spain among the most savage tribes, but nowhere could they be subdued by any race, however barbarous. Thence they came, twelve hundred years after the people of Israel crossed the Red Sea, to their home in the west where they still live today. The Britons they first drove out, the Picts they utterly destroyed, and, even though very often assailed by the Norwegians, the Danes and the English, they took possession of that home with many victories and untold efforts; and, as the historians of old time bear witness, they have held it free of all bondage ever since. In their kingdom there have reigned one hundred and thirteen kings of their own royal stock, the line unbroken [by] a single foreigner. The high qualities . . . of these people, were they not otherwise manifest, gain glory enough from this: that the King of kings and Lord of lords, our Lord Jesus Christ, after His Passion and Resurrection, called them, even though settled in the uttermost parts of the earth, almost the first to His most holy faith. Nor would He have them confirmed in that faith by merely anyone by the first of His Apostles . . . the most gentle Saint Andrew, the Blessed Peter's brother, and desired him to keep them under his protection as their patron forever.

Greater Scythia: the area north of Greece—
modern-day Bulgaria
Pillars of Hercules: the Straits of Gibraltar

The Most Holy Fathers your predecessors gave careful heed to these things and bestowed many favors and numerous privileges on this same kingdom and people, as being the special charge of the Blessed Peter's brother. Thus our nation under their protection did indeed live in freedom and peace up to the time when that mighty prince the King of the English, Edward [I], the father of the one who reigns today, when our kingdom had no head and our people harbored no malice or treachery and were then unused to wars or invasions, came in the guise of a friend and ally to harass them as an enemy. The deeds of cruelty, massacre, violence, pillage, arson, imprisoning prelates, burning down monasteries, robbing and killing monks and nuns, and yet other outrages without number which he committed against our people, sparing neither age nor sex, religion nor rank, no one could describe nor fully imagine unless he had seen them with his own eyes.

But from these countless evils we have been set free, by the help of Him Who though He afflicts yet heals and restores, by our most tireless Prince, Kind and Lord, the Lord Robert. He, that his people and his heritage might be delivered out of the hands of our enemies, met toil and fatigue, hunger and peril, like another Macabaeus or Joshua and bore them cheerfully. Him, too, divine providence, his right of succession according to our laws and customs which shall maintain to the death, and the due consent and assent of us all have made our Prince and King. To him, as to the man by whom salvation has been wrought unto our people, we are bound both by law and by his merits that our freedom may be still maintained, and by him, come what may, we mean to stand. Yet if he should give up what he has begun, and agree to make us or our kingdom subject to the King of England or the English, we should exert ourselves at once to drive him out as our enemy and a subverter of his own rights and ours, and make some other man who was well able to defend us our King; for, as long as but a hundred of us remain alive, never will we on any conditions be brought under English rule. It is in truth not for glory, or riches, nor honors that we are fighting, but for freedom—for that alone, which no honest man gives up but with life itself.

Therefore it is, Reverend Father and Lord, that we beseech your Holiness with our most earnest prayers and suppliant hearts, . . . [that] you will look with the eyes of a father on the troubles and privation brought by the English upon us and upon the Church of God. May it please you to admonish and exhort the King of the English, . . . to leave us Scots in peace, who live in this poor little Scotland, beyond which there is no dwelling-place at all, and covet nothing but our own. We are sincerely willing to do anything for him, having regard to our condition, that we can, to win peace for ourselves. . . . [The author declares that the pope should demand that all aggressors go on Crusade to the Holy Land instead of attacking their smaller and weaker neighbors.] But if your Holiness puts too much faith in the tales the English tell and will not give sincere belief to all this, nor refrain from favoring them to our prejudice, then the slaughter of bodies, the perdition of souls, and all the other misfortunes that will follow, inflicted by them on us and by us on them, will, we believe, be surely laid by the Most High to your charge.

To conclude, we are and shall ever be, as far as duty calls us, ready to do your will in all things, as obedient sons to you as His Vicar; and to Him as the Supreme King and Judge we commit the maintenance of our cause, casting our cares upon Him and firmly trusting that He will inspire us with courage and bring our enemies to naught. May the Most High preserve you in his Holy Church in holiness and health and grant you length of days.

Source: *The Declaration of Arbroath.* 1320. Translated by John Prebble. Reprinted with permission from Jan Prebble. Accessed online at http:www.constitution.org/scot/arbroath.htm

AFTERMATH

Unlike the *Remonstrance*, Pope John XXII did respond to the *Declaration* and the letter from King Robert Bruce that accompanied it. He lifted the ban of excommunication on the king (who no doubt was compelled to do penance for the murder of his competition) and urged the kings of England and Scotland to meet and enact a peace treaty between them. Edward II was uninterested in making peace, especially after the humiliating defeat at Bannockburn, and a treaty—that of Northampton—was not enacted until 1328 by the regency council of King Edward III following the deposing of Edward II. Even this treaty did not settle the conflict between the kingdoms, as it demanded the forfeiture of Scottish estates by nobles who were loyal to England. King Edward III, after he attained his majority in 1330, re-engaged the Bruce kings in a second "Scottish War of Independence." A final treaty between the two kingdoms was not enacted until 1357, with the Treaty of Berwick, in which the kings of England relinquished their claim to controlling the throne of Scotland. Edward III, however, never returned the Stone of Scone, the traditional coronation seat of Scottish kings, which had been taken by King Edward I in 1296.

ASK YOURSELF

1. Why would the pope respond to this petition when he did not respond to the *Remonstrance*?
2. What is the role of ethnic or national identity in formulating a protest against foreign influence?
3. Why did the Scots nobles consider it necessary to write this petition to the pope?

TOPICS TO CONSIDER

1. Compare the *Remonstrance* and the *Declaration of Arbroath*.
2. Analyze the ways in which the English kings are presented in the document and compare them to the ways in which Scotland and its king are presented.
3. Compare the *Declaration of Arbroath* and the Declaration of Independence (1776) and consider how Jefferson might have been influenced in his drafting of the latter document.

Further Information

Menache, Sophia. "The Failure of John XXII's Policy toward France and England: Reasons and Outcomes, 1316–1334." *Church History* 55, no. 4 (1986): 423–437.

Simpson, Grant G. "The Declaration of Arbroath Revitalised." *The Scottish Historical Review* 56, no. 161, pt. 1 (1977): 11–33.

30. KING ROBERT BRUCE AND DIPLOMACY IN SCOTLAND (1321)

INTRODUCTION

Once Robert Bruce was crowned and had removed any other competitors for the Scots throne (such as the murder of John Comyn of Badenoch), he consolidated his authority through the expansion of the royal chancery and engaged in the kinds of international diplomacy that would establish him as the monarch in Scotland. Although now a part of Scotland, the Orkney Islands, which had been settled by Norsemen since sometime in the eighth century, was still part of the Kingdom of Norway in the fourteenth century, but jurisdiction was somewhat contested. Moreover, Bruce, as the victor of the Scottish wars of succession, was in a delicate position with respect to the kings of Norway, because they had a tenuous claim to the kingdom through Margaret of Scotland, who married King Eric II of Norway, and whose granddaughter Margaret's death in 1290 precipitated the Great Cause. The letter to the baillies (royal officials) of Orkney reflects the delicacy of Bruce's position even in 1321, seven years after the battle of Bannockburn drove the English from the kingdom.

KEEP IN MIND AS YOU READ

The multiethnic region of Scotland was not united in its current borders until the middle of the fifteenth century. Kings of the Scots had worked diligently to gain sovereignty over the "southern isles"—the islands of the Irish Channel and the Inner and Outer Hebrides—in the thirteenth century but were unable to gain an advantage over the kings of Norway with respect to the "northern isles" of Orkney, Shetland, and Lewis. The population of those regions was largely Scandinavian, with Gaelic Scots merging into the dominant group. Even today the modern dialects in the northern isles are blends of Scots Gaelic and Norwegian.

Document 1: Letter of King Robert I to the Baillies of the King of Norway in Orkney. Dated at Cullen, 4 August 1321, Regnal Year 16 Robert I

Robert by grace of god king of Scotland to the baillies of the lord king of Norway [Magnus VII, r. 1319–1343] in Orkney, greetings. Among the many and varied treaties made between the predecessors of the king of Norway and our royal progenitors, the kings of Scotland, and also renewed between King Hakon of good memory, the previous king of Norway, and ourselves to be observed under penalty of ten thousands marks, was one that no king of either kingdom should receive or harbor fugitives from the other's lands, unless under the hope of procuring reconciliation . . . We have heard truly that Alexander Brown, our enemy [who is] convicted of treason against our crown [the term used is guilty of *lese maiestas*] was received by your baillies at Orkney, and that [even though] Sir Henry Sinclair, our bailly in Caithness, demanded his return, you refused to deliver him, contrary to the aforementioned treaty . . . Wherefore we . . . wish and desire to know . . . whether this entertainment and abovementioned breach of the treaty has been done by you on the instruction of the King of Norway aforesaid or on your own authority . . . Moreover, we understand by the information received from certain trustworthy persons . . . that you not only rashly violate the said treaties in this matter . . . [but that you also admit other wrongdoers to dwell in Orkney and send your own men to do injury to us, so that] our enemies are not prohibited from sojourning among you, while the faithful men of our kingdom whose natural and human right it is to be protected and cherished wherever they be, are not received; concerning which we also desire [to know] whether the same is on your own authority or by royal command.

Source: *Regesta Regum Scottorum.* Vol. V. *The Acts of Robert I: King of Scots, 1306–1329.* Edited by Archibald A. M. Duncan. Edinburgh: Edinburgh University Press, 1988. Translated by editor.

AFTERMATH

Although King Robert Bruce was successful in securing his dynastic hold over most of Scotland, continuing conflict between Scotland and England during the reign of Edward III, as well as between Scotland and Norway, prevented the monarchy from being entirely independent of outside influence. In 1468, as part of the marriage negotiations between King Christian I of Norway and King James III (Stewart) of Scotland, in which Christian's daughter Margaret was betrothed to James, King Christian pledged the northern isles as security for Margaret's dowry. The dowry never materialized, so the northern isles were effectively joined to Scotland.

ASK YOURSELF

1. How would engaging in this kind of diplomacy assert Robert Bruce's legitimacy to the throne of Scotland?
2. Why would the residents of Orkney resist any influence from King Robert Bruce?
3. In what ways could this letter be construed as an attempt by the king of Scots to interfere in the sovereignty of Orkney?

TOPICS TO CONSIDER

1. Consider the reign of Robert I Bruce and compare it to that of King Edward I of England.
2. Investigate the ways in which the Bruce monarchy utilized English administrative techniques to consolidate royal authority and power.

Further Information

Barrow, G. W. S. *Robert Bruce and the Community of the Realm of Scotland.* Edinburgh: Edinburgh University Press, 2005.

Helle, Knut. "Norwegian Foreign Policy and the Maid of Norway." *The Scottish Historical Review* 69, no. 188, pt. 2 (1990): 142–156.

WARFARE, CONQUEST, AND DIPLOMACY

31. King Alfred, War, and Diplomacy (Ninth Century)

INTRODUCTION

King Alfred's life and reign were notable in several respects: he gained a reputation for being a clever tactician and a brave warrior despite some significant physical ailments (which included possibly Crohn's disease and definitely a very bad case of hemorrhoids) as well as a respected leader of soldiers and an esteemed and flexible ruler. Several episodes are remarked upon in the *Anglo-Saxon Chronicle*, as well as mentioned in Asser's *Life of Alfred*, that were formative to his development as a monarch: the battle of Ashdown, which was the first major victory of the Wessex army over the Danes, and Alfred's successful fight against the armies of the Danelaw at Edington seven years later, which led to the baptism of the king of the Danelaw, Guthrum, and Alfred standing as his godfather in the ceremony. The baptism was part of the diplomatic negotiations following the battle, in which the borders of the kingdom of Wessex and the Danelaw were established and a peace treaty was signed between the two leaders.

KEEP IN MIND AS YOU READ

Anglo-Saxon armies did not fight on horseback, unlike the armies led by knights in later years. When they confronted their enemies, they did so behind a "shield wall": a defensive strategy in which the infantry was protected by interlocking their shields, which made it possible for them to move forward in formation or to stand and withstand an oncoming army. Although accounts of battles often mention a significant slaughter of soldiers, the use of numbers in medieval sources usually simply indicate that a host was "large" or "really large."

The strategy of requiring the baptism of the vanquished was one that had been employed by Charlemagne against the Saxons early in the ninth century, but with only limited success. Although Guthrum did accept baptism, it is not clear how sincerely such a conversion could be, and it did not include the wholesale Christianization either of his army or of the Danish and Norse rulers of the Danelaw.

Document 1: Alfred at Ashdown and Edington

871 In this year the army came into Wessex to Reading, and three days later two Danish earls rode farther inland. Then Ealdorman Aethelwulf encountered them at Englefield, and fought against them there and had the victory, and one of them, whose name was Sidroc, was killed there. Then four days later KING ETHELRED [I] and his brother Alfred led a great army to Reading and fought against the army; and a great slaughter was made on both sides and Ealdorman Aethelwulf was killed, and the Danes had possession of the battlefield.

And four days later King Ethelred and his brother Alfred fought against the whole army at Ashdown; and the Danes were in two divisions: in the one were the heathen kings Bagsecg and Healfdene, and in the other were the earls. And then King Ethelred fought against the kings' troop, and King Bagsecg was slain there; and Ethelred's brother Alfred fought against the earls' troop, and there were slain Earl Sidroc the Old, and Earl Sidroc the Younger and Earl Osbearn, Earl Fraena, and Earl Harold; and both enemy armies were put to flight and many thousands were killed, and they continued fighting until night.

And a fortnight later King Ethelred and his brother Alfred fought against the army at Basing, and there the Danes had the victory. And two months later, King Ethelred and his brother Alfred fought against the army at *Meretun*, and they were in two divisions; and they put both to flight and were victorious far on into the day; and there was a great slaughter on both sides; and the Danes had possession of the battlefield. And Bishop Heahmund was killed there and many important men. And after this battle a great summer army came to Reading. And afterwards, after Easter, King Ethelred died, and he had reigned five years, and his body is buried at Wimborne **minster**.

Then his brother Alfred, the son of Aethelwulf, succeeded to the kingdom of the West Saxons. And a month later King Alfred fought with a small force against the whole army at Wilton and put it to flight far into the day; and the Danes had possession of the battlefield. And during that year nine general engagements were fought against the Danish army in the kingdom south of the Thames, besides the expeditions which the king's brother Alfred and ealdormen and king's thegns often rode on, which were not counted. And that year nine (Danish) earls were killed and one king. And the West Saxons made peace with the army that year.

. . .

878 In this year in midwinter after twelfth night the enemy army came stealthily to Chippenham, and occupied the land of the West Saxons and settled there, and drove a great part of the people across the sea, and conquered most of the others; and the people submitted to them, except King Alfred. He journeyed in difficulties through the woods and *fen-fastnesses* with a small force.

And the same winter the brother of Ivar and Healfdene was in the kingdom of the West Saxons [in Devon], with 23 ships. And he was killed there and 840 men of his army with him. And there was captured the banner which they called "Raven."

And afterwards at Easter, King Alfred with a small force made a stronghold at Athelney, and he and . . . the people of Somerset . . . nearest to it [fought] from that stronghold against the enemy. Then in the seventh week after Easter he rode to "Egbert's stone" east of Selwood, and there came to meet him all the people of Somerset [and] Wiltshire and the part of Hampshire which was on this side of the sea, and they rejoiced to see him. And then after one night he went . . . to Iley, and after another night to Edington, and there fought against the whole army and put it to flight, and pursued it as far as the fortress, and

Meretun: Marton, in either Wiltshire or Dorset; exact location unknown
fen-fastnesses: marshes and wetlands

stayed there a fortnight. And then the enemy gave him preliminary hostages and great oaths that they would leave his kingdom, and promised also that their king should receive baptism, and they kept their promise. Three weeks later King Guthrum with 30 of the men who were the most important in the army came [to Alfred] at Aller[ton], which is near Athelney, and the king stood sponsor to him at his baptism there; and the unbinding of the chrism took place at Wedmore. And he was twelve days with the king, and he honored him and his companions greatly with gifts.

Source: "Ashdown and Other Engagements." In *The Anglo-Saxon World: An Anthology.* Translated by Kevin Crossley-Holland. © 1982 Boydell Press, reprinted with the permission of Boydell and Brewer Ltd.

AFTERMATH

The peace between the kingdom of Wessex and the Danelaw did not last long. Although Alfred was able to secure a measure of stability in his kingdom, his successors continued to fight against the Scandinavian-held Danelaw, with the unification of the northern region and the kingdom of Wessex being achieved by King Athelstan (r. 924–939), King Alfred's grandson. This did not end competition between English and Danish kings, as the successful invasion of Cnut in the next century attests.

ASK YOURSELF

1. What would Alfred have learned about battle techniques between the time when his brother was on the throne and the time when he confronted the Danes as king?
2. Why was it so difficult for the armies of Wessex to withstand attacks from the Danes and northerners?
3. How could the forced conversion to Christianity of their enemies help the kings of Wessex both militarily and diplomatically?

TOPICS TO CONSIDER

1. Compare Alfred's battles at Ashdown and Edington to that of his grandson at Brunanburh, not only in the ways they are described but also in military tactics.
2. Compare Anglo-Saxon fighting techniques to those of the Normans at the battle of Hastings in 1066.
3. Imagine in what ways in which the use of a shield wall would be effective as a battle strategy.

Further Information

Brooks, N. P. "England in the Ninth Century: The Crucible of Defeat." *Transactions of the Royal Historical Society* 29 (1979): 1–20.
Nelson, Janet L. " 'A King across the Sea': Alfred in Continental Perspective." *Transactions of the Royal Historical Society* 36 (1986): 45–68.
Sturdy, David. *Alfred the Great.* London: Constable, 1998.

32. King Athelstan and the Battle of Brunanburh (937)

INTRODUCTION

The battle of Brunanburh was one of the great victories of King Athelstan and his brother Edmund Atheling over an alliance of Olaf Guthfrithson, King of Dublin and York, Owain of Strathclyde, and Constantine, king of the Scots. This victory consolidated Athelstan's hold over all of England: the first time the region was actually united as a single kingdom, albeit with regional and localized differences in law and governance. The description of the battle in the *Anglo-Saxon Chronicle* is in the form of an alliterative heroic poem.

KEEP IN MIND AS YOU READ

If taken as a single event, the battle was not necessarily all that significant, as all the participants on the opposing side had earlier sworn oaths to King Athelstan and had attended his royal court several times, thus suggesting that they had accepted positions as subkings to Athelstan as "high" king. The battle, therefore, was more of a large skirmish in the ongoing territorial conflicts among rulers in the British Isles. In terms of national pride, however, the battle and Athelstan's victory loomed large in the English psyche. The fact that the author of the entry in the *Anglo-Saxon Chronicle* rendered it in heroic verse is a testament to the emotional power of the victory.

Document 1: The Battle of Brunanburh

In this year King Aethelstan, Lord of Earls,
ring-giver to men, and his brother also,
Prince Eadmund, won eternal glory
in battle with sword edges
around Brunanburh. They split the shield-wall,
they hewed battle shields with the remnants of hammers.
The sons of Eadweard, it was only befitting their noble descent
from their ancestors that they should often
defend their land in battle against each hostile people,

> *hoary:* white-haired

horde and home. The enemy perished,
Scots men and seamen,
fated they fell. The field flowed
with blood of warriors, from sun up
in the morning, when the glorious star
glided over the earth, God's bright candle,
eternal lord, till that noble creation
sank to its seat. There lay many a warrior
by spears destroyed; Northern men
shot over shield, likewise Scottish as well,
weary, war sated.
The West-Saxons pushed onward
all day; in troops they pursued the hostile people.
They hewed the fugitive grievously from behind
with swords sharp from the grinding.
The Mercians did not refuse hard hand-play to any warrior
who came with Anlaf over the sea-surge
in the bosom of a ship, those who sought land,
fated to fight. Five lay dead
on the battle-field, young kings,
put to sleep by swords, likewise also seven
of Anlaf's earls, countless of the army,
sailors and Scots. There the North-men's chief was put
to flight, by need constrained
to the prow of a ship with little company:
he pressed the ship afloat, the king went out
on the dusky flood-tide, he saved his life.
Likewise, there also the old campaigner through flight came
to his own region in the north–Constantine–
hoary warrior. He had no reason to exult
the great meeting; he was of his kinsmen bereft,
friends fell on the battle-field,
killed at strife: even his son, young in battle, he left
in the place of slaughter, ground to pieces with wounds.
That grizzle-haired warrior had no
reason to boast of sword-slaughter,
old deceitful one, no more did Anlaf;
with their remnant of an army they had no reason to
laugh that they were better in deed of war
in battle-field—collision of banners,
encounter of spears, encounter of men,
trading of blows—when they played against
the sons of Eadweard on the battle field.
Departed then the Northmen in nailed ships.
The dejected survivors of the battle,
sought Dublin over the deep water,
to return to Ireland, ashamed in spirit.
Likewise the brothers, both together,
King and Prince, sought their home,

West-Saxon land, exultant from battle.
They left behind them, to enjoy the corpses,
the dark coated one, the dark horny-beaked raven
and the dusky-coated one,
the eagle white from behind, to partake of carrion,
greedy war-hawk, and that gray animal
the wolf in the forest.
Never was there more slaughter
on this island, never yet as many
people killed before this
with sword's edge: never according to those who tell us
from books, old wisemen,
since from the east Angles and Saxons came up
over the broad sea. Britain they sought,
Proud war-smiths who overcame the Welsh,
glorious warriors they took hold of the land.

Source: "The Battle of Brunanburh 937 AD." http://www.brunanburh.org.uk/asc-poems/asc-poem-english. Copyright © 2015 The Battle of Brunanburh 937 AD.

AFTERMATH

Athelstan's victory and his annexation of the kingdom of York unified the territory of England for the first time since the Viking invasions. In addition, he was able to claim—although not necessarily enforce—overlordship as king of the English over HYWEL DDA, king of Deheubarth in south Wales, as well as over Constantine of Scotland and Owain of Strathclyde. Olaf, in the meantime, returned to Dublin. Nevertheless, historians consider Athelstan's success to be ephemeral. When his brother Edward succeeded, he was unable to retain control over northern England, which was again ruled by Olaf, and the Viking kings ultimately achieved total success against the kings of Wessex during the reign of Ethelred II "the Redeless" (r. 978–1013, 1014–1016).

Anglo-Saxon poetry used adjectives known as "kennings" to describe nouns as a way of enhancing the alliterative and rhythmic aspects of the verse. A common kenning to describe a king was "ring-giver" even though by the reign of Aethelstan, it was rare for the king's troops, or "war band," to be rewarded in this way. Can you locate other kennings in this poem?

ASK YOURSELF

1. Why would the author of this poem insert it into a historical chronicle?
2. How does the poet describe the battle?
3. Why was this battle so important for the Anglo-Saxons?

TOPICS TO CONSIDER

1. Compare the battle of Brunanburh to those described in the Alfred readings above.
2. Consider the political as well as emotional resonance of the battle in poetic form as written in the *Anglo-Saxon Chronicle*.

3. Consider the ways in which the Anglo-Saxons and the Danes are presented in the poem: as heroic, as cowardly, as venal, and so on, and analyze these presentations as propaganda.

Further Information

Foote, Sarah. *Athelstan: The First King of England.* New Haven: Yale University Press, 2011.

Halloran, Kevin. "The Brunanburh Campaign: A Reappraisal." *The Scottish Historical Review* 84, no. 218, pt. 2 (2005): 133–148.

33. Two Views of the Battle of Hastings (1066)

INTRODUCTION

The invasion of William, Duke of Normandy, and the ensuing battle near the town of Hastings in Kent on October 14, 1066, was a watershed in British history. Duke William's success and the death of KING HAROLD GODWINSON in the battle changed utterly England's relation to the continent and to the other regions of the British Isles. The crowning of William also ushered in a completely new kind of political structure, with an administration that was recorded in Latin, rather than the vernacular, and with very different views on everything from land ownership to taxes, to dispute resolution.

Depictions of the battle of Hastings in various chronicles differ significantly not only in their political stance—whether they supported the Anglo-Saxon king Harold Godwinson or the Duke of Normandy—but also in their descriptions of the battle itself. This can make it quite difficult to reconstruct a complete chronology of the battle. Nevertheless, two elements are agreed upon by most, if not all, the depictions: that Harold's troops were driven in some way to "break" their defensive shield wall, which protected them from William's mounted knights, and that William employed radically different tactics—such as pretending to retreat or even flee—in order to lure the Anglo-Saxon soldiers into traps prepared for them.

KEEP IN MIND AS YOU READ

As mentioned above, the Anglo-Saxons did not fight on horseback and they relied on their training and shield wall to defend against enemy attacks. These tactics served them well against the armies of Harald Hardrada, the king of Norway, who invaded England and whom Harold Godwinson met in battle at Stamford Bridge, Yorkshire, on September 25, 1066—a mere three weeks before engaging William's army. The routing of the Scandinavian invaders and the death of Harald Hardrada was a great victory, but it was a tired and footsore army that met Duke William's fresh troops at Hastings in October.

Document 1: The Battle of Hastings According to the Anglo-Saxon Chronicle

Meantime Earl William came up from Normandy into Pevensey on the eve of Michaelmas; and soon after his landing was made, they constructed a castle at the port of Hastings. This was then told to King Harold; and he gathered a large force, and came to meet him at the estuary of Appledore. William, however, came against him unawares, before his army was collected; but the king, nevertheless, very bravely encountered him with the men that would support him; and there was a great slaughter made on either side. There was slain King Harold, and Leofwin his brother, and Earl Girth his brother, with many good men; and the Frenchmen gained the field of battle, as God granted them for the sins of the nation. Archbishop Aldred and the corporation of London desired to have the child Edgar [Edgar the Atheling] as king, as he was the most appropriate candidate [as the last surviving male of the House of Wessex]; and Edwin and Morkar promised them that they would fight with them. But the more prompt the business should ever be, so was it from day to day the later and worse; as in the end it all fared. This battle was fought on the day of Pope Calixtus: and Earl [*sic*: Duke] William returned to Hastings, and waited there to know whether the people would submit to him. But when he found that they would not come to him, he went up with all his force that was left and that came since to him from over sea, and ravaged all the country that he overran, until he came to Berkhampstead; where Archbishop Aldred came to meet him, with child Edgar, and Earls Edwin and Morkar, and all the best men from London; who submitted then for need, when the most harm was done. It was very ill-advised that they did not so before, seeing that God would not better things for our sins. And they gave him hostages and took oaths; and he promised them that he would be a faithful lord to them; though in the midst of this they [the Normans] plundered wherever they went. Then on midwinter's day [December 21st] Archbishop Aldred consecrated him as king at Westminster, and gave him possession with the books of Christ, and also made him swear, before he would set the crown on his head, that he would so well govern this nation as any before him best did, if they would be faithful to him. Nevertheless he laid very heavy tribute on men, and in Lent went over sea to Normandy, taking with him Archbishop Stigand, and Abbot Aylnoth of Glastonbury, and the child Edgar, and the Earls Edwin, Morkar, and Waltheof, and many other good men of England. Bishop Odo and Earl William lived here afterwards, and built castles widely through this country, and harassed the miserable people; and ever since has evil increased very much. May the end be good, when God will!

Source: *The Anglo-Saxon Chronicle*, Part 5: A.D. 1052–1069. Online Medieval and Classical Library Release #17. http://omacl.org/Anglo/. Text based on *The Anglo-Saxon Chronicle*, translated by James Ingram. London: Everyman Press, 1912. Modernized by editor.

Document 2: The Battle of Hastings According to Henry of Huntingdon

[After the Battle of Stamford Bridge] Harold, king of England, returned to York . . . But while he was at dinner, a messenger arrived with the news that William, duke of Normandy, had landed on the south coast, and had built a fort at Hastings. The king hastened southwards to oppose him, and drew up his army on level ground in that neighborhood. Duke William commenced the attack with five squadrons of his splendid cavalry, . . . but first he addressed them to this effect:

[William exhorts his troops in a lengthy speech extolling the martial prowess of the Normans and reminding them—"the race of ROLLO"—of their successful conquests in France and Italy. He goes on to excoriate the English for their lack of military skill on horseback and their lack of archers.]

Duke William had not concluded his harangue, when all the squadrons, inflamed with rage, rushed on the enemy with indescribably impetuosity, and left the duke speaking to himself! Before the armies closed for the fight, one *Taillefer*, sportively brandishing swords before the English troops, while they were lost in amazement at his gambols, slew one of their standard-bearers. A second time one of the enemy fell. The third time he was slain himself. Then the ranks met; a cloud of arrows carried death among them . . . But Harold had formed his whole army in close column, making a rampart, which the Normans could not penetrate. Duke William, therefore, commanded his troops to make a feigned retreat. . . . they happened unawares on a deep trench . . . into which numbers fell and perished. . . . Duke William also commanded his bowmen not to aim their arrows directly at the enemy, but to shoot them in the air . . . this occasioned great loss to the English. [A small force of knights break through the shield-wall and capture the English standard.] Meanwhile, a shower of arrows fell round King Harold and he himself was pierced in the eye. A crowd of horsemen now burst in, and the king, already wounded, was slain. With him fell Earl Gurth and Earl Leofric, his brothers. After the defeat of the English army . . . the Londoners submitted peaceably to William and he was crowned at Westminster by Aldred, archbishop of York. Thus the land of the Lord brought to pass the change which a remarkable comet had foreshadowed in the beginning of the same year . . . [Indeed, as depicted on the Bayeaux Tapestry and verified scientifically, Halley's Comet made a pass in early 1066.]

> *Taillefer:* possibly Duke William's fool or court jester

Source: *The Chronicle of Henry of Huntingdon.* Translated and edited by Thomas Forester. London: Henry G. Bohn, 1853. Pp. 209–212.

Henry of Huntingdon (ca. 1080–1160) was archdeacon of Lincoln during the reigns of Henry I (r. 1100–1135) and Stephen (r. 1135–1155) and, shortly before his death, witnessed the succession of Henry II to the throne. Unusually for the period, Henry was not a monk, but rather a member of the secular clergy: it was rare for writers of chronicles to operate outside the cloister. Henry's histories are written in a very personal style, full of anecdotes and long speeches, none of which are reliable as accurate. He is the source of the legend that King Henry I died from overindulging in his favorite food, lamprey eels.

Henry's presentation of the battle of Hastings is characteristic of his writing, which differs significantly not just in style but also in substance from other accounts of the battle.

AFTERMATH

The results of the battle of Hastings were profound, not just in the replacing of one elite community by another, in addition to the replacing of one royal dynasty by another. The relationship between king and subject; the legal, fiscal, and judicial systems under which all people in

England lived; and the relationship between the British Isles and continental Europe, all were transformed. Although King William I (r. 1066–1087) claimed to be retaining the "good old laws" of Anglo-Saxon England, in fact he created a radical break between the political, legal, and social systems before the conquest and those that developed after.

ASK YOURSELF

1. Why were the Normans successful in the end?
2. What features of the battle are emphasized by the authors? Why do you think that is?
3. What would medieval people have thought about the comet: what would it have signified for them?

TOPICS TO CONSIDER

1. Compare the accounts of the battle and consider the significance of one coming from an Anglo-Saxon author and the other from a Norman author.
2. Imagine what might have happened if Harold Godwinson had not died in the battle but still had been defeated.
3. Consider the differing battle tactics of the Anglo-Saxons and the Normans and analyze why the Normans' strategies were more effective.

Further Information

Chibnall, Marjorie. *The Debate on the Norman Conquest.* Manchester: Manchester University Press, 1999.

Hollister, C. Warren. "The Norman Conquest and the Genesis of English Feudalism." *The American Historical Review* 66, no. 3 (1961): 641–663.

Morris, Marc. *The Norman Conquest: The Battle of Hastings and the Fall of Anglo-Saxon England.* New York: Pegasus Books, 2013.

34. The Competing Reigns of King Stephen and Empress Matilda and the Siege of Newbury (1153)

INTRODUCTION

England experienced a period of civil war in the years after the death of King Henry I (r. 1100–1135). Henry's heir was his daughter, Matilda, widow of Emperor Henry V and wife of Geoffrey "Plantagenet," count of Anjou. Although his barons swore to honor Henry's wish for his daughter to succeed him on the throne, a large faction broke away upon Henry's death and declared themselves supporters of Count Stephen of Blois, whose mother, ADELA, was Henry's sister (and thus daughter of William the Conqueror). The ensuing war between the followers of Stephen, who was crowned by the Archbishop of Canterbury a mere four days after King Henry I's death, and those of Empress Matilda, who called herself "Lady of the English" rather than queen, occupied the majority of the next 20 years.

John Marshal, the father of William Marshal, was a supporter of the empress. In 1153, King Stephen's army laid siege to John Marshal's castle; in the *History of William Marshal*, it is referred to as Newbury (Newtown), but it is likely to have been the castle of Hampstead Marshal in Berkshire. The success of the castle's inhabitants in defending themselves by trickery and guile led directly to the release of little William Marshal into the custody of King Stephen as a hostage.

KEEP IN MIND AS YOU READ

Sieges were far more common in medieval warfare than outright battles. They were often lengthy campaigns—and destructive, as the besiegers laid waste to the countryside around the castle and those being besieged often suffered from dwindling supplies of food, water, and defensive weapons. The poem's description of the siege, and the ways in which the inhabitants of Newbury defended themselves against the king's army, is a rare—and useful—glimpse into the typical workings of such a military endeavor.

Document 1: The Siege of Newbury

[T]he King [Stephen] besieged Newbury
at the head of a mighty force of men.
But he did this so much by surprise
that those inside the castle
were not aware at all of it
until they saw their soldiers,
their archers and their scouts,
indeed the whole army, which dismounted
and set to pitching tents.
When those within the walls saw them,
they knew full well that they had been taken unawares.
This surprise attack was particularly disagreeable
since they had little in the way of provisions.
The King sent a formal request by messenger,
asking the **constable**
whether he was prepared to surrender the castle
or wished to defend it against him.
No time was lost in reaching a decision:
"We are not so beleaguered
that we have no wish to put up a stout defense;
we have no intention of surrendering the castle.
Things have now gone so far
that there will be many a blow received,
many a skull split, and many otherwise wounded
by blade of spear of lance,
and many trampled underfoot so that
all that will be needed after that are the biers."
The King directed his anger against their side,
and he swore by the birth of Christ:
"I'll be sure to take my revenge on the low villains,
they will all fall into my hands.
Now, to arms, my valiant **squires**,
my valiant men-at-arms and archers!
Snarl as they might, we'll capture them.
To the first man to get inside
I shall give such wealth
that he will never be poor again in his lifetime."
You should have seen those squires
start to clamber with great daring
over the ditches and up the embankments.
And those within the walls defended themselves
courageously and furiously;
they hurled down slabs of stone, sharpened stakes,
and massive pieces of timber to knock them to the ground.
They made them pay a horrible price
for their attempt on them;

if it was in their power, they would thwart it.
Many could be seen to topple upside down
and fall headlong on to their backs;
many were wounded and many knocked unconscious.
Those in the castle could not be blamed
for defending themselves,
for they expected no immediate help.
Those outside had the worst of it.
Thereupon the assault was suspended,
an assault that had been very dangerous.
The King was greatly troubled by events,
and swore that he would not let things rest there
and that he would never leave that place
until he had taken the towerand punished those within.
The people in the castle decided,
good folk that they were,
they would ask for a truce,
and in the meantime would relay
to their lord and master
all the information about their situation.
They asked for the truce and were given it,
and, as fast as they could,
they informed their lord that they had only one day's truce,
therefore, if he could, would he come and rescue them,
for inside they had nothing to live on.

Source: *History of William Marshall.* Edited by A. J. Holden, translated by S. Gregory, and notes by D. Crouch. Volume I. London: Anglo-Norman Text Society, 2002. Lines 400–472; pp. 23–25. Reprinted with permission.

AFTERMATH

Although King Stephen had two sons at the beginning of the civil war, Eustace, his eldest, died in 1153. In 1151, Count Geoffrey of Anjou died, and his son Henry succeeded him as count of Anjou and duke of Normandy, which Count Geoffrey had seized and held during the long war. Henry soon landed in England to continue his mother's fight; a stalemate between his forces and those of Stephen ensued. The two contenders ultimately signed the Treaty of Wallingford in 1152, in which Stephen ceded the Crown of England to Henry after his death—in effect adopting him as his son and heir for England—while his younger son, William, retained the title and lands of Blois. King Stephen died in October 1154; Henry succeeded to the throne and was crowned in April 1155. Those barons who had remained loyal to his mother were significantly rewarded by the young Henry II; among those was John Marshal.

ASK YOURSELF

1. Who would be at best advantage: the besieger or the besieged?
2. Why would besieging castles lead to long-term anxieties or enmity?
3. Why might sieges be more effective than battles in prosecuting a war?

TOPICS TO CONSIDER

1. Most discussions of medieval warfare focus on battles, but the reality of war in the Middle Ages is that significant levels of noncombatant activity occurred, especially in sieges, where most of the victims were not soldiers. Consider the nature of warfare in the Middle Ages and how civilian populations were affected.

2. Consider the long-term implications of a civil war: how would the former enemies be reconciled? How would rewards and punishments be distributed?

Further Information

Albion 6, no. 3 (1974) [special issue on the reign of King Stephen].

Chibnall, Marjorie. *The Empress Matilda: Queen Consort, Queen Mother, and Lady of the English*. Oxford: Basil Blackwell, 1991.

King, Edmund. *King Stephen*. New Haven: Yale University Press, 2011.

35. CONFLICT AND CONSOLIDATION IN SCOTLAND (TWELFTH CENTURY)

INTRODUCTION

The royal dynasty descended from Malcolm III Canmore survived to rule in Scotland until 1290, when the principal line died out with the demise of PRINCESS MARGARET, "Maid of Norway." KING WILLIAM I "THE LION" (r. 1165–1214) was the grandson of King David I; he succeeded to the throne after the death of his brother Malcolm IV. King William was determined to consolidate royal power throughout Scotland and to extend his influence into northern England: he hoped to annex Northumberland. Although he was able to gain control of some English territory by helping to fund King Richard I's crusade, the native leaders of western Scotland resisted his encroachments, and there were two rebellions, in 1179 and 1181, against him. The second rebellion was led by Donald MacWilliam, a descendent of King Duncan II (son of Malcolm III and his first wife—or concubine—Ingibiorg Finnsdottir, who ruled briefly in 1094), who was also known, like his ancestor, as Donald *Ban* (Donald the Fair). King William put down such rebellions brutally—a technique of rule that did not always mete criticism in the chronicle sources.

KEEP IN MIND AS YOU READ

Scotland was an ethnically diverse portion of Britain with a highly decentralized political structure. The earls, especially those on the outer fringes of the kingdom, had virtual sovereign authority in their regions and it is unclear how effectively the kings of Scotland could interfere or intervene in them. Nevertheless, the kings from the eleventh century maintained an agenda to consolidate royal rule throughout Scotland, by either fortuitous marriages, diplomacy, or warfare. They were also, for much of the time between the Norman Conquest and the fourteenth century, considered to be subject to the overlordship of the king of England, although English kings varied in their demands of homage and fealty.

Document 1: The Revolt of Donald MacWilliam

Also in this year William king of Scotland, together with his brother David earl of Huntingdon and a great army, advanced into Ross against MacWilliam, whose real name was Donald *Ban*. There he fortified two castles, Dunskeath and Etherdouer. Having fortified these, he returned to the southern parts of his realm. But seven years after that, since Donald *Ban* continued in his customary wickedness, the king advanced into Moray with a large army, a very strong force, against this same adversary Donald *Ban*. Donald [boasted] that he was of royal descent, the son of William, the son of Duncan the Bastard, who was the son of the great king Malcolm, the husband of St. Margaret. Relying on the treachery of some disloyal subjects, he had first of all by insolent usurpation forcibly removed from his king the whole earldom of Ross. He subsequently held the whole of Moray for a considerable time, and by employing fire and slaughter had seized the greater part of the kingdom, moving all about all of it, and aspiring to have it under his control.

While the king with his army was staying in the town of Inverness, and had been harrying Donald *Ban* and his supporters with daily raids for booty and plunder, it chanced one day that when he had sent out his men as usual, up to two thousand strong, to reconnoiter and take booty across the **moors** and the countryside, some of those who were serving with the king's army suddenly and unexpectedly came upon MacWilliam as he was resting with his [exhausted] troops on a moor near Moray called "Mam Garvia." When MacWilliam saw that the king's troops were few in comparison with his own, he hurriedly joined battle with them, and charged the royal forces. They bravely resisted all his efforts, and because they trusted in their righteousness of their cause, continued to resist courageously. With God's help they cut down MacWilliam and five hundred of his men, and put the rest to flight, on Friday 31 July, thus repaying him with a just reward for his evil deeds. They sent his head to the king to be displayed to the whole army.

Source: Bower, Walter. *A History Book for Scots*. Edited by D. E. R. Watt. Edinburgh: Mercat Press, 1998. P. 111.

AFTERMATH

King William I's reign was very long—indeed, long enough to span the rebellions against King Henry II in England, as well as the reigns of Richard I and John, before the baronial rebellion of 1215. His longevity made it possible for him to stretch royal authority farther into the northern and western reaches of Scotland than any of his predecessors, but it was still only a partial victory. The native earls—those, at least, whose marriages did not connect them to the king or to his Anglo-Norman-based court—remained significantly independent and the northern isles remained in the nominal control of Scandinavian kings. However, William I took significant steps to associate the kings of Scotland more closely with their English royal neighbor, especially through marriage. His son ALEXANDER II was married to Joan of England, daughter of King John and ISABELLE OF ANGOULÊME; Alexander's son by his second wife, Marie de Coucy, King ALEXANDER III, married Margaret of England, daughter of King Henry III and ELEANOR OF PROVENCE. These royal connections helped stabilize relations between the two kingdoms in profitable ways in the thirteenth century. They were to be destabilized by the dynastic conflict that followed the death of Alexander III's designated heir, his granddaughter Margaret of Norway.

ASK YOURSELF

1. Why would there be regionally based rebellions in Scotland against the king?
2. How would sending Donald MacWilliam's head to the king be considered a politically astute act?
3. In what way was the church in Scotland involved in this conflict, according to the chronicler?

TOPICS TO CONSIDER

1. Compare the description of these battles in Scotland to those in England, as presented in the readings above.
2. Consider the level of violence directed at elites in the battles between the competing Scots armies. Battles by the late eleventh century often included the ransoming of elites rather than their deaths. Why is this not happening in Scotland?
3. Would William I be considered a strong king or a weak king on the basis of this excerpt? Consider the political implications of his victory over Donald MacWilliam.

Further Information

Oram, Richard. *Domination and Lordship: Scotland, 1070–1230.* Edinburgh: Edinburgh University Press, 2011.

Owen, D. D. R. *William the Lion, 1143–1214: Kingship and Culture.* East Linton: Tuckwell Press, 1997.

Stevenson, J. H. "The Law of the Throne: Tanistry and the Introduction of the Law of Primogeniture: A Note on the Succession of the Kings of Scotland from Kenneth MacAlpin to Robert Bruce." *The Scottish Historical Review* 25, no. 97 (1927): 1–12.

36. King Edward of England and Prince Llywelyn ap Gruffudd of North Wales (1275–1278)

INTRODUCTION

Relations between the kings of England and the princes of Wales were always complicated, made even more so by the Norman Conquest and subsequent expansion of Anglo-Norman rule across the Welsh March and into Wales itself. By the thirteenth century, almost all the greatest magnates of the realm—the earls of Pembroke, Hereford, Norfolk, Gloucester, and Lincoln—controlled territory in Wales and pitted themselves regularly against the native princes. Throughout the thirteenth century, a stalemate essentially occurred, with no one group—Anglo-Norman or Welsh—able to permanently gain an upper hand. The most important Welsh princes, those of Gwynedd (North Wales), Deheubarth (Southwest Wales), and Powys (Mid-Wales), shifted frequently in their alliances, sometimes joining together against the English kings and sometimes turning against each other and allying with England.

The most prominent political group among the native Welsh was the House of Gwynedd, especially the two key figures of the thirteenth century, LLYWELYN AB IORWERTH (aka Llywelyn Fawr—the Great) and his grandson LLYWELYN AP GRUFFUDD. Gwynedd's princes demanded fealty from those of Deheubarth and Powys, which drove them into alliances with the English kings, especially Henry III and Edward I. At the same time, the "marcher" baronage—those controlling the borderlands between Wales and England as well as most of the southern region, especially by the 1270s—operated as yet another political body whose loyalties lay not always with their sovereign king and whose internal disputes threatened to destabilize Wales and the Marches even further.

The political situation in Wales came to a head soon after the crowning of King Edward I (r. 1272–1307) because of destabilizing conflicts among all the stakeholders in the region, Welsh and English. King Edward's demands that the Welsh princes take oaths of homage and fealty to him were met with resistance. His response was to invade. The conquest of Wales and the establishment of the "principality" as a subsidiary of the English Crown (Edward of Caernarvon, future Edward II, was the first English prince of Wales) took decades to accomplish, with localized rebellions appearing into the fifteenth century. The bulk of the conquest, however, occurred between 1277 and 1283.

KEEP IN MIND AS YOU READ

The only "historical" chronicle (as opposed to the largely mythic *History of the Kings of Britain* by Geoffrey of Monmouth) of the medieval period in Wales, the *Brut y Tywysogion*, or *Chronicle of Princes*, seems to have been compiled from a variety of monastic chronicles and collected possibly at the royal foundation of Strata Florida Abbey. The chronicle records events from the mid-ninth century to the early fourteenth century, suggesting that it was compiled soon after that time. The Latin original has disappeared, but Welsh versions are extant. The chronicle presents a decidedly "native" Welsh slant on events during the years of war with King Edward I, which provides a contrast to the perspectives of English historians.

Document 1: The Welsh Princes and King Edward I

1275. In the ensuing year, a little before Ascension Thursday [the Feast of the Ascension of Christ], King Edward [I] appointed a council in London; and then he established new institutions over the whole kingdom. In that year, on the fifteenth day of August, Owain, son of Maredudd, son of Owain, son of Gruffudd, son of the lord Rhys, died, and was buried at Strata Florida, in the chapter house of the monks, near his father. That year, about the feast of St. Mary in September, King Edward came from London to Caerleon, and summoned to him Llywelyn, son of Gruffudd, prince of Wales, to do homage to him. And the prince summoned unto him all the barons of Wales; and by general consent, he did not go to the king, because the king harbored his fugitives, namely David, son of Gruffudd, and GRUFFUDD, SON OF GWENWYNWYN. And on that account the king returned to England in anger, and Llywelyn returned to Wales. . . . That year, after the feast of St. Michael, Emri, son of Simon Montford, with Eleanor his sister, sailed for Gwynedd. And upon that journey they were seized by the gate-keepers of Haverford, and conveyed to the prison of King Edward. And this Eleanor had been betrothed to Llywelyn for his wife by representative words. And she, through the intercession and advice of Pope Innocent [IV] and the gentry of England, was set at liberty. And then, on the Feast of St. Edward, the marriage of Llywelyn and Eleanor was solemnized at Winchester, Edward, king of England himself bearing the cost of the banquet and nuptial festivities liberally. And of that Eleanor there was a daughter to Llywelyn, called Gwenllian; and Eleanor died in childbirth, and was buried in the chapter house of the *barefooted friars*, at Llanvaes in Mona. The said Gwenllian, after the death of her father, was taken as a prisoner to England, and before she was of age, she was made a nun against her consent. Emri was liberated from the king's prison, and he took a journey to the court of Rome.

barefooted friars: the Spiritual Franciscans
Midland District: the central counties of England
St. Ynys: unknown—*ynys* is Welsh word for island

1276. The ensuing year, the Lord Llywelyn sent frequent messengers to the court of the king about forming a peace between them, but he did not succeed. And at length, about the feast of Candlemas [February 2, also known as the Feast of the Purification of the Virgin], the king appointed a council at Worcester; and there he designated three armies against Wales; one for Caerleon, and himself to lead it; another for Castle Baldwin, led by the Earl of Lincoln [Edmund de Lacy] and Roger Mortimer. Gruffudd, son of Gwenwynwyn, had fixed upon them to reconquer his territory, which he had previously lost, . . . The third army he sent to Caermarthen and Ceredigion, led by Pain, son of Patrick de Says.

1277. The ensuing year, the Earl of Lincoln and Roger Mortimer besieged the castle of Dolvorwyn, and at the end of a fortnight they obtained it, through want of water. Then Rhys, son of Maredudd, son of Owain, son of Gruffudd, son of the lord Rhys, and Rhys Wyndod, son of young Rhys, son of Rhys Mechell, son of Rhys the Hoarse, son of the lord Rhys, nephew, sister's son, to the prince, became reconciled to Pain, son of Patrick. Llywelyn, his brother, and Howel, and Rhys the Hoarse, quitted their territory, and went to Gwynedd, to Llywelyn; Rhys, son of Maelgwn, son of the lord Rhys, went to Roger Mortimer, and made submission to the king, by the hand of Roger. And last of all, from South Wales, Gruffudd, and Cynan, the sons of Maredudd, son of Owain, son of Gruffudd, son of the lord Rhys, and Llywelyn, son of Owain, his nephew, became reconciled to the king. And thus all South Wales became subjected to the king. Then Pain, son of Patrick, subjugated to the king three **commotes** of Upper Aeron—Anhunog, and Mevenydd, and the middle commote. And Rhys, son of Maredudd, and Rhys Wyndod, and the two sons of Maredudd, son of Owain, son of Gruffudd, son of the lord Rhys, from Ceredigion, went to the court of the king, to offer their homage and oath of allegiance to him. But the king delayed accepting their homage until the next council; sending Rhys, son of Maredudd, and Gruffudd, son of Maredudd, home, and retaining with him Cynan, son of Maredudd, son of Owain, and Rhys Wyndod. And then Pain placed Llywelyn, son of Owain, as a youth in guardianship, because of a deficiency of age. After that, on the octave of the feast of St. John [the Baptist—June 24th], Rhys, son of Maelgwn, and the four above named barons, did homage to the king in the council at Worcester. The same year, the feast of St. James the Apostle [July 25th], Edmund, the king's brother, came with an army of Llanbadarn; and began to build a castle at Aberystwyth. And then the king, having his force with him, came to the *Midland District*, and fortified a court at Flint, surrounded with vast **dykes**. From thence he proceeded to Rhuddlan, and this he also fortified, by surrounding it with dykes; and there he tarried some time. That year, the Saturday after August [probably the feast of St. Augustine of Hippo, August 28th], Rhys, son of Maelgwn, son of the lord Rhys, retired to Gwynedd, to Llywelyn, for fear of being taken by the English who were at Llanbadarn; and thereupon the English took possession of his whole territory. And along with him the men of Genau y Glyn all retreated to Gwynedd, leaving the whole of their [grain crops] and land waste. On the eve of St. Matthew [September 20th], Edmund and Pain went to England, and left Roger Myles to be constable at Aberystwyth, and to protect the country. The day after the feast of *St. Ynys*, Rhys Wyndod, and Cynan, son of Maredudd, returned from the court of the king to their own country. That year, in the beginning of harvest, the king sent a great part of his army into Mona, which burned much of the country, and took away much of the [crop]. And on the **calends** of winter [possibly December 21st] after that, Llywelyn came to the king at Rhuddlan, and made his peace with him; and then the king invited him to come to London at Christmas, and he went there, and there he made his homage to the king. And after he had remained in London a **fortnight**, he returned to Wales. About the feast of St. Andrew, Owain the Red, and Owain, son of Gruffudd, son of Llywelyn, son of Iorwerth, and Gruffudd, son of Gwenwynwyn were released from the prison of Llywelyn, by the command of the king. And then Owain the Red obtained from his brother Llywelyn the **cantref** of Lleyn, with his full consent.

Source: *Brut y Tywysogion or The Chronicle of the Princes*. Ed. The Rev. John Williams Ab Ithel. Rolls Series. London: Longman, Green, Longman, and Roberts, 1860. Pp. 363–371.

Pronouncing Welsh names can be quite confusing! The double-l is pronounced as if there is an "h" in front of it, almost like a whistled-l. A double-d is pronounced as a soft "th" and a double-f is pronounced as a "v." Thus, "Daffydd ap Llywelyn" is pronounced "Dáh-vith ap Hlew-él-in."

AFTERMATH

Although Llywelyn was not without resources—especially with respect to his extensive castle-building throughout Gwynedd—he was never a real match for the manpower King Edward could deploy, and the treaty of Aberconwy of 1277 placed significant limits on his ability to raise an army. In addition, Llywelyn alienated other native princes, especially the lord of Powys, Gruffudd ap Gwenwynwyn, who turned to Edward in order to resist the prince of Gwynedd's invasion of his lands. Finally, although re-allied with his brother Dafydd, Llywelyn was unable to regulate his behavior or his loyalty, which waffled between the English king and the Welsh prince. This led to a confrontation between the Welsh and the English that was perhaps inevitable, but the outcome of which was not. In 1282, a new rebellion led by Dafydd ap Gruffudd broke out and Llywelyn lent his support. He was killed after being isolated from his troops and the main portion of the revolt collapsed. King Edward set upon occupying and rebuilding Gwynedd's castles, in time establishing royal military dominance up and down the western coast.

ASK YOURSELF

1. Wales is a tiny country; why was the political situation so volatile there?
2. Why would the king of England want control over Wales?
3. Why would Welsh lords, as well as English marcher barons, choose to swear oaths of loyalty to King Edward I rather than to Llywelyn ap Gruffudd?

TOPICS TO CONSIDER

1. Compare the conflicts between King William I, the Lion of Scotland, and the northwest territorial lords and those between King Edward I and the Welsh barons and consider the political motives behind a desire to consolidate sovereignty in such remote territories.
2. Consider the ways in which royal power is expressed through military action, in the context of both Edward I and Llywelyn ap Gruffudd.

Further Information

Given, James. "The Economic Consequences of the English Conquest of Gwynedd." *Speculum* 64, no. 1 (1989): 11–45.
Morris, J. E. *The Welsh Wars of Edward I.* Stroud: Sutton Publishing, 1996 [1901].
Turvey, Roger. *The Welsh Princes, 1063–1283.* London: Longman, 2002.

37. Edward I in Scotland, Prisoners of War, and the Countess of Buchan (1306)

INTRODUCTION

The political circumstances that led to what is popularly known as the **Great Cause** are extremely complicated because of the ways in which the Anglo-Norman and native Scots families intermarried in the years between the reign of David I (r. 1124–1153) and the death of Alexander III (r. 1249–1286). Alexander's heir was Margaret of Norway, his granddaughter, the child of King Eric II of Norway and Margaret of Scotland, who was only three years old at the time of his death in 1286. The kingdom of Scotland was placed in the hands of six "Guardians": William Fraser, bishop of St Andrews; Robert Wishart, bishop of Glasgow; Alexander Comyn, earl of Buchan; John II Comyn "the Black," lord of Badenoch; James Stewart, high steward of Scotland; and Duncan [Donnchadh] III, earl of Fife (or mormaer of Fife). They negotiated with King Edward I concerning maintenance of the kingdom during the lengthy projected minority of Princess Margaret of Norway, including an agreement to betroth her to Edward's son and heir, Edward of Caernarvon. Margaret's death in 1290, in transit to visit Scotland for the first time, threw the political community of Scotland into chaos, and brought forward all of the competitive hostilities that had developed among the lay Guardians and their fellow magnates, especially Robert Bruce, earl of Carrick, and the Comyns of Badenoch. King Edward claimed the right to determine the next king of Scotland, based on heredity and lineage; he chose John Balliol, who was duly crowned in 1292, only to be forced to abdicate by King Edward in 1296; the wars that erupted between England and Scotland were therefore connected to conflicts between competing members of the extended Canmore lineage and their allies.

In 1306, one of the "Competitors," Robert Bruce earl of Carrick, murdered another "Competitor," John III Comyn "the Red," Lord of Badenoch. The killing occurred moreover in a religious space: the church of the Greyfriars of Dumfries. As soon as King Edward learnt of John Comyn's death, he sent an army into Scotland led by John Comyn's brother-in-law, Aymer de Valence. Bruce, who had been crowned by ISABELLA MACDUFF, countess of Fife (and daughter of the Guardian), whose husband, John Comyn, earl of Buchan, supported King Edward against Bruce, was defeated in the Battle of Methven in June 1306. He sent his female relations and Countess Isabella north away from the fighting, but they were captured by Aymer de Valence's troops and imprisoned.

KEEP IN MIND AS YOU READ

The two accounts are different kinds of sources: one is from official letters sent between the army and King Edward, and the other is a chronicle. They therefore present different perspectives on the same event.

The use of hostages—including women—at times of war was extremely common in the Middle Ages, as attested to by the experiences of William Marshal as a child-hostage in the reign of King Stephen. King Edward's methods of imprisonment, which might have involved a certain level of public spectacle, were not necessarily unusual—although they are presented as such in the chronicle source—but they were effective.

Document 1: 34 Edward I (1306): Orders for Custody of Scottish Prisoners

[6] It is ordained and commanded by letters of the **privy seal** to the **Chamberlain** of Scotland or his representative at Berwick on Tweed, that in one of the turrets inside the castle, where it is most appropriate, he is to build a cage of strong lattice, well reinforced with bars, in which he should place the Countess of Buchan, who should be assiduously guarded in that cage so that she can in no way escape. And he should assign a lady or two from Berwick, who is English and upon whom no suspicion falls, to attend to the Countess concerning her food and drink, and other things that she requires. And whoever is guarding the cage should not allow her to speak with any man or woman who is of the nation of Scotland, nor any others except the woman or women who are assigned to attend her. And the cage should have every comfort appropriate to the Countess's station, but it is nevertheless commanded that the guard of the Countess never be lessened, but that guards be replaced [so that she is never not under guard].

[7] In the same manner it is ordained and commanded that Mary, sister of Robert de Bruce former Earl of Carrick be held at Rokesburgh [Roxborough] under guard in the castle in a cage.

[8] Item: Margery the daughter of Robert de Bruce be held at the Tower of London placed in a cage in the manner aforementioned, and that she not be allowed to talk to any man except the man whom the Constable of the Tower has assigned to guard her.

Source: *Documents and Records Illustrating the History of Scotland and the Transactions between the Crowns of Scotland and England.* Edited by Sir Francis Palgrave. London, 1837. 1: 358–359. Translated by editor.

The "cage of strong lattice" has been mythologized in the chronicles to become an iron cage that King Edward had hung over the battlements of Berwick Castle. This is clearly not the case: it was common for prisoners to be confined to a structure that could be locked easily and afforded the guards the visual reinforcement they needed, without endangering the physical safety of a woman prisoner. The "cage" in which the Countess of Buchan was placed was, therefore, the size of a room, luxuriously appointed, but open to view of the men guarding her in the tower.

Document 2: The Westminster Chronicle Describes the Aftermath of the Murder of John Comyn (1306)

After these events, the king of England marched into Scotland, with the Prince of Wales and the nobles of his kingdom, and some Scots received him honorably, some retreated backwards, and some sought the secret recesses of the woods. But the king's army traversed the whole kingdom of Scotland, and began to pursue the fugitives, and slew many of them, and took some alive, as the bishops and the abbot who have been mentioned above, having on breastplates and armor beneath their outer garments. The fault of both the bishops was great, but that of the bishop of Saint Andrew was the greater; for on the day of the battle between the English and Scots at Methven, near Saint John's, he sent all his retainers armed to the assistance of the Scots. But he himself, in the meantime, cunningly surrendered himself to the English, in order that, if the Scots triumphed over the English, they might deliver him from their power, as having been taken by force for want of sufficient protection, but that, if the English triumphed, they might spare him, because he had been deserted by his family, as not consenting to their actions. Therefore those perjured prelates were thrown into very close prisons, in the same garb and dress in which they had been taken, until it should be decided by the Apostolic See what was to be done with them. Also, that impious conspiratress, the countess of Buchan, was taken prisoner, respecting whom the king was consulted, when he said, "Because she has not struck with the sword, she shall not die by the sword; but, on account of the unlawful coronation which she performed, let her be closely confined in an abode of stone and iron, made in the shape of a crown, and let her be hung up out of doors in the open air at Berwick, that both her life and after her death she may be a spectacle and eternal reproach to travellers."

Source: *The Flowers of History, Especially Such as Relate to the Affairs of Britain. From the Beginning of the World to the Year 1307.* Collected by Matthew of Westminster. Translated from the original by C. D. Yonge, B. A. Volume II. London: Henry G. Bohn, 1853. Pp. 588–589.

AFTERMATH

The Edwardian "triumph" over Bruce and his Scottish allies was short-lived. During the reign of Edward II (r. 1307–1327), King Robert Bruce regained the upper hand and destroyed an English army at the battle of Bannockburn in 1314. Nevertheless, King Robert did not get his womenfolk back until a prisoner exchange after the battle of Bannockburn, and Isabella MacDuff Comyn seems to have died in prison.

ASK YOURSELF

1. If women were actively engaged in defending castles against armies, how is it that they are not often considered by historians to have been combatants in war?
2. Edward I clearly considered women such as Countess Isabella MacDuff to have been an enemy combatant; how does this change your view of medieval warfare?
3. Members of the clergy, too, are often not considered as fellow-combatants, but the chronicler clearly considers them to have engaged actively in warfare. How does this change your view of war in the Middle Ages?

TOPICS TO CONSIDER

1. Compare the description of the conquest of Wales with the invasion of Scotland.
2. Consider the political reasons why Edward I wanted to gain control of Scotland as a subordinate kingdom to England.
3. Consider the role of elite women in both the political and the military cultures of medieval Britain.

Further Information

Barrow, G. W. S. *Scotland and Its Neighbours in the Middle Ages.* London: Hambledon Press, 1992.

Neville, Cynthia J. "Widows of War: Edward I and the Women of Scotland during the War of Independence." In *Wife and Widow in Medieval England.* Edited by Sue Sheridan Walker. Ann Arbor: University of Michigan Press, 1993.

Young, Alan. *Robert the Bruce's Rivals: The Comyns, 1212–1314.* East Linton: Tuckwell Press, 1997.

CRIME, DISORDER, AND DEVIANCE

38. Crime and Violence in Early and Later Medieval Scotland (Eighth and Thirteenth Centuries)

INTRODUCTION

Later medieval Scottish chroniclers, such as WALTER BOWER, often had few written sources on which to rely, and so made use of orally transmitted tales and supposed eyewitness accounts that were passed down through the generations. What comes to be emphasized, especially in the early history of the Scots, is a level of violence and disorder that seems custom-designed to contrast with the civilized and orderly society of later medieval Scotland.

Two examples, one from the eighth century and the other from the thirteenth, demonstrate the ways in which such oral testimonies became mythologized and narratized into lessons for later Scots folk. This is particularly the case with the description of the death in 1222 of Adam, Bishop of Caithness, who, after attending the Fourth Lateran Council of 1215, attempted to impose the same kinds of ecclesiastical rights in his diocese of Caithness (in the far north of Scotland) as were permitted in other parts of Scotland. Earl Jon Haraldsson of Caithness, whose loyalties were divided between the King of Scotland and, as the Earl of Orkney, the King of Norway, failed to protect his bishop against the angry mob. His lack of action spurred King Alexander II to threaten to invade Caithness, prompting Earl Jon to travel to the king's Christmas court at Forfar to swear to his innocence.

KEEP IN MIND AS YOU READ

Chroniclers have multiple motives for including specific events in their histories, and these two examples demonstrate the competing motives of historical narration and lessons in ethical and moral behavior. Both are designed as well to demonstrate the savagery of the north in comparison to the civilization and security of the south, a common trope in Scottish chronicles.

Document 1: Mayhem in Medieval Scotland

The Murder of King Fergus Son of Aed Find of Dál Riata (r. 778–781) by His Wife

[Fergus] is said to have been poisoned by his wife and queen who was excessively jealous of him because of his affairs with other women. She afterwards openly admitted to the deed, although she was suspected by no one of such a crime. When she looked upon the dead king's body, with mournful cries and tearing her hair, she burst out with these or similar words: "Most wretched of women, more savage than any wild beast, basest betrayer, what have you done? Have you not wickedly killed with a most cruel king of treachery, most like in this respect to the asp and urged on by wanton madness, your lord the king, most loving of all husbands and handsome beyond the love of women, whom alone you loved with the innermost love of your heart more than all men now living? But this wicked crime will not go unpunished. I shall be avenged upon myself. Accordingly do you, accursed hand, hasten to prepare and do not let pass this same cup with which you drank the health of your lord, not long ago your sweetest lover, or boldly prepare an even more bitter cup for my lips too!" Then after she had drained the lethal draught she immediately began: "But that witch's potion ought not to suffice as full atonement for me who committed such a great crime. No! rather should I be tied to the tails of horses and dragged off to be hanged and this unspeakable body should be burnt to ashes in fires of thorns and the ashes scattered to the wind."

The Murder of Adam, Bishop of Caithness (1222)

This year that illustrious pastor Adam bishop of Caithness, formerly abbot of Melrose, along with Serlo his monk earned the fellowship of the saints after much suffering. For after the savage threats of impious men, after the bruising of injuries and bloody wounds, after the clubs of James and the stones of Stephen, at length he suffered the fire of Laurence by being burnt in his own house called Halkirk. His body scorched by the fire and bruised by the stoning was found whole beneath a heap of stones after the fire, and was given an honorable burial in the church. All this happened because he demanded *teinds* [tithes] and other ecclesiastical rights from those in his jurisdiction. They became inflamed with rage, and more than 300 men assembled in one place on the Sunday within the week after the [feast of the] Nativity of the Blessed Mary [September 8th]. And he was stoned by them, seized, beaten, bound, wounded, stripped and thrown into his own kitchen, which had been set on fire, and there he was burnt to death. Before this they killed the monk who was his companion, as well as one of his servants. But Earl John of Caithness, although he stayed nearby and had seen the people in arms converging from all sides, when asked by some of the bishop's servants to come and help, ignored what was going on, saying: "If the bishop is afraid, let him come to me." And it was because of this that many believed him to be party to this crime.

But our lord king Alexander, as he was on the point of setting out for England and had halted at Jedburgh to settle some business of his realm, was brought the news of this crime by trustworthy messengers. So he put that business aside and, raising an army as became a catholic man and a prince ordained by God, he set out for Caithness. Though the aforesaid earl proved on the testimony of good men that he was innocent and had offered no support or advice to those ruffians, yet because he had no immediately south to take appropriate vengeance on them, had to give up a great part of his lands and [pay] a large sum of money to the king in order to win his favour. He likewise handed over for punishment many of those who had done this deed; and the king had their limbs cut off and subjected them to various tortures.

While the lord king celebrated Christmas at Forfar, the earl of Caithness came to meet him, and there after handing over money recovered from the king the land which he had made over the year before [as reparation] for the death and burning of the bishop already mentioned. However the earl did not escape punishment for that crime, for when seven years had elapsed that same earl was hemmed in by his foes in his own house, killed and burnt. Which only goes to show the truth of the following lines:

There is no juster law in human affairs

Than that of the murderer perishes by violent death himself.

Source: Bower, Walter. *A History Book for Scots*. Edited by D. E. R. Watt. Edinburgh: Mercat Press, 1998. Pp. 26, 135–137.

AFTERMATH

According to legend, King Fergus's grandson was Kenneth MacAlpin, who is traditionally counted as the first king of a united Scots people, having conquered the Pictish lands and joined them to Dál Riata, the western region of Scotland, to create the kingdom of the "Scots." The alleged murder by and suicide of a Scots queen out of jealousy for her husband's mistresses does not seem to have deterred future kings of the Scots from engaging in similar behavior, as many were known to have numerous illegitimate children, including the important king Malcolm III.

The death of Bishop Adam was a useful excuse for King Alexander II (r. 1214–1249) to push his sovereign boundaries northward into lands at least nominally controlled by the kings of Norway. His were the first truly successful inroads into the northern reaches of Britain. However, the bishops of Caithness continued to struggle to gain the kind of control over their diocese as the bishops of southern Scotland enjoyed.

ASK YOURSELF

1. How reliable do you think orally transmitted histories might be, even when they are not filled with supernatural elements?
2. Why would the men of Caithness—who professed to be Christian, after all—be so hostile to the idea of a bishop exercising jurisdiction over them?
3. In what way was King Alexander II's intercession into the religious conflict in Caithness a politically astute move?

TOPICS TO CONSIDER

1. North–south conflicts in Scotland were an enduring situation throughout the medieval period (and beyond). Consider this reading in light of the excerpt on King William the Lion's invasion of the same region of Caithness and the revolt of Donald MacWilliam.
2. Although the murder of King Fergus occurred three centuries before the reign of Macbeth, King of Alba (r. 1040–1057), their stories came to feature legendary depictions of wives who are murderous—neither of which are factual or verifiable.

Consider the role of the ambitious or vengeful wife in popular legends about kings, and the possible influence of the story of King Fergus's wife on William Shakespeare's depiction of Lady MacBeth.

Further Information

Cowan, Edward J. "Myth and Identity in Early Medieval Scotland." *The Scottish Historical Review* 63, no. 176, pt. 2 (1984): 111–135.

Hammond, Matthew H. "Ethnicity and the Writing of Medieval Scottish History." *The Scottish Historical Review* 85, no. 219, pt. 1 (2006): 1–27.

39. The Development of English Courts of Law in the Thirteenth Century: Courts in Eyre and Local Complaints (1256)

INTRODUCTION

One of the most important developments in dispute resolution and adjudication in the British Isles was the development, beginning in the twelfth century but considerably expanded in the thirteenth, of permanent courts of law in both Westminster and Dublin, the seats of the royal court, and in the counties and "shires" of England, Wales, and Ireland. The expansion of royal jurisdiction in local disputes led to a standardization of legal procedure, placing the responsibility for the maintenance of order on local officials, such as the sheriff and his associates.

Developed in the twelfth century and utilized regularly during the reigns of King John and Henry III (from 1199 to 1272), a court "in **eyre**" was a royal court of law—the *curia regis*—sent on a traveling circuit to investigate cases locally, rather than requiring them to be heard at Westminster. The court in eyre superseded the local county courts of assize, to which they were linked, and all local cases were supposed to be introduced to it. Originally designed to rotate in a seven-year circuit, in which one region of England would be in eyre at a time, the popularity of the fixed Court of Common Pleas at Westminster eventually made the courts in eyre redundant.

KEEP IN MIND AS YOU READ

Records from courts of law by their very nature emphasize disruptions in the countryside rather than stability. It is important not to assume that mayhem was occurring all the time, but it is also important to be aware that lawlessness and local disputes were a common feature of medieval life, ones which were sometimes very difficult to adjudicate.

Some forms of legal procedures were extremely popular among the population subject to English Common Law. One form in particular was the assize of novel disseisin, which was a cheap and fast way of settling disputes over land, rather than resulting to forms of "self-help": that is, engaging in reciprocal acts of violence. If someone forcibly ejected a landholder—"disseised" him—from his land, the victim had a year to introduce a writ of novel disseisin into the court, either at Westminster or at Dublin (depending on whether the disseisin occurred in England or Ireland) or the county courts of assize. The jury summoned were charged with investigating whether a disseisin had taken place and had to report quickly back to the court yes or no. If yes, then the victim immediately regained seisin of his land, regardless of any claims of rightful ownership on the part of the perpetrator. The goal of this litigation was to prevent local disputes erupting into violence.

Document 1: Civil and Crown Pleas from the Shropshire Eyre, 1256

Writ of Novel Disseisin

Did Thomas Corbet disseise Fulk fitzWarin the younger of about 120 acres of arable [land] in Alberbury? Thomas says that he did not disseise him, for the land the complaint is about is part of his, Thomas's, own fee, and Fulk renounced his homage to him in front of several magnates and faithful subjects to the king, and returned the land and said in definite terms that he would never hold it or any other land from him. For that reason he, Thomas, placed himself in **seisin**, as he was entitled to, once Fulk had abandoned it. Fulk says that he never renounced the land or his homage. Even if he had, in anger and emotion, renounced his homage in words, but did not alter his status, rather remaining in continuous seisin, he demands judgment whether Thomas could disseise him on account of his word only. He puts himself on the assize that he never renounced the land spontaneously and voluntarily.

The jurors say that at a love-day between Thomas and Griffith son of Wennonwyn [Gruffudd ap Gwenwynwyn] to settle a number of disputes, several magnates assembled and Fulk also was there; and Thomas and Fulk became angry with each other, and Thomas called Fulk, this Fulk's father, a traitor. Fulk, roused by this to violent anger told Thomas that since he attributed such a stain to his father and himself, he would renounce his homage and never hold land from him. Asked if Fulk renounced his homage to Thomas in person, the jurors say no, but through a go-between, namely a certain Hamon Strange [Hamo Lestrange]. Asked if Fulk, after speaking to Thomas thus, returned to seisin of the land, they say yes, and that Fulk is now in seisin of the castle of Alberbury, the chief manor-house pertaining to that land, and caused the land to be ploughed and cultivated for about eight days before Thomas ejected him. So Fulk recovers seisin by view, and Thomas is in mercy. Damages, if there are any: 40 shillings.

Crown Pleas in Eyre Courts

Henry Moyses stabbed Philip Welsh in the stomach with a knife in the township of Down so that he died on the spot. Henry fled and is of ill repute, so let him be **exacted** and **outlawed**. He had no chattels. The townships of Down, Kempton, Bromlow and Clunton did not make pursuit and are in mercy. The same townships buried the body without the coroners' view and are in mercy. Judgment on Richard Tyrel, who would not come but sent his clerk instead.

487.

Douce wife of Llewelyn hanged herself with her **wimple** at her home in Kempton. The woman who found her first has died. Judgment: suicide. The township of Purslow buried her without the coroners' view. So it is in mercy.

488.

Roger de Cadigan of Burton stabbed Llewelyn of Obley to the heart with his knife so that he died on the spot. Roger fled and is of ill repute, so let him be exacted and outlawed. He had no chattels. The township of Brampton and the townships mentioned above are in mercy for not making pursuit.

489.

Simon Miller of Broadward stabbed William son of Philip of Abcott right through the body with a lance, and William instantly struck back at Simon with an axe and then cut his throat, so that they both died on the spot. Cecily, wife of Simon and the one who found him first, has not appeared, and she was attached by William son of Richard of Jay and his son William from the same township. They are in mercy. The other finder, that is of William, has died. William's chattels, 9 pence, for which the sheriff is answerable. Simon's chattels, 11 shillings, 2 pence, for which the sheriff is answerable. The townships of Clungunford, Jay, Beckjay and Broadward buried the body without the coroners' view and are in mercy.

541.

William son of Robert Seys, a boy of eight or nine years, threw a javelin which by accident struck Thomas of Worthen beneath the eye, so that he died eight days later. William promptly fled and is of ill repute, so let him be exacted and outlawed. He had no chattels. The five jurors of the manor falsely presented the case and are in mercy. Worthen, where this happened did not arrest William, and is therefore in mercy.

542.

Isabel daughter of Iseult, who has died, appealed Henry of Gydesay in the shire court of the rape of her virginity. Henry does not come, so let him be arrested, and his pledges, Richard Catchpole of Cause, Hugh Potter of Habberly, Baldwin of Westbury and Ralph Buffard, are in mercy.

Source: *The Roll of the Shropshire Eyre of 1256.* Edited by Alan Harding. London: Selden Society, 1981. Pp. 138, 197, 209. Modified by editor. Reprinted with permission.

AFTERMATH

Eyres were problematic in a number of ways, in particular because the revenue generated by them went directly into royal coffers, rather than into the sheriff's operating budget. In addition, cases could be delayed an inordinate amount of time, preventing the kind of swift justice that was intended by the use of the assizes. Eventually, most of the cases that might have been heard by an eyre court came to be located in county courts presided over by sheriffs, appointed officials such as coroners, and justices of the peace.

Although communities were required by law to contact the authorities when a crime had been committed, especially a violent one, they often did not do so—even to the point of burying bodies of people who had died under suspicious circumstances in order to avoid a coroner's inquest. When communities failed in their obligations of policing themselves, they were adjudged to be "in mercy": subject to monetary penalties called amercements.

ASK YOURSELF

1. Why would suing someone in court over a local land dispute be more useful than engaging in "self-help" (that is, resolving local disputes through violence)?
2. Why would the men of the village be fined (be "in mercy") for failing to pursue wrongdoers? What reasons would communities have for trying to avoid official notice of crimes that had been committed?
3. What kinds of activities are local people expected to engage in to help police their communities?

TOPICS TO CONSIDER

1. Consider the problems of easy access to sharp implements in the seeming frequency of disputes resulting in stabbings and other forms of violence.
2. If the *assize of novel disseisin* was one of the most popular writs to be heard in court, this means that there were frequent and sometimes violent disputes between neighbors and co-claimants over land. Consider the relationship between such disputes and the royal courts, in particular the likelihood that even suing in court seems not to have stemmed the tide of "self-help."
3. Consider the relationship between notions of the king as the fount of justice and the popularity of the courts of law for dispute resolution.

Further Information

Biancalana, Joseph. "For Want of Justice: Legal Reforms of Henry II." *Columbia Law Review* 88, no. 3 (1988): 433–536.

Burt, Caroline. "The Demise of the General Eyre in the Reign of Edward I." *The English Historical Review* 120, no. 485 (2005): 1–14.

Butler, Sara M. "Women, Suicide, and the Jury in Later Medieval England." *Signs* 32, no. 1 (2006): 141–166.

Green, Andrew Thomas. *Verdict According to Conscience: Perspectives on the English Criminal Trial Jury, 1200–1800.* Chicago: University of Chicago Press, 1985.

Hudson, John. *The Formation of the English Common Law: Law and Society in England from the Norman Conquest to Magna Carta.* London: Longman, 1996.

40. Conflicts between and among Welsh and English after the Edwardian Conquest: The Welsh Assize Roll, 1277–1284

INTRODUCTION

Before the conquest of North Wales by King Edward I in the 1270s, Welsh people were not subject to English Common Law. If a Welshman or -woman lived in one of the regions controlled by a marcher baron, the so-called Liberty of the **March** prevented the king's writ from "running" in the barony. If the Welsh person lived in a part of Wales controlled by a native prince, then Welsh law (collected as the *Laws of Hywl Dda*) prevailed. Welsh law was based on custom and oral transmission down to the thirteenth century. It did not have the administrative infrastructure seen in the English common law courts and differed significantly from English law procedurally.

After the conquest and the establishment of the English principality of Wales, King Edward extended both English law and legal procedure into the regions of Wales where it had not appeared before. The first assizes heard in Wales, beginning in 1277, thus represented a new form of dispute resolution in a region that had retained customary procedures.

KEEP IN MIND AS YOU READ

Although Welsh people might not have appeared in English royal courts in Wales itself, they were not unfamiliar with the kinds of procedures maintained in those courts—as the novel disseisin case in the Shropshire Eyre attests. Welsh people who lived on the border between England and Wales probably had some access to English courts, especially if they held land from English lords. Nevertheless, the use of the English-style courts to resolve violent disputes between Welsh people was a new development after the Edwardian conquest.

Document 1: Cases from the Welsh Assize Roll

Membrane 12. Pleas Heard at Rhuddlan, Sunday after the Nativity of the Blessed Virgin, 6 Edward I [1278] before Sirs Reginald de Grey, Roger Lestrange, Walter de Hopton, Hywel ap Meurig, and Gronw ap Heilyn, Justices.

Merig ap Madog, Ieuan ap Madog, and Ithel Vychan complain that certain thieves, after the peace made between the King and Llewelyn, Prince of Wales, about the feast of St. Martin, 5 Edward I [1277], robbed them of 30 oxen and cows, 23 pigs and led away the animals to the castle of Flint and that Guncelin de Badlesmere, then Justice of Chester, took these animals from them, and although he had a mandate from the King that they should be delivered, he detained them and still detains them.

Guncelin, called and questioned by the Justices on the matter, answers that he did not receive these animals after the making of the peace, and puts himself on an **inquisition of the country**. [The jurors conducting the inquisition] say that Meurig, Ieuan, and Ithel were in the King's peace when the animals were taken but, nevertheless, it was before the common proclamation of the peace between the King and the Prince of Wales. And Meurig and his followers acknowledge that they had come to do homage and **fealty** the day after the robbery was committed on them.

Membrane 25. Pleas Heard at Montgomery, a week from St. John the Baptist, 7 Edward I [1279] before Walter de Hopton and his associates, Justices.

Einon Llwyd and Rhydderch Kavernethy appeal Roger Impias of the death of Owain Foel, their brother, killed in the town of Oswestry, which Roger Impias evilly and feloniously killed the same Owain Foel, their brother, against the King's peace, etc.

Roger comes and denies all felony and all death and whatsoever is against the King's peace, etc. And for good and ill **puts himself upon the country**. And 12 jurors say upon their oath that Roger is not guilty of the said death. Therefore he is acquitted of it.

Membrane 30. Pleas Heard at Montgomery, Wednesday after St. Andrew the Apostle, 9 Edward I [1280]

Richard de Camera, who sues for the King and his men, and [for] Isabella Mortimer and her men of Oswestry [acts as their attorney], complains of Llewelyn Vychan that Hwfa ap Heilyn, Madog Treydras, and others named in the writ, by previous consent and sending of Llewelyn, maliciously burnt, against the peace, etc., the King's mill of Coedgoch and certain houses of Isabella Mortimer and her men of Oswestry with the goods and chattels within the mill and houses, by which they say they are injured and suffered the loss of £100. The trespass was done them on Friday after Michaelmas, 8 Edward I [just a few weeks before]. And on it they produce suit, etc. Llewelyn comes and denies previous consent and sending and all wrong and puts himself on the country. Therefore let the country of the neighboring and nearest, etc., be summoned, namely Knockin, Ellesmere, Wem, Deuddwr.

Source: *The Welsh Assize Roll, 1277–1284.* Edited by James Conway Davies. Cardiff: University of Wales Press, 1940. Pp. 259–260, 296, 309. Reprinted with permission.

AFTERMATH

The Welsh countryside was persistently subject to upheaval and disruption throughout the Middle Ages, with numerous small revolts against English dominance and English rule occurring after the Edwardian conquest, and one major revolt, that of OWAIN GLYNDWR (Owen Glendower) in 1400–1412. Kings of England who attempted to take control of Wales through a centralized court system found themselves competing with local landlords as well, with conflicted jurisdictions a common problem. Even so, as the system of English law advanced in Wales, the establishment of local courts to adjudicate disputes became more common and more efficient.

ASK YOURSELF

1. Why would Welsh people use English law courts to resolve disputes?
2. The disputes excerpted here demonstrate a certain level of lawlessness, especially on the border. What benefit would people derive from engaging in litigation instead of simply resorting to self-help?
3. Why weren't the Welsh princes able to stem the tide of violence in their regions in Wales?

TOPICS TO CONSIDER

1. Compare the cases heard in the Welsh assizes to those heard at the Shropshire eyre.
2. Consider the possible conflicts that could arise in mixed communities of Welsh and English residents and how they might have been adjudicated in assize courts.
3. Analyze the potential benefits of adopting English law or of retaining Welsh customary law in resolving disputes.

Further Information

Davies, R. R. "Colonial Wales." *Past & Present* 65, no. 1 (1974): 3–23.

Price, Huw. "Lawbooks and Literacy in Medieval Wales." *Speculum* 75, no. 1 (2000): 29–67.

41. Examples of Crimes Prosecuted in Local Courts: Gaol Delivery Rolls (Fourteenth Century)

INTRODUCTION

Criminal proceedings under medieval English law contained a number of different jurisdictions and procedural hurdles. When a violent crime had been committed, the men in the community were required to **raise the hue and cry** upon its discovery (women could do this only in cases of rape or if their husbands were attacked). All adult men of the community were subject to service in the **view of frankpledge**: a body that identified evildoers and catalogued crimes committed between court sessions. If a death occurred, the royal coroner in the county was obligated to investigate and determine the cause of death. The coroner's inquest was a public hearing held several times a year. Those who were summoned to court after being accused of criminal activity were arrested and *gaoled* and the sheriff then had to "deliver" the prisoners to the court of the King's Bench or the circuit court of Assize in order to be adjudged. This system remained remarkably consistent until the middle of the fourteenth century, when King Edward III began to replace central courts with more local jurisdictional courts, specifically for the adjudication of noncapital crimes. The system of "gaol delivery" however, continued.

KEEP IN MIND AS YOU READ

Courts of law proceedings, especially the criminal courts, required severe penalties for crimes we would consider fairly minor. Indeed, death sentences were more common than other kinds of penalties for crimes such as robbery, burglary, and assault. As a result, many people accused of crimes fled before being arrested. When trials did occur, very often juries would refuse to convict their neighbors and acquaintances, accepting pleas such as poverty or mental incompetence as excuses to acquit.

Document 1: Proceedings from Cambridgeshire

2. William le Aunblour of Sutton in Holland, in the diocese of Lincoln, confessed before Roger de Abyton and William Waryn, coroners, [that] he had stolen a mare and a horse,

gaoled: English spelling of "jail"—pronounced the same

ordinary: the archdeacon's court

[valued at] 10 shillings, from Henry Watte of Histon at Impington on 4 September 1331. He appealed [accused] Hugh Colyn for [of] aiding him and receiving his share. Later William le Aunblour, escorted by the sheriff, comes and withdraws his accusation; he is sentenced to be hanged; he has no chattels. Hugh Colyn, questioned at the demand of the king, pleads not guilty and puts himself on the country; the jurors of Northstow and Chesterton **hundred**s find him not guilty; he is acquitted.

6. Margaret daughter of Robert de Stanton [was] arrested on indictment before William Waryn coroner on 3 February 1332 at Tadlow, for on Saturday, 1 February 1332, at Tadlow feloniously killing her daughter Alice. [She] comes escorted by the sheriff, pleads not guilty, puts herself on the country, and offers a **writ of *bono et malo*** from the king, instructing the justices to release Margaret if she has been imprisoned for the death of Alice, and not by special order. The jurors of Armingford hundred say that from 29 January 1332 to 4 February 1332 Margaret was mad and on Saturday at the hour of vespers she killed Alice with a knife; being asked if the killing was malicious or premeditated they say it was due to the madness. Margaret is returned to prison to await the king's pardon.

27. Agnes Wendont of Cavenham [Suffolk] [is] indicted before the sheriff of Cambridge at his tourn at Swaffham on 10 November 1332, for on 21 June 1332 entering the house of John le Wyse at Isleham, binding his wife Alice, and feloniously robbing her of woolen and linen cloth valued at 5 shillings; she comes and pleads not guilty, and puts herself on the country. The jurors of Staine hundred say that Agnes robbed Alice at Isleham on the said day of a surcoat, [worth] 9 pence; let her remain in prison for 3 weeks and be released under suitable conditions.

71. William de Hildersham **scrivener**, [is] arrested for the death of John son of Robert Ace of Girton, [who was] feloniously killed in Cambridge on 7 February 1334, whence he was indicted before Adam de Bungeye coroner of Cambridge. He comes, escorted by John Putok mayor of Cambridge, says he is a clerk and [cannot be indicted in the royal court, but must be tried through the bishop's court as a clergyman]. John vicar of St. Edward's, acting for the bishop of Ely, comes and offers the bishop's letter as enrolled on membrane 1; finding by examination that William is a clerk he seeks William's release; after the jury has found William guilty he is released to the *ordinary* as a convicted clerk to await the king's permission for **purgation**; the jury [value] his chattels at 4 shillings, the mayor and bailiffs of Cambridge are responsible for these which are confiscated for the king.

41. Nicholas le Souter of St. Ives [Huntingdonshire], is arrested on the appeal of John Shirlok, **approver,** for receiving him at St. Ives on 10 February 1331 with a brass pot, price 2 shillings, [even though he knew] him to be a thief and the pot stolen. Nicholas comes escorted by the sheriff, pleads not guilty, and puts himself on the country; the sheriff of Hunts is ordered to summon for 26 July 1334 from the neighborhood of St. Ives 18 free and lawful men unrelated to Nicholas; Nicholas is returned to prison.

A4. Nicholas Souter of St. Ives [Huntingdonshire] and Simon Molendinarius of Stilton [Huntingdonshire] [were] arrested on appeal by the said John [Shirlok], hanged approver, for receiving him at Stilton with divers goods stolen at divers places, linen and woolen cloth and various utensils valued at 20 shillings, on 21 June 1332, [although they knew] he was a thief and the goods stolen. The sheriff reports both have died in prison of natural causes according to the coroner's report. The cases are closed.

Source: *A Cambridgeshire Gaol Delivery Roll 1332–1334.* Edited and translated by Elisabeth G. Kimball. Cambridge: Antiquarian Records Society, 1978. Pp. 33, 37, 49–50,

59–60, 77, 80. Translations modified by editor. Reprinted with permission from the Cambridgeshire Records Society.

AFTERMATH

Criminal activity in the countryside waxed and waned depending on how secure the population felt and how reliable and fair they considered the keepers of the peace to be. In addition, it is difficult to determine the exact rates of conviction of alleged perpetrators of crimes such as burglary, assault, and homicide but the suggestions in the records are that most people were either acquitted or they fled, and so were outlawed. One reason for the low rate of conviction might have been the fact that the punishments for crime were very severe, ranging from mutilation—cutting off of hands, ears, or nose or other forms of disfigurement—to death. Local communities might have been reluctant to punish neighbors to such an extent, and so turned a blind eye to those who fled the region and the realm.

ASK YOURSELF

1. How typical are the crimes presented in these extracts, and if typical, what does this say about crime in the medieval English countryside?
2. Would villagers who served on local courts be more likely or less likely to convict their fellow townspeople for criminal activity?
3. Would villagers resent having to serve on juries to investigate these kinds of crimes? Why or why not?

TOPICS TO CONSIDER

1. Compare the procedures outlined in the gaol delivery rolls to those in the crown pleas in eyre.
2. Consider the frequency with which villagers in the gaol delivery cases failed—like those in the eyre records—to follow through with investigating and capturing wrongdoers. Analyze reasons why this might be the case.
3. Consider the possibility: was medieval England more violent or less violent than modern England? Consider the kinds of weapons available and the apparent frequency of modes of self-help in engaging in disputes.

Further Information

Hanawalt, Barbara A. "Violent Death in Fourteenth- and Early Fifteenth-Century England." *Comparative Studies in Society and History* 18, no. 3 (1976): 297–320.

Musson, Anthony. "Twelve Good Men and True? The Character of Early Fourteenth-Century Juries." *Law and History Review* 15, no. 1 (1997): 115–144.

[Westman], Barbara Hanawalt. "The Peasant Family and Crime in Fourteenth-Century England." *Journal of British Studies* 13, no. 2 (1974): 1–18.

42. DEATH AND MISADVENTURE: EXAMPLES FROM THE CORONERS' ROLLS (FOURTEENTH CENTURY)

INTRODUCTION

The coroners' rolls are one of the most interesting document collections of medieval English law and procedure. Every county was assigned at least one coroner—and by the end of the thirteenth century, there were usually at least two assigned to each county—who worked with the sheriff to determine the circumstances surrounding deaths that occurred in the county, and that were brought to the court through the view of frankpledge or the raising of the hue and cry. Coroners were required to investigate all deaths that were not obviously natural, and to determine who might potentially be responsible. The coroner's inquest was a public hearing presided over by the coroner, in which the sheriff summoned witnesses to court and deaths were either determined accidental (that is, no person's fault) or needing an indictment. The system continues to this day in the United Kingdom.

KEEP IN MIND AS YOU READ

The entire community, especially the men who were in tithing-groups known as hundreds, was required to police itself and to make note of misbehavior and acts of violence in the community. The most common act was the raising of the "hue and cry": the public alert made by an individual or individuals that a crime had occurred. Once this had occurred, it was the obligation of the community to round up the suspects and keep them secured until such time as the coroner or the county court could adjudicate. The raisers of the hue and cry were expected to testify in court to their discovery; they too could be jailed if they failed to appear.

Document 1: Coroners' Rolls

Accidental Deaths

[1] It happened at Wick on Sunday after Candlemas, 19 Richard II [6 February 1396], that Edith Rogers of Wick, who was demented or insane, was drowned in a little well filled with rain-water in the highway called Rose Street in Wick, and was found dead. The first finder

of her body was Henry Redhood; John Bond and Nicholas Northland are pledges for his appearance before the itinerant justices when they come into these parts. Edith was viewed by the said coroner on the following Tuesday.

Inquest was taken at Dursley before John Trye on the said Friday of that year on the oath of John Trotman, John Bond, John Dangerville, and Elias Spark, jurors of the township of Wick, and John Cowley, William at the Elm, John Browning, and Robert Browning, jurors of the township of Cam, and Richard Halling, John Cokes, John Dorney, and Walter Jordan, jurors of the township of Slimbridge. They say on their oath that Edith by reason of her own negligence and insanity fell into the well and thus by misadventure was drowned, and they can ascertain nothing more. And they say that she had no goods.

[2] It . . . happened at Cowley on Wednesday after the feast of the Nativity of Blessed Mary, 20 Richard II [13 September 1396], that a small boy, Robert of Cowley, was there found dead. The first finder of his body was Henry Lawes of Cowley; John Brinkworth and William Shire are pledges for his appearance before the itinerant justices when they came into these parts. The body was viewed on the following Friday by the aforesaid John Trye.

Inquest was taken at Crowley on the said Friday on the oath of twelve jurors of the said townships of Wick, Cam, and Slimbridge; they say on their oath that Robert, a little boy only three years of age, fell into a pan full of milk and thus was drowned by misadventure. The pan is worth six pence and remains in charge of the township of Cowley. And [the jurors] can ascertain nothing more, etc.

[3] It also happened at Cam on Friday next before the feast of St. Leonard in the twentieth year of the present king [3 November 1396] that William Bachelor, who was ten years of age, was found dead in a certain field near the Woodend. The first finder of his body was Henry Allport; the pledges [for his appearance] before the itinerant justices, etc. are Henry Draycot and John Hart. The body was viewed by the aforesaid coroner on the following Saturday.

Inquest was made at Cam on that same Saturday before the said coroner on the oath of twelve jurors of the aforesaid townships of Wick, Cam, and Slimbridge; they say on their oath that the said William sat sleeping in a certain sand-pit under an overhanging bank of the said pit, which suddenly fell upon him, and thus by misadventure he was crushed by the falling sand. [The jurors say] that they can ascertain nothing more, and that he has no goods.

A Case of Homicide

Inquest was taken [at Stepney] before the coroner on Sunday on the eve of St. Lawrence's day [9 August] in the aforesaid year of King Edward the Third [1366], on view of the body of a certain John Clerk, tiler, on the oath [of twelve men]. They say on their oath that on Friday next before St Lawrence's day in the said year Adam Case, an inhabitant of London, came to the ville of Stepney, namely to a certain field below that ville, and there insulted the said John Clerk, tiler, with opprobrious words, and forthwith drew a certain knife thirteen inches long, with which he had feloniously stuck John Clerk, making a severe wound on

> *by the abetment or procurement of any person:* with the assistance of any accomplices
> *sparthe:* a long-handled combination of spear and battle-axe

his left shoulder one inch long and thirteen inches deep, and this wound at once caused his death. Being asked whether [Adam] did this *by the abetment or procurement of any person*, they say, No. Being also asked whither the felon had gone, they say that he was arrested forthwith and taken to Newgate gaol. Being also asked what his good and chattels are worth and who has them, they say that he has nothing in this lordship but only in the city of London. Being also asked who first found him dead, they say that Thomas Clerk of Aldgate Street first found him, and he raised the hue. And the four men and the reeves of four neighboring townships, to wit, Bromley, East Smithfield, Hackney, and Shoreditch, say the same. Thomas Clerk, the finder, was **mainprised** by John Green, a butcher of London, and Henry Baker of Holywell Street.

A Case of Overzealous Administration

[Northamptonshire].

It happened at Polebrook on Saturday next after Ascension Day 29 Edward I [13 May 1301] that a certain Reginald Porthors and Ralph Chapman, both of Polebrook, went after dinner to the house of John of Weldon of Polebrook, by order of Sir Ralph Porthors of Polebrook, to bring the said John to Sir Ralph's court alive or dead, and they found John asleep. They said Reginald struck him on the left side of the head with a certain sword, [which penetrated] to the brain, and thus he came to his death. And Ralph Chapman struck him on the back with a certain axe called a *sparthe* but he lived until Tuesday next after the following Trinity Sunday [30 May], when he died after confessing and partaking of the communion.

Inquest was made before John of Ashton by four neighboring townships to wit, Oundle with Elminton, and Aston, Hemington, and Warmington. They say on their oath that they know nothing more thereof except as is aforesaid. And they say that the said Reginald and Ralph Chapman took from the said John and carried away ten shillings and a farthing; and then they went forthwith to the court of Sir Ralph Porthors. The **tithing-men** of Polebrook followed them thither with the hue, intending to attach them. And Sir Ralph would not allow the tithing-men to enter his court, but he received the said Reginald and Ralph before and after the act; and they afterward fled to some unknown place. They had no chattels. The sword was worth twelve pence, the axe four pence; the township of Polebrook will answer for these. Also the township of Polebrook by itself says that the said Reginald and Ralph Chapman went to the house of John of Weldon, by order of Sir Ralph Porthors, to bring Joan, [John's] wife, to Sir Ralph's court and to place her in his stocks, and for no other purpose. R. de Vere, sheriff of Northamptonshire is ordered to arrest Sir Ralph Porthors, Reginald Porthors, and Ralph Chapman.

Source: Gross, Selden, ed. *Select Cases from the Coroners' Rolls. A.D. 1265–1413.* Selden Society. London, 1896. Pp. 49–59. Modified by editor.

AFTERMATH

The majority of deaths investigated by medieval coroners were cases of "death by misadventure" rather than homicide. Accidents were all too common, and many could result in death or serious disfigurement. This is particularly the case for children who were often in charge of younger siblings while themselves very young: a six-year old in charge of an infant was not an uncommon occurrence. Child deaths by accident were all too frequent in an environment of open fires, top-heavy cooking cauldrons, and uncovered wells. Adults also were subject to accidental death, especially when working at jobs that could be dangerous. Finally, the lack of effective medical care probably rendered injuries deadly in the Middle Ages that today would be fairly easily cured. This all meant that the coroners' job was a busy one!

ASK YOURSELF

1. Why were all deaths—even accidents—investigated by the coroner?
2. What information can you derive from cases such as these that tell you about how medieval people lived?

TOPICS TO CONSIDER

1. Compare the information you gain from the coroners' rolls and those you gain from eyres, assizes, and gaol deliveries and analyze how historians might utilize all three to develop a clearer picture of criminal activity and violence in medieval England and Wales.
2. Consider other uses for these kinds of documents, such as determining, by knowing where and how people died, how nonelite people in the British Isles might have lived.

Further Information

Hanawalt, Barbara A. *The Ties That Bound: Peasant Lives in Medieval England.* Oxford: Oxford University Press, 1988.

Hunnisett, H. F. "The Medieval Coroners' Rolls." *The American Journal of Legal History* 3, no. 2 (1959): 95–124.

Musson, A. J. "Turning King's Evidence: The Prosecution of Crime in Late Medieval England." *Oxford Journal of Legal Studies* 19, no. 3 (1999): 467–479.

43. Chronicles of the Great Rising of 1381

INTRODUCTION

The Great Rising (also known as the English Peasants' Revolt) was a revolt of people from a variety of social levels against the hated **poll tax** of 1380, which was supposed to help fund a war with France. The main counties involved were the most heavily populated and among the richest in the kingdom: Essex, Sussex, and Kent in the southeast and Norfolk and Suffolk in the northeast. These counties were also the most heavily embedded in a system of feudal and manorial tenancies in which the estates were controlled by wealthy and influential monasteries and church officials, who were noted for their efficient exploitation of the local populace.

The group who led the revolt comprised men of different social standing: JOHN BALL, a defrocked priest who was associated with the Lollard movement; and two men whose names were probably aliases: JACK STRAW and WAT TYLER. Indeed, it is difficult to determine who these latter two men were, as they cannot be identified in any sources of the time.

The chronicle sources, most of them written in monastic scriptoria—among them St. Albans, which was attacked by the rebels—vilify the rebels as traitors to the king and to society. Nevertheless, the stated aims of the revolt seem reasonable to modern people: to abolish villeinage, to establish rents at reasonable levels, to allow wages to be market-driven in the postplague era, to gain some kind of parliamentary representation, and to abolish regressive and extraordinary taxation such as the poll tax. Their methods, which included murder, mayhem, and the burning down of the Duke of Lancaster's Savoy Palace, led, however, to their demise and the collapse of the rebellion.

The chronicle excerpted here is one of the most famous of those written in the reign of Richard II. Penned by the St. Albans chronicler THOMAS WALSINGHAM, this account details of the rebels' attack on Walsingham's own monastic house. While the author was too young to experience the attack personally, it had a long-term effect on the monastery.

KEEP IN MIND AS YOU READ

The Great Rising was only one of a number of uprisings of the lower and middle classes that occurred in the fourteenth century, especially after the Black Death. The drastic population decline and attempts on the part of the elites and the church to retain their privileges over the peasantry and the urban poor sparked many of these revolts. Anger at the aristocracy was accompanied by significant levels of anger directed at the clergy, a situation that also sparked the growth of Lollardy in England. Similar expressions of discontent can also be seen in literature of the period, including Langland's *Piers Plowman* and John Gower's *Vox Clamantis*.

One of the most iconic, but possibly also apocryphal, images of the Great Rising is the speech of John Ball in which he utters the immortal rhyme "When Adam delved [plowed] and Eve span [spun thread], who was then the gentleman?" There is no way to verify whether Ball invented the rhyme or if it was a common sentiment among the disaffected peasantry, but it typifies the spirit of protest that was common in the decades following the Black Death.

Document 1: The Great Rising According to Thomas Walsingham

[The "peasants" in London]

[T]he squads of the peasants had split up into three parts. One of them . . . was intent on destroying the estate at Highbury [the manor of the head of the Knights Hospitaller in London, Sir Robert Hales]. Another was waiting near London, at a place called Mile End. [the Essex rebels, at the eastern gate of the City] A third actually seized Tower Hill. This crowd near the Tower showed itself to be so . . . lacking in respect that it shamelessly seized goods belonging to the king . . . And besides this, it was driven to such a pitch of madness that it forced the king to hand over to them the archbishop [of Canterbury, Simon Sudbury], the Master of the Hospital of St. John [Hales] and others hiding in the Tower itself, all of whom they called traitors. They told the king that if he was unwilling to do this they would deprive even him of his life.

So the king, being in a very tight spot, allowed them to enter the Tower and search its most secret recesses, as their wicked wills dictated, since he himself could not in safety refuse any of their requests. . . .

[W]ho would ever have believed that not just peasants but the lowest of them . . . would have dared with their worthless *staves* [quarter-staffs, which they used for fighting] to force a way into the bedroom of the king or of his mother, scaring all the nobles with their threats and even touching and stroking with their rough, filthy hands the beards of some of the most eminent of them? . . . And, besides all this, several of them . . . had the effrontery to sit and lie on the bed of the king joking merrily, with one or two even asking the king's mother [dowager princess of Wales, Joan of Kent] for a kiss.

[The men of St. Albans plot against the Abbey]

[W]hen . . . the townspeople of St Albans and the servants of the abbot arrived at the manor of Highbury . . . and got to London, the townspeople soon separated from the abbot's servants [who remained loyal to the abbot] and turned to deeds of wickedness. For they . . . began to discuss their enslavement to the monastery and how they might effect the wishes which they long harbored in secret. These were that they should enjoy new boundaries around the town in which they could graze their animals freely, have places assigned to them in which they could fish without blame and similar places assigned for hunting and hawking, and set up their hand-mills wherever they liked at their own wish and whim. They also wanted to suffer no interference from the bailiff of the liberty inside the town boundaries, and to claim back the bonds which their parents had once made to abbot

Richard of Wallingford [abbot of St Albans from 1327 to 1355] . . . any other charters which were prejudicial to them, and, in a word, all records in the abbey which were a support to them or involved loss for the monastery.

Source: *The Chronica Maiora of Thomas Walsingham (1376–1422)*. Translated by David Preest. Woodbridge: Boydell Press, 2005. Pp. 124–125, 131–132.

AFTERMATH

The revolt was brutally suppressed, with the leaders being charged and punished for treason: their heads were affixed to spikes on London Bridge after being paraded through the city. Any reforms that King Richard II had offered in order to quell the mob were quickly retracted and the status quo before the rebellion reinstated. Nevertheless, popular dissent against elite exploitation and anticlericalism continued to appear throughout the fifteenth century, erupting in a series of smaller revolts, as well as one significant one, led by Jack Cade, in 1450 during the reign of King Henry VI.

ASK YOURSELF

1. What were the "peasants" revolting against?
2. Why did the rebels attack monasteries and administrative offices?
3. In what way was the Great Rising a revolt, and in what way was it more of an extended riot?

TOPICS TO CONSIDER

1. The leaders of the Great Rising were interested in gaining liberties denied them, especially the abolition of villeinage. Consider the reasons why this would have been resisted by the elites and why they might have been willing to respond so violently to such ideas.
2. Analyze the effects of the pillaging, looting, and burning of law offices and record repositories and how this might affect the maintenance of the social fabric in the countryside after the revolt. For example, if all contracts between landlords and peasants were destroyed in a particular village, how would the relationship between them be re-established, and to whose advantage?

Further Information

Barker, Juliet. *1381: The Year of the English Peasants' Revolt*. Cambridge, MA: Belknap Press, 2014.

Ormrod, W. M. "The Peasants' Revolt and the Government of England." *Journal of British Studies* 29, no. 1 (1990): 1–30.

Prescott, Andrew. "Writing about Rebellion: Using the Records of the Peasants' Revolt of 1381." *History Workshop Journal* no. 45 (1998): 1–27.

POPULAR CULTURE
AND LITERATURE

44. THE IRISH CLAIM EARLIEST CHRISTIAN ADHERENCE: THE DEATH OF CONCHOBHAR (EARLY NINTH CENTURY)

INTRODUCTION

The collection of stories known as the "Ulster Cycle," which has at its core the stories comprising the *Táin Bó Cúailgne* (The Cattle Raid of Cooley), might owe its origins to the early ninth century, a time when the Irish were experiencing invasion from the Danes and the Norse for the first time, but they are identified with a much earlier time shrouded for the Irish in myth: the first century CE. These tales introduce one of the great heroes of Irish legend, the king CÚ CHULAINN (pronounced "Koo-koollin"). Conchobhar (pronounced "Conover") was another great mythic hero, an associate of Cú Chulainn and other Ulstermen. His death—like the death of most mythic heroes such as those of ancient Greece and the Anglo-Saxon legendary warrior Beowulf the Geat—comes about because of fate.

The tales created about Ireland's heroic past mix the fantastical with elements of the historical. In particular, the Irish—especially in the twelfth century, the time when many of these texts were written down for the first time—staked a claim to being the first nation to convert to Christianity, thereby giving them precedence over Rome and its pope.

KEEP IN MIND AS YOU READ

Irish heroes were larger than life in every way: blonder, taller, stronger, and capable of prodigious consumption of food and drink. The tales seem extreme, even bizarre, to modern ears, but they were known by heart by every man, woman, and child of medieval Ireland. Moreover, the resonance of these tales and their nationalistic overtones have continued in the Irish imagination to the present day.

Document 1: The Death of Conchobhar

The Ulstermen were very drunk, once, in Emhain Macha. Great disputes and contentions arose between them—Conall, Cú Chulainn, and Leoghaire. "Bring me," said Conall, "the brain of Meis-Geghra, so that I can talk to the warriors who are contending." It was the custom among the Ulstermen in those days to take out the brains of any warrior whom they killed in single combat, out of his head, and to mix them with lime, so that they became hard balls. And when they used to be disputing or contending, these would be brought to them so that they had them in their hands. "Well now, Conchobhar," said Conall, "until the warriors who are contending do a deed like this one in single combat, they are not worthy to contend with me." "That is true," said Conchobhar.

The brain was put then on the shelf on which it used always to be.... Now Cet son of Madu came on a tour of adventures in Ulster. This Cet was the most troublesome monster in Ireland.... While the buffoons were playing with the brain of Meis-Geghra, ... Cet heard that [it was identified as Meis-Geghra's brain]. He snatched the brain from the hand of one of them and carried it off with him, for Cet knew that it was foretold that Meis-Geghra would avenge himself after his death.... One day this Cet came east and drove a [herd of stolen] cattle from Fir Ros. The Ulstermen pursued and caught up with him, but the men of Connaught arrived from the other side to rescue him. A battle was fought between them; Conchobhar himself came into the battle. Then the women of Connaught begged Conchobhar to come aside so that they might look at his figure, for there was not on earth the figure of a man like the figure of Conchobhar in form and shape and dress, in size and straightness and symmetry, in eye and hair and whiteness, in wisdom and good manners and speech, in garments and splendor and array, in weapons and amplitude and dignity, in habits and feats of arms and lineage.... Now it was through the prompting of Cet that the women made this appeal to Conchobhar. He went on one side by himself, to be looked at by the women.

Cet came, then, so that he was in the midst of women. Cet fitted Meis-Geghra's brain into the sling, and slung it so that it struck Conchobhar on the top of his skull, so that two-thirds of it were in his head, and he fell headlong on the ground. The men of Ulster leaped towards him and carried him off from Cet.... The fight was kept up till the same hour the next day, after what happened to the king; and then the Ulstermen were routed. Conchobhar's doctor, Fínghin, was brought to him.... "Well," said Fínghin "if the stone is taken out of your head you will die immediately. If it is not taken out, however, I could heal you; but it will be a disfigurement to you." "We would rather have a disfigurement than death," said the Ulstermen.

His head was healed then, and was sewn up with a golden thread, for the color of Conchobhar's hair was like the color of gold. And the doctor told Conchobhar he should take care that anger should not seize him, and that he should not mount on horseback, and should not have to do with a woman, and should not eat food gluttonously, and should not run. So he remained in a dangerous state, as long as he lived, for seven years, and he was not able to be active but to stay in his seat only; until he heard that Christ was crucified by the Jews. A great trembling came on the elements at that time ... "What is this?" said Conchobhar to his druid, "what great evil is being done today?" "It is true," said the druid, "it is a great deed that is done there, Christ the Son of the Living God crucified by the Jews." "That is a great deed," said Conchobhar. "That man," said the druid, "was born the same night that you were born, that is, on the eighth day before the calends of January, though the year was not the same."

Then Conchobhar believed; and he was one of the two men in Ireland who believed in God before the coming of the Faith, and the other was Morann. "Well now," said Conchobhar, "a thousand armed men shall fall at my hand in rescuing Christ." He leaped for his two spears then, and brandished them violently so that they broke in his fist; and he took his sword in his hand next and attacked the forest around him, so that he made an open field of the forest ... And he said, "Thus would I avenge Christ on the Jews and those who crucified Him, if I could get at them." With that fury, Meis-Geghra's brain sprang out of his head, so that his own brains came out, and he died of it ...

Source: *A Celtic Miscellany: Translations from the Celtic Literatures.* Translated by Kenneth Hurlstone Jackson. Middlesex, England: Penguin Books, 1976. Pp. 53–56. Modified by editor.

AFTERMATH

The Irish claims to being the first true Christians, along with the legend of St. Patrick, compelled them into breaking out of their island sanctuary and engaging in missionary activity throughout the British Isles. The stories of Cú Chulainn and Conchobhar, as well as of the heroes of the "Fenian Cycle," also made their way to Wales and Scotland to form part of those regions' legendary histories. When the Anglo-Normans invaded Ireland and settled there as conquerors, they came to adopt the Irish origin tales as their own just as they came to adopt Irish cultural attributes that would eventually separate them to some extent from their English neighbors and kin.

One of the most pervasive themes in ancient Irish stories, especially concerning the great heroes such as Cú Chulainn, was the cultural importance of "cattle raiding"—the stealing of cattle, which was both the main form of currency and the visible sign of wealth in the era before minted coins in Ireland. Cattle raiding was not only a pastime, of sorts; it was also a rite of passage into manhood and a symbol of heroic activity, much as tournaments and jousts were for later medieval knights.

ASK YOURSELF

1. Why would the Irish creators and consumers of this literature consider it important to identify themselves as the first Christians?
2. How does this story fit very uncomfortably into a Christian context?
3. What does this tale tell you about notions of heroism in early medieval Ireland?

TOPICS TO CONSIDER

1. Compare notions of the hero and heroism in this excerpt and the one following.
2. Compare notions of the hero in this excerpt with other cultural notions of the hero—Greek and Roman, Anglo-Saxon, and others.
3. Consider the process of oral transmission of such stories and how their Christianization could have been inserted and when.

Further Information

Carney, James. "Language and Literature to 1169." In *A New History of Ireland*, edited by Dáibhí Ó Cróinín, 451–510. Oxford: Oxford University Press, 2005.

Cormier, Raymond J. "Cú Chulainn and Yvain: The Love Hero in Early Irish and Old French Literature." *Studies in Philology* 72, no. 2 (1975): 115–139.

McManus, Damian. "Goodlooking and Irresistible: The Hero in Early Irish Saga to Classical Poetry." *Ériu* 59 (2009): 57–109.

45. Nationalism and Ancient Tales of Heroism in Ireland

INTRODUCTION

The *Tales of the Elders of Ireland* (*Acallam na Senórach* or "Fenian Cycle") is the earliest written "history" of Ireland, produced in the twelfth century in the region of Ireland still ruled by native kings. It combines myth, legend, and heroic tales about the warriors of the *Fían*—the followers and progeny of the legendary hero Finn mac Cumaill (Finn Mac Cool)—to produce a cultural foundation for Irish identity and nationalism. Tales such as these were transmitted for centuries orally by professional **bards** attached to the courts of Irish kings and chieftains. They also formed the core of Irish popular history and heritage and continue to be referenced by poets and novelists to this day, along with another foundational collection of early texts, the *Táin Bó Cúailgne* (The Cattle Raid of Cooley, also known as the "Ulster Cycle"), which introduced the great Irish hero Cú Chulainn.

The Fenian cycle combined not only a pre-Christian consciousness but also incorporated tales of St. Patrick, who according to legend converted the Irish to Christianity. This linked a fundamentally mythic story to a historically contextualized one.

KEEP IN MIND AS YOU READ

The names of the great mythic heroes of the past, while unfamiliar to most of us in the modern age, would have been utterly familiar to the common person in Ireland who had heard these tales passed down for generations. Like all legendary histories, the combination of reality—such as the use of cattle as currency—and fantasy—the inclusion of supernatural elements—would have seemed perfectly reasonable at the time.

Document 1: Extracts from the Tales of the Elders of Ireland

Prologue

After the battles of *Commar, Gabair, and Ollarba,* the *Fían* was destroyed. The survivors scattered, in small bands, across Ireland and, by the time our story begins, only two of the nobles of this ancient *Fían* were still alive: Oisín, the son of Finn mac Cumaill "the son of Cumall," and Caílte, the son of Crundchú, son of Rónán. . . . Sixteen of the *Fían* warriors travelled with them across the wooded and flower-covered slopes of the Fews. By evening they had reached the Bright Herb Gardens, now called Louth, and sat down there, at the setting of the sun, in great sorrow and despair.

Caílte then said to Oisín, "Well, good Oisín, where shall we go, before day's end, to find some hospitality for the night?" "That I do not know," said Oisín, "since, of the elders of *Fían*, the old companions of Finn mac Cumaill, only the three of us remain; you, Caílte, and I, and the Lady and Guardian Cáma, who watched over Finn from his boyhood until the very day of his death." "We can certainly expect hospitality from her tonight," said Caílte. . .

Cáma gave them lodging for the night and asked them who they might be. When they told her their names she shed long and bitter tears. Each asked the other about the many years that had passed since their last meeting; afterwards the *Fían* went to the guest hall she provided. The Lady Cáma, the old guardian of Finn mac Cumaill, had the freshest of foods brought to them, with the oldest of wines. . . . Weak and infirm though she was, she spoke with them of the *Fían* and of Finn mac Cumaill, . . . Caílte then said, "Just as painful for us as these memories is the fact that the eighteen of us, the only survivors of that great and noble fellowship, must now part with one another." Oisín replied, "I swear there will be little fight or strength left in me when the others have gone." And though they were manly warriors, they, together with Lady Cáma, wept deeply and disconsolately. They received their fill of food and drink there, and stayed on for three days and nights. As they took leave of Cáma, Oisín recited the following lines:

"Cáma is weary today, she is at the end of her journey;
Childless, heirless, old age is upon her."

They went outside onto the grassy lawn to take counsel and decided that they must now part, one from the other, and their parting was at the parting of the soul from its body. Oisín went on to the *Síd* of the Breast of Cleitech, where his mother, Blaí, daughter of Derg Díanscothach "the Quick of Speech," lived. Caílte went to the Estuary of Bec the Exile, now the site of the monastery of Drogheda. It had been named after Bec the Exile who died there. He was the son of Airist, King of the Romans. He had come to conquer Ireland, but a great wave drowned him at that place. From the estuary Caílte went on to the Pool of Fíacc, on the bright-flowing Boyne, then southwards across the Old Plain of Brega [a part of county Meath] to the Fortress of the Red Ridge, where Patrick, son of Capurn, then happened to be.

Chapter VII

They went to the fortress and the boy lodged Patrick and his people in Coscrach's splendid dwelling where they were well attended to. Meanwhile Caílte went along the south side of the fortress to the Rock of the Weapons, the great stone on which the *Fían* used to sharpen their weapons every year. Standing there on top of the rock he wept flowing tears of great sadness, remembering the great people that often stood on that rock with him in earlier times. Before long he saw a warrior approaching wearing a purple cloak with a pin of gold in it. . . . Quite unexpectedly the warrior sat at the end of the rock near him. "What is your name, warrior?" asked Caílte. "Coscrach na Cét is my name," he said "and I think I know who you are." . . . "It seems to me . . . that you are Caílte, son of Rónán." "Truly I am," said Caílte. "I am happy to meet with you," said Coscrach, "whenever it is time to reap the crop a very fierce and wild stag comes, and destroys and devastates everything so that we have no benefit of it. Dear Caílte, by the truth of your valour and prowess," said Coscrach na Cét, "give help and assistance to me in warding off that stag."

. . . Caílte asked Coscrach whether messengers might be found to travel to the fair Meadow of the Parish in the province of Munster and to Oakgrove of the Kin-Slaying. "My seven hunting-nets are in that place, and they cover seven **cantreds** of cliff and cataract, of river and level plain."

The messengers went after the nets and brought them back to Caílte and Coscrach. Caílte organized the hunt and placed a host of men and a multitude of hounds facing the direction from which he expected the stag to come, arranging his nets over the cliffs and streams and estuaries of the land. The great stag came towards them as it had every year. Caílte watched it approaching the Ford of the Stag on the Slaney. He took his spear *In Coscarach* "The Victorious" and cast it at the stag that was caught in his net. The shaft of the spear went though him the length of a warrior's arm. "You seem to have bloodied the stag," said Coscrach, "and what better name for the ford than the Ford of Bloodying of the Stag?" This is the name of the ford ever since. They carried the chine of the stag to the Broad Ridge, now called the Red Ridge of the Herd. . . .

Coscrach and Caílte went to meet with Saint Patrick, and Coscrach, with his seven sons and seven daughters, put his head in Patrick's lap and paid homage to him. He received two benefits that evening: Patrick saved his soul and Caílte protected his wealth and his grain by killing the troublesome stag that was destroying it. They spent that night in drinking and pleasure and in the morning all of the host, together with Patrick, went out from the fortress onto the lawn.

Coscrach na Cét asked Caílte, "Why is this mighty stone here on the lawn called the Rock of the Weapons?" "This is the rock," said Caílte, "on which the *Fían* used to sharpen their weapons each year on the day of *Samhain* and the edges that they put on them did not dull in battle, in skirmish, or in

> *Síd:* fairy mound
> *Samhain:* the Celtic festival of the dead

fighting. On that rock was the best token of peace that existed in Ireland and Scotland in the reigns of Conn and Art and Cormac and Cairbre Lifechair, the ribbed arm-ring containing eight score ounces of red gold. There was a hole in this rock in which the arm-ring was placed, and such was the excellence of the rule of these kings that no one dared to steal it. Such was the excellence of the knowledge of their druids that no one dared to move it, given the authority of the kings. . . . We, the remnants of the *Fían*," said Caílte, "came as far as this place and I turned the stone over and put the top half of it against the ground as you now see it." . . . All that were there went to the rock but were unable to move it. Caílte came, put his two forearms about it and drew it from the earl. Thus it was, with the gold arm-ring in the hole that had been underneath. Caílte took the arm-ring and divided it in two, giving half to Patrick and half to the people of the region. The Meadow of the Arm-ring is still the name of that meadow and the Stone of the Weapons the name of that rock. . . .

"May you have victory and blessing, dear Caílte," said Patrick, "the story and the eknowledge you have told us are good."

Source: *Tales of the Elders of Ireland (Acallam na Senórach)*. Translation and Introduction by Ann Dooley and Harry Roe. Oxford: Oxford University Press, 1999. Pp. 3–4, 124–126.

AFTERMATH

The "memory" of Ireland's heroic past was very important to the Irish who were experiencing conquest and occupation by the Anglo-Normans in the twelfth and thirteenth centuries.

The writing down of these tales beginning in the twelfth century and their transmittal through many stages of Irish language were in part an exercise of national pride and in part an attempt to preserve the stories for posterity and future generations.

ASK YOURSELF

1. Why would it be important to Irish people to connect their legendary heroes to early Christian religious figures such as St. Patrick?
2. In the "Prologue" the timeframe is at the end of the era, where the *Fían* are destroyed and they are at the end of their lives. The tales that follow are in the form of memory. Why would this structure be appealing to an Irish audience?
3. What are the implications and significance of the removal of the arm-ring and the moving of the Stone of Weapons? What would an Irish audience understand that significance to be?

TOPICS TO CONSIDER

1. Magical or mystical artifacts, such as swords, stones, and jewelry, are common tropes in medieval literature, from this tale of the Stone of Weapons and the golden arm-ring, to King Arthur's sword Excalibur being drawn out of a stone (or an anvil in the original tales). In both circumstances, the objects regulate war and peace. Consider this relationship between mystical objects and the conducting of war or peace in the medieval imagination.
2. Compare this selection to the excerpt on the death of Conchobhar.
3. Place this tale in relation to other legendary tales of heroes at their ends. Consider how these stories would be useful in inculcating certain social and cultural values in a population.

Further Information

CELT: Corpus of Electronic Texts. University College Cork. http://www.ucc.ie/celt/

Donahue, Annie. "The Acallam na Senórach: A Medieval Instruction Manual." *Proceedings of the Harvard Celtic Colloquium* 24/25 (2004/2005): 206–215.

Nagy, Joseph Falaky. "Fenian Heroes and Their Rites of Passage." *Béaloideas* 54/55 (1986/1987): 161–182.

46. Strange Tales about the Welsh (Twelfth Century)

INTRODUCTION

Gerald of Wales, a member of the Barry family who were lords of Manorbier, Pemrbokeshire, accompanied Baldwin, the archbishop of Canterbury, to Wales in 1188 to preach the Third Crusade. Gerald was part Welsh—his grandmother was the (in)famous Nest, daughter of Rhys ap Tewdr of Deheubarth and mistress of King Henry I—and proud of both sides of his parentage. Nevertheless, he considered the Welsh to be largely in need of civilizing, especially in the Norman manner.

Gerald enjoyed including legends and bizarre stories in his descriptions of the Celtic lands of Wales and Ireland. He had a particular interest in the flora and fauna of both regions (although he often repeated the same stories for one as for the other) and considered the eccentric behavior of mythically large toads and hardworking beavers to be symbolic of human behavior in the same regions.

KEEP IN MIND AS YOU READ

In the twelfth century, the competition between native Welsh princes and the Anglo-Norman barons of the Welsh march was fierce. Nevertheless, through intermarriage, the two elite groups were becoming mingled. This is not the case with the nonelite population, which remained significantly separated. The novelty of an English archbishop coming to Wales to preach to the local population must have been somewhat surprising and Gerald was enlisted to provide assistance in dealing with the native Welsh.

Although Gerald of Wales's works were read only in elite intellectual circles in the Middle Ages, his legacy continued far into the modern age. Indeed, his book on the Norman invasion of Ireland, *Expugnatio Hibernia*, was used as a justification for the seventeenth-century suppression of the Irish by Oliver Cromwell and his army. Gerald's biases against the Celtic populations, despite his own Celtic ancestry, thus entered into the general culture of a formative period in British history.

Document 1: Book II, Chapter 2:
Our Journey through Cemais and Our Stay in St Dogmael's Monastery

I want to tell you about two events which happened in the cantref of Cemais, one fairly recently and the other some time ago. In our days a young man who lived in this neighborhood, and who was lying ill in bed, was persecuted by a plague of toads. It seemed as if the entire local population of toads had made an agreement to go visit him. Vast numbers were killed by his friends and by those looking after him, but they grew again like the heads of the Hydra. . . . In the end the young man's friends and the other people who were trying to help were quite worn out. They chose a tall tree, cut off all its branches and removed all its leaves. Then they hoisted him up to the top in a bag. He was still not safe from his venomous assailants. The toads crawled up the tree looking for him. They killed him and ate him right up, leaving nothing but his skeleton. His name was Seisyll Esgairhir, which means Longshanks. . . .

In the same cantref, in the time of King Henry I, a rich man who lived on the northern slopes of the Prescelly Mountains dreamed three nights in succession that if he put his hand in a stone which stuck out above the gusting water of a near-by spring called the Fountain at Saint Bernacus, he would find there a gold torque. On the third day he did what he had been told to do in his dreams. He was bitten in the finger by a viper and died from the wound. It is true that many treasures have been discovered as a result of dreams, and in all sorts of circumstances. It seems to me that dreams are like rumors: you must use your common sense, and then accept some but refuse to believe others.

I must tell you about an extraordinary event, which occurred in our own time in Llanhyver Castle [Nanhyver or Nevern Castle], which is the chief stronghold in Cemais. After besieging it with a force of armed men, Rhys ap Gruffudd captured Llanhyver Castle from his own son-in-law, a young nobleman called William FitzMartin [married to Angharad, Rhys's daughter]. He did this at the instigation of his son Gruffudd, a cunning artful man. It was a direct contravention of a series of oaths that he had sworn in person on the most precious relics to the effect that William should be left in all peace and security in his castle. Rhys then handed the castle over to Gruffudd. In doing so he broke another oath that he had sworn, mentioning Gruffudd by name and promising that he would never permit him to hold Llanhyver Castle. . . . "Vengeance is mine; I will repay, saith the Lord," through the mouth of His prophet. [Romans 10:19] God ordained that soon afterwards the castle should be taken away from Gruffudd, . . . and handed over to his brother Maelgwn, the man he hated most in all the world. About two years later Rhys was planning to disinherit his own daughter [wife of William fitzMartin], his grandsons and his two granddaughters. Instead he was made prisoner in a battle with his sons [in 1194] and locked up in this very same castle. God took vengeance on him in the most apposite way, for, as he well deserved, he was disgraced and discountenanced in the very place where he had perpetrated a base and shameful crime.

At the time when he suffered this misfortune, and this is well worth bearing in mind, he had stolen the torque of Saint Cynog of Brecknockshire and had it hidden in Dinevor. For this act alone he deserved to be captured and locked up, as an example of the judgment of God.

Source: Gerald of Wales. *The Journey through Wales and the Description of Wales*. Introduction and translation by Lewis Thorpe. London: Penguin Books, 1978. Pp. 169–172. Modified by editor.

AFTERMATH

Gerald's interest in what he considered the cultural and ethnic peculiarities of the Welsh and the Irish, as well as his enthusiastic appropriation of stories of fantastical creatures, bizarre human malformations, and similar sensationalist lore, provided reading audiences for centuries with "proof" of the subordinate status of the Celtic people of those regions. Although Gerald's motivations for including such stories is not really known, he presents the Welsh and Irish in ways that promote Anglo-Norman dominance as appropriate and right, even if the Celtic population being subordinated were, in his estimation, pious and hospitable.

> The paragraph "in the same cantref . . . to believe others" appears also in *The Conquest of Ireland* in a slightly different form. This is typical of Gerald, who also repeated an elaborate story about how and why beavers build dams in both his *Description of Wales* and his *Conquest of Ireland*.

ASK YOURSELF

1. Why would Gerald include stories about giant murderous toads in an otherwise sober text?
2. The family of Rhys ap Gruffudd seems unusually bellicose. What is Gerald's explanation for the intrafamily fighting?
3. What is the significance of the golden torque?

TOPICS TO CONSIDER

1. Like the reading from the Fenian Cycle (above) there is a golden torque—an arm-ring—that holds mystical qualities, although its exact powers are not articulated by Gerald. Compare the two stories and discuss what the golden arm-ring might signify.
2. Consider the ways in which locally and orally transmitted tales could be used as a propaganda tool for promoting the values of a conqueror.

Further Information

Bartlett, Robert. *Gerald of Wales: A Voice of the Middle Ages*. Stroud: Tempus Publishing, 2006.

Faletra, Michael A. *Wales and the Medieval Colonial Imagination: The Matters of Britain in the Twelfth Century*. New York: Palgrave Macmillan, 2014.

Holden, Brock. " 'Feudal Frontiers?' Colonial Societies in Wales and Ireland 1170–1330." *Studia Hibernica* 33 (2004/2005): 61–79.

47. Attitudes in Popular Culture about the Sexes and Marriage (Fourteenth Century)

INTRODUCTION

It is common to encounter in medieval literature a wide range of attitudes about women, men, and marriage. Some of these are deliberately satirical; others are designed as moralistic warnings about maintaining proper behavior. Although it is more common to read texts that are critical of women than those in praise of women, medieval attitudes were not entirely misogynistic, as the phrase "A woman is a worthy wight" (person)—used as the title for a collection of sources about medieval women—demonstrates.

Beginning in the fourteenth century, a series of texts began to be produced that formed a collection known as the *Querelles des femmes*: the Debate about Women. In these stories, moralistic fables, and poems, the relative merits of females were weighed against their presumed defects. Some of these texts were incredibly misogynistic, while others presented women as the sum of all virtues; almost all were written by men. At the end of the century, and in the early fifteenth, three texts in this so-called debate stood out: Boccaccio's *De mulieribus claris* (*On Famous Women*), Geoffrey Chaucer's *The Legend of Good Women*, and Christine de Pizan's *The Book of the City of Ladies*.

KEEP IN MIND AS YOU READ

It is very hard to gauge the degree to which medieval people accepted the ideas about women embedded in the "Debate." It has to be assumed that writing both admiringly and satirically about women and men was a popular pastime because so many of these texts survive, and the structure of the *querelles des femmes* persisted well into the eighteenth century. The deliberately extreme contrasts in these kinds of texts might have shaped social and cultural attitudes about the sexes through the years, but the personal experiences of individuals with their families, neighbors, and friends had to influence day-to-day attitudes as well.

Document 1: Praising and Damning Women

In Praise of Women

I am as swift as any roe [deer]
To praise women where'er that I go.
To unpraise women it were a shame,
For a woman was your dame [mother];
Our Blessed Lady bears the name
Of all women where'er that they go.
A woman is a worthy thing—
They do the wash and do the wringing;
"Lullaby, lullaby," she does to thee sing,
And yet she has both care and woe.
A woman is a worthy wight [person],
She serves [her] man both day and night,
To serve them she puts all her might,
And yet she has both care and woe.

The Trials of Marriage

What, why did you wink [blink, or shut eyes] when you a wife took?
You never had your eyes more wide open to look!
A man that weds a wife when he winks,
Will stare afterwards, I do now think!

The Bawd and the Adulterers

A woman there was some time ago, who was a *bawd* between a farmer and another man's wife, and often since she brought them together in the sin of adultery; and they continued for a long time through the help of this bawd. At last this woman, the procuress, fell sick and was about to die. She thought in her heart as how she had been a sinful wretch, and was sorry in her heart that she had offended God, and thought she would make amends, as holy church decreed. She sent for her priest [to receive communion] and confessed [her sins] and took her penance, . . . and swore never to turn again to sin; and wept profusely and prayed to Christ, for the virtue of his blessed Passion, that he have mercy on her, and also prayed to his blessed Mother and all the saints; and so she passed out of this world. And soon after, the man and woman who lived in sin died without repentance.

bawd: a procuress or pimp

The bawd's husband prayed profusely for his wife, that God would show him how his wife fared [in the afterlife]. Afterward on a certain night, as he lay in bed, his wife appeared to him and said, "Husband be not afraid, but rise up and go with me, for you will see marvels." He rose and went with her, until they came into a fair plain. Then she said, "Stand still here, and be not afraid, for you will have no harm [come to you], and wisely behold what you will see." Then she went a little ways from him until she came to a great stone that had a hole in the middle; and as she stood before the stone, suddenly she was a long adder [a snake], and put her head in the hole in the middle of the stone, and crept through, but she left her skin outside the stone, and soon she stood up a fair woman. And soon after came two devils yelling and bringing a cauldron full of hot boiling brass, and set it down beside the stone; and after them came other devils, crying, and bringing a man; and after them came other devils, with great noise, and bringing a woman. Then the two devils took both the man and the woman that they had brought, and cast them into the cauldron and held them there, until the flesh was boiled from the bone. Then they [the devils] took out the bones and laid them beside the cauldron; and soon they were made man and woman [again]. And the devils cast them again into the cauldron; and thus they were treated many a time. And then the devils went from where they had come.

The woman who had crept through the stone went again to her husband and said, "Do you know this man and this woman?" He said, "Yes, they were our neighbors." Did you see, though," she said, "what pain they experienced?" He said, "Yes, a hideous pain." "This pain," she said, "will they have in hell forever, for they lived in adultery and did not make amends. And I was the bawd between them, and brought them together; and I should have been with them in the cauldron forever, had I not amended my life with contrition, confession, and satisfaction [penance], through the mercy of God; and I crept through the stone and left my skin behind."

"The stone is Christ; the hole his blessed wound on His side; and the skin is my sins that I left behind me, through the merits of Christ's passion; and therefore I will be saved. Go home now and beware of sin, and make amends for you will live but a short while; and do charity for you[rself] and for me."

Then the husband went home and did as she told him, and within a short time after he died and went to the bliss [of Heaven].

Source: *The Trials and Joys of Marriage.* Edited by Eve Salisbury. Kalamazoo, MI: Medieval Institute Publications, 2002. Pp. 247, 249, 177–178. Text translated from Middle English and/or modernized by editor. Reprinted with permission.

AFTERMATH

As the literary conceit of the "Debate about Women" expanded in the following centuries, the misogynistic elements began to outweigh the works praising women; moreover, those that did praise women usually took the form of historical minibiographies, such as found in Christine de Pizan's works about women, that presented women of the past as noble and self-sacrificing, but did little to present women of the day as worthy of respect for their abilities, rather than for their willingness to be martyrs to religion or to their families. Indeed, one of the most popular texts concerning a "woman worthy" was the story of "Patient Griselda" who suffered unspeakable tortures from an abusive husband and thereby "won" his love. The presentation of women's personalities as constituting a rigid dichotomy—virgin/whore; martyr/hedonist—was challenged by only a few authors over the centuries between the Middle Ages and the modern era.

ASK YOURSELF

1. How do you think medieval people—male and female—reacted to the ideas about women in the satirical texts about them?
2. What is the moral of the story about the bawd and her husband?
3. What activity do you think would be socially more unacceptable: engaging in adultery or helping adulterers succeed in cuckolding their spouses?

TOPICS TO CONSIDER

1. Compare the presentation of women in these texts with the character of Noah's wife in the Play of Noah (see below).
2. Consider how modern-day cultural notions about women and the sexes might have been influenced by medieval notions as expressed in these texts.

Further Information

Kelly, Joan. "Early Feminist Theory and the 'Querelles des Femmes', 1400–1789." *Signs* 8, no. 1 (1982): 4–28.

Meale, Carol M., ed. *Women and Literature in Britain, 1150–1500.* 2nd ed. Cambridge: Cambridge University Press, 1996.

48. Welsh Entertainers, Welsh and English Audiences (Fourteenth to Fifteenth Centuries)

INTRODUCTION

In the later Middle Ages, although secular audiences still enjoyed and appreciated the traditional literary entertainments of medieval Romance—such as stories of King Arthur and his court—and lives of the saints—such as appeared in the popular compilation known as *The Golden Legend*—they were also enjoying new and more profoundly secular forms of literature. These poems, songs, and stories presented contemporary life and social interactions in more realistic ways, poking fun at the foibles of people everywhere and presenting their surroundings in a more personal way. Authors such as Geoffrey Chaucer, John Gower, and William Langland blended religious sensibilities and secular themes in ways that made them more relevant to their audiences.

As Wales became more interconnected with the English kingdom, and as the populations along the borders blended more and more, the forms of entertainment also blended. One such entertainer was the poet DAFYDD AP GWILYM (ca. 1315–1370), considered by many scholars to be one of the leading poets of the later Middle Ages, and certainly the foremost poet writing in Welsh in the fourteenth century. He wrote in the "court poet" tradition: focusing on secular themes of love, nature, and daily life in aristocratic households. Dafydd often placed himself at the center of his poetry, rather than writing about legendary heroes and heroic events. Other poets and balladeers, many whose names are unknown to us, commented on the ways in which the hybrid culture of the Welsh March presented challenges to all professional entertainers.

KEEP IN MIND AS YOU READ

In the following poem by Dafydd ap Gwilym, he complains about the women he encounters in the church of Llanbadarn (an ancient town in northern coastal Wales near Aberystwyth), which is, according to legend, the place of his birth. Dafydd has gone to church only to look at, and possibly flirt with, women but they are aware of his flirtatious tendencies and spurn him. In the second extract, a Welsh harper complains about the need to compete with hated English bagpipers for scarce pennies earned as entertainers.

Both texts rely on the audience being aware of a number of social conventions, and both bring the audience into the author's personal space by engaging in a good dose of self-deprecatory humor and exaggeration. Dafydd is aware of his reputation as an unreliable flirt, but he revels in it until spurned by the wiser and more sensible women; the harper shakes his head at the lack of taste of English lords living on the border for choosing bagpipes over the Welsh harp.

Document 1: Merched Llanbadarn
[The Girls of Llanbadarn]

I am bent with wrath,
a plague upon all the women of this parish!
for I've never had (cruel, oppressive longing)
a single one of them,
neither a virgin (a pleasant desire)
nor a little girl nor hag nor wife.
What hindrance, what wickedness,
what failing prevents them from wanting me?
What harm could it do to a fine–browed maidento have me in a dark, dense wood?
It would not be shameful for her
to see me in a bed of leaves.
There was never a time when I did not love —
never was any charm so persistent —
even more than men of Garwy's ilk,
one or two in a single day,
and yet I've come no closer to winning one of these
than if she'd been my foe.
There was never a Sunday in Llanbadarn church
(and others will condemn it)
that my face was not turned towards the splendid girl
and my nape towards the resplendent, holy Lord.
And after I'd been staring long
over my feathers across my fellow parishioners,
the sweet radiant girl would hiss
to her companion, so wise, so fair:
"He has an adulterous look—
his eyes are adept at disguising his wickedness—
that pallid lad with the face of a coquette
and his sister's hair upon his head."
"Is that what he has in mind?"
says the other girl by her side,
"While the world endures he'll get no response,
to hell with him, the imbecile!"
I was stunned by the bright girl's curse,
 meagre payment for my stupefied love.
I might have to renounce
this way of life, terrifying dreams.

Indeed, I'd better become
a hermit, a calling fit for scoundrels.
Through constant staring (a sure lesson)
over my shoulder (a pitiful sight),
it has befallen me, who loves the power of verse,
to become wry–necked without a mate.

Source: The Girls of Llanbadarn, translated from the Welsh by A. Cynfael Lake. http://dafyddapgwilym.net/eng/3win.htm. Reprinted with permission.

Document 2: The Welsh Harper and the English Bagpiper

Welsh; authorship uncertain; fifteenth century.

Last Sunday I came—a man whom the Lord God made—to the town of Flint, with its great double walls and rounded bastions; may I see it all aflame! An obscure English wedding was there, with but little mead—an English feast! and I meant to earn a shining solid reward for my harper's art. So I began, with ready speed, to sing an ode to the kinsmen; but all I got was mockery, spurning of my song, and grief. . . . They all called for William the Piper to come to the table, a low fellow he must be. He came forward as though claiming his usual rights, though he did not look like a privileged man, with a groaning bag, a paunch of heavy guts, at the end of a stick between chest and arm. He rasped away, making startling grimaces, a horrid noise, from the swollen belly, bulging his eyes; he twisted his body here and there, and puffed his two cheeks out, playing with his fingers on a bell of hide—unsavoury conduct, fit for unsavoury banqueters. . . . The pigmy puffed, making an outlandish cry, blowing out the bag with a loud howl; it sang like a buzzing hornet, that devilish bag with the stick in its head, like a nightmare howl, fit to kill a mangy goose, like a sad bitch's hoarse howl in its hollow kennel; a harsh paunch with monotonous cry, throat-muscles squeezing out a song, with a neck like a crane's where he plays, like a stabbed goose screeching aloud. There are voices in that hollow bag like the ravings of a thousand cats; a monotonous, wounded ailing, pregnant goat—no pay for its hire. After it ended its wheezing note, that cold songstress whom love would shun, Will got his fee, named bean-soup and pennies (if they paid) and sometimes small halfpennies, not the largesse of a princely hand; while *I* was sent away in high vexation from the silly feast all empty-handed. I solemnly vow, I do forswear wretched Flint and all its children, and its wide, hellish furnace, and its English people and its piper! That they should be slaughtered is all my prayer, my curse in their midst and on their children; sure, if I go there again, may I never return alive!

Source: *A Celtic Miscellany: Translations from the Celtic Literatures.* Translated by Kenneth Hurlstone Jackson. Middlesex, England: Penguin Books, 1976. Pp. 216–217.

AFTERMATH

Cultural differences between the English and their Celtic neighbors persisted, especially among the people of the countryside who had little contact with the more cosmopolitan urban regions. Nevertheless—and despite a considerable amount of nationalist feeling in all the different populations of the British Isles—hybrid cultures and societies grew in the borders between regions, in the cities and towns governed using English administrative structures, and in the international trade conducted by merchants and manufacturers. This can be seen in the development of court poetry in Wales, the employment of Irish bards by English nobles settled in Ireland, and the building of English "gothic" buildings throughout the isles.

ASK YOURSELF

1. Is Dafydd ap Gwilym making fun of himself, or making fun of the women who spurn him?
2. In "The Girls of Llanbadarn," Dafydd presents himself in a romantic role of courtly knight who is misunderstood by the women of the town. Is he really misunderstood, or is his self-image a ploy for sympathy?
3. The Welsh harper's complaint about the English bagpiper is not just aesthetic; it is also financial. In what ways would the hybrid culture of the late medieval March promote and make active the cultural blending of music and other art forms; in what ways would it limit such a blending?

TOPICS TO CONSIDER

1. Compare Dafydd ap Gwilym's presentation of the women of Llanbadarn and the poem "In Praise of Women" and consider the contrast between satire and sentiment in presenting women in a positive light.
2. Consider the ways in which the blending of cultures in lands with diverse populations, such as Ireland and Wales, could result in significant cross-cultural fertilization, such as in styles of poetry, aesthetics, and lifestyle. Also consider how this might be threatening to people living outside those blended communities.

Further Information

Fulton, Helen. "The *Encomium Urbis* in Medieval Welsh Poetry." *Proceedings of the Harvard Celtic Colloquium* 26/27 (2006/2007): 54–72.

Luft, Diana. "Genre and Diction in the Poetry of Dafydd ap Gwilym: The Revelation of Cultural Tension." *Proceedings of the Harvard Celtic Colloquium* 18/19 (1998/1999): 278–297.

49. Theatrical Drama for a Christian Audience: The Play of Noah (Fifteenth Century)

INTRODUCTION

The development of Christian-themed theatrical performances in the later Middle Ages in England led the way to a more sophisticated form of secular theater in the sixteenth and seventeenth centuries that exhibited plays by the likes of John Kidd, Christopher Marlowe, and William Shakespeare. The medieval plays, usually referred to as "mystery" plays (when referencing the Bible, especially the Passion) or "miracle" plays (often having to do with the lives of saints), were acted at certain times of year and the acting troupe was usually local or locally itinerant, producing the plays on the back of carts in the outdoors. The Play of Noah is one of the Wakefield or Townley Mystery cycle, which was compiled in the mid-fifteenth century, although the plays themselves might have been performed for many years before being written down. It was probably performed during the Feast of Corpus Christi, which celebrates the mystery of the Eucharist.

A typical component of many of these Middle English plays is the combination of social commentary and humor—often in the form of slapstick antics and gender inversion. The Play of Noah is a good example of the ways in which popular culture viewed the problems and challenges of marriage and family, as well as presenting a well-known story in a dramatic way to populations unable to read it for themselves.

KEEP IN MIND AS YOU READ

As in Shakespeare's day, only men were permitted to perform as actors in public (although there is evidence that nuns, in the privacy of their convents, did sometimes act out plays for their own personal enjoyment). This means that all female roles were played by men, who were costumed in women's clothes. The audience for the plays—comprising both men and women—would have been well aware of this double gender inversion (a man playing a woman who refuses to be subordinated to "her" husband), and it might have heightened the comedic aspects of the plays for them, much as the cross-dressing roles assumed by the Monty Python comedy troupe were designed to push the absurdity of human behavior to an extreme.

The style of the poetry is a basic four-line alternating "tail-rhyme" (ABAB/CDCD/etc.), which cannot be preserved entirely in modern English.

Document 1: The Play of Noah

[Preface: the reason for God's anger at humanity is detailed; Noah, a righteous man, bewails the evil of humanity.]
  [God descends and comes to Noah]

Noah, my friend, I thee command
From cares thee to [cool],
A ship that thou ordained
Of nail and board, full well.
Though was always well working,
To me true as steel,
To my bidding [be] obedient,
Friendship shall thou feel
As a reward;
Of length thy ship be
Three hundredth cubits, warn I thee,
Of height even thirty,
Of fifty also in breadth.
. . .
One cubit on height
a window shall thou make;
On the side a door with slight
Beneath shall thou take;
With thee shall no man fight,
nor do thee no kin harm.
When all is done thus right,
thy wife, that is thy mate,
Take in to thee;
Thy sons of good fame,
Sem, Japhet, and Came,
Take in also Hame,
Their wives also three.
. . .
[Noah is convinced of the urgency of the situation, but worries about what his wife will say.]
Noah: Lord, homeward will I haste
as fast as that I may;
My wife will I ask
what she will say,
And I am aghast
that we get some fray
Betwixt us both;
For she is full tetchy,
For little [things] oft angry;
If anything wrong be,

Soon is she wroth.
[Noah goes to his wife]
God speed, dear wife,
how fare ye?
Noah's Wife: Now, as ever might I thrive,
the wars I thee see;
Do tell me believe,
where has thou thus long be?
To deed may we drive
or live because of thee,
For want.
When we sweat or toil,
Thou does what thou think,
Yet of meat and of drink
Have we very little.

. . .

[Noah and his wife fight—both verbally and physically—about the ark, but he builds it and convinces his sons and their wives to enter it. His wife, however, remains adamantly in denial.]
Noah: Now are we there
as we should be;
Do get in our gear,
our cattle and possessions
Into this vessel here
my noble children.
Noah's Wife: I was never barred up here
As ever might I prosper,
In such an hostelry as this.
In faith I cannot find
Which is before, which is behind;
But shall we here be confined,
Noah, as have thou bliss?
[The wife leaves the ark]
Noah: Dame be reasonable,
here must us abide grace;
Therefore, wife, with good will,
come into this place.
Noah's Wife: Sir, for Jack nor for Jill
will I turn my face
Till I have on this hill
spun for a while
On my distaff;
Well were he, might get me.
Now will I down set me,
Yet I allow no man to prevent me,
For dread of a knock.
Noah: Behold to the heavens
the cataracts all,
That are open even,
great and small,

And the planets seven
Have left their stall,
This thunder and lightning
begin to fall
Full stout,
Both halls and bowers,
Castles and towers;
Full sharp are these showers,
That run all about;
Therefore, wife, have done!
Come into ship fast!
Noah's Wife: Yee, Noah, go mend thy shoes,
the better will they last.

. . .

[*The three sons and their wives plead with their mother to enter the ship, but she refuses, and continues her spinning.*]
Noah: Now is this twice Come in,
dame, on my friendship.
Noah's Wife: Whether I lose or I win
in faith, thy fellowship,
Set I not a pin.
This spindle will I slip
Upon this hill,
Before I stir one foot.
Noah: Peter! I think we are fools;
Without any more talk
Come in if you will.
Noah's Wife: Yea, water comes so near
that I sit not dry,
Into ship with a byre
Therefore will I hie
For dread that I'll drown here.
Noah: Dame, securely,
It'll be bought full dear,
ye abode so long by
Out of ship.
Noah's Wife: I will not, fat thy command,
Go from door to dunghill.
Noah: In faith, and for your long tarrying
Ye shall accept the whip.
Noah's Wife: Spare me not, I pray thee,

but even as thou think,
These great words shall not flay me.
Noah: Abide, dame, and drink,
For beaten shall thou be
with this staff until thou stink;
Are strokes good? say me.
[Noah strikes his wife]
Noah's Wife: What say ye, *Wat Wink*?

Ye shall accept the whip: accept your punishment
Wat Wink?: Silly Dope
Nicholl Nedy!: Lincoln Log! (Nicholl was another spelling of Lincoln, from the Latin form of the town's name)

Noah: Speak!
Cry me mercy, I say!
Noah's Wife: To that say I nay.
Noah: Unless thou do, by this day
Thy head shall I break.
Noah's Wife: Lord, I would be at ease
and heartily contented,
If I had a bowl
of widow's pottage;
For thy soul, without less,
should I a penny gladly pay
So would more, no matter
that I see in this place
Of wives that are here,
For the life that they lead,
Would that their husbands were dead,
For, as ever ate I bread,
So would I wish my husband were.
Noah: You men that have wives
while they are young,
If you love your lives,
chastise their tongue!
Me think my heart splits,
both liver and lung,
To see such strife wedded men have;
But I,
As have I bliss,
Shall chastise this.
Noah's Wife: Yet may you miss,
Nicholl Nedy!
[Noah and his wife fight, ad lib.]
. . .

[The fight ends with the wife sitting atop Noah]
Noah [addresses audience]: See how she can groan,
and I lie under [her];
But, wife,
In this haste let us stop,
For my back is near [broke] in two.
Noah's Wife: And I am bet so bruised
That I may not thrive.
First Son: A! Why fare ye thus,
Father and mother both?
Second Son: Ye should not be so spiteful,
standing in such peril.
Third Son: These are so hideous,
with many a dire disease.
Noah: We will do as ye bid us;
we will no more be wroth,
Dear bairns!

Now to the helm will I hasten,
And to my ship go.
Noah's Wife: I see on the firmament,
Me think, the seven stars show.
[All go aboard the Ark]

Source: *The Play of Noah: The Townley (Wakefield) Mystery Plays.* The President and Fellows of Harvard College. Maintained by L. D. Benson. Accessed online http://sites.fas.harvard.edu/~chaucer/special/litsubs/drama/noah.html. Middle English modernized by editor.

AFTERMATH

The medieval miracle and mystery plays were one of the most important elements of popular expressions of piety in the later Middle Ages in England. Their popularity persisted until the church reformers—both Protestant and Catholic—began to condemn them for including too many extrabiblical elements: precisely the elements of pathos and comedy that drew audiences to the plays.

ASK YOURSELF

1. Why might the story of the flood be a popular subject for medieval playwrights?
2. Why is Noah's wife depicted as a raging harridan? How would having a man portray Noah's wife affect the way she is depicted?
3. How do you think this play would have been received by a medieval audience?

TOPICS TO CONSIDER

1. Compare the depiction of women here and in the poems about marriage and discuss them in terms of the "Debate about Women" that evolved in the late Middle Ages.
2. Consider the relationship between the flood texts in the Bible and the embellishments of the story in the play and analyze the reasons why (what purposes they might serve beyond entertainment value) they would have been added.
3. Consider ways in which plays such as this might influence the growing anticlericalism movement in England in the late Middle Ages.

Further Information

Daniels, Richard J. "*Uxor* Noah: A Raven or a Dove?" *The Chaucer Review* 14, no. 1 (1979): 23–32.
Sponsler, Claire. *Drama and Resistance: Bodies, Goods, and Theatricality in Late Medieval England.* Minneapolis: University of Minnesota Press, 1997.
Tolmie, Jane. "Mrs Noah and Didactic Abuses." *Early Theatre* 5, no. 1 (2002): 11–35.

50. Pessimism in an Age of Anxiety: The Wars of the Roses

INTRODUCTION

From the deposition of Richard II in 1399 to the overthrow of Richard III by Henry Tudor in 1485, England in particular and the British Isles in general experienced a significantly heightened period of anxiety marked by almost constant warfare (although usually on a low or localized level), economic problems, and periodical outbreaks of the bubonic plague. In particular, competition between competing branches of the royal family—the House of York, descended from two sons of Edward III, on the paternal side Edmund of Langley duke of York, and on the maternal side, Lionel of Antwerp duke of Clarence, and the House of Lancaster, descended from John of Gaunt duke of Lancaster—spent most of the second half of the fifteenth century battling over who would attain the throne. The war between England and France known as the Hundred Years' War did not end until King Henry VI (a Lancastrian) renounced his claim in 1453. He did so in the aftermath of a serious rebellion of the Commons and the peasantry in 1450, led by Jack Cade (likely a pseudonym), which erupted in the counties surrounding London and which also enveloped the city itself. The loss of any claims to France was also an impetus for the House of York to stake a claim to the throne and led to the civil war known as the Wars of the Roses.

By the fifteenth century, the population of England was more literate, more cosmopolitan, and more weary of the political upheavals of the day than their thirteenth- and fourteenth-century predecessors. The result was an outpouring of political balladry that highlighted the complaints of the common folk: the weakness of the king and the corruption of his officials; the stagnating economy, especially due to the loss of France; the worries over continuing outbreaks of plague as well as other diseases such as smallpox. The poem included here, which appears in a manuscript found at Corpus Christi College Library, Oxford, presents the common person's view of the conflict between the "Lancastrians"— the party of King Henry VI—and the "Yorkists"—the party of King Edward IV—as they fought an unproductive civil war over the Crown. Unlike the wars of the thirteenth century, which many consider to have been helpful in the development of laws protecting the liberties of the commons and of the lower levels of the baronage against incursions of the crown, the so-called Wars of the Roses were both destabilizing and ultimately pointless, as they were the direct precursor to the invasion and conquest of Henry Tudor, earl of Richmond, future King Henry VII, who claimed the throne of England by right of conquest, even though he was in no way eligible to inherit the throne (his grandmother was Katherine of

France, widow of Henry V and mother of Henry VI; his mother was Margaret Beaufort whose family line was barred because of illegitimacy from claiming the English Crown; his wife was one of the daughters of King Edward IV and Elizabeth Woodville, whose line Henry VII officially deposed).

KEEP IN MIND AS YOU READ

The British Isles had been a hotbed of popular political balladry for many years, including doggerel verses about King Edward I and Queen Eleanor of Castile ("the king desires to get our gold/the queen our manors fair to hold") but the anxieties of the fifteenth century, especially in the wake of the Great Rising of 1381 and the second deposing of a king within a century (Edward II in 1327 and Richard II in 1399), produced an unusual outpouring of protest and political dissent created by common people. In addition, it was an era of religious upheaval, with Lollardy competing with orthodoxy in the same counties where political rebellion seems to have occurred more readily.

Document 1: On the Times

Now is England all in fight;
Many people of conscience light;
Many knights, and little of might;
Many laws, and little right;
Many acts of parliament,
And few kept with true intent;
Little charity, and few to please;
Many a gallant is penniless;
And many a wonderful disguising,
By imprudence and misadvising;
Great countenance, and small wages;
Many gentlemen, and few pages;
Wide gowns, and large sleeves;
Well dressed, and strongly scented;
Much padding [or boasting] of their clothing,
But well I know they trifle with their oaths [their duties].

Source: *Political Poems and Songs Relating to English History.* Edited by Thomas Wright. London: Longman, Green, Longman, and Roberts, 1861. Pp. 2: 252–253. Translated from Middle English by editor.

AFTERMATH

The poem expresses the frustrations of common people, who saw the ever-widening disparity between rich and poor, typified by faddish clothing and wasteful spending, as emblematic of the corruption at the top of the political system. Although Jack Cade's rebellion was put down brutally, and there were no other major rebellions in the fifteenth century until Henry Tudor's harrowing of the northern counties, these sentiments seem to have dogged the royal administration even after the overthrow of Richard III at Bosworth Field in 1485 by Henry Tudor, future Henry VII.

ASK YOURSELF

1. Considering the tone of the poem, to whom do you think it is directed and why?
2. What complaints does the poet have against the government and the elites?
3. Do the complaints of the poet sound familiar to you as a modern reader? Why and in what ways?

TOPICS TO CONSIDER

1. Explore the relationship between religious and political dissent in the fifteenth century, especially during the "Wars of the Roses."
2. Investigate the specific issues at play in the rebellion of Jack Cade and compare to the reasons behind the Great Rising of 1381.
3. Consider the reception of a poem such as this and how its circulation might be considered dangerous by the royal administration.

Further Information

Aston, M. E. "Lollardy and Sedition 1381–1431." *Past & Present* 17, no. 1 (1960): 1–44.

Ellis, Steven G. "Nationalist Historiography and the English and Gaelic Worlds in the Late Middle Ages." *Irish Historical Studies* 25, no. 97 (1986): 1–18.

Horrox, Rosemary, ed. *Fifteenth-Century Attitudes: Perceptions of Society in Late Medieval England*. Cambridge: Cambridge University Press, 1994.

Kaufman, Alexander L. *The Historical Literature of the Jack Cade Rebellion*. Farnham: Ashgate Publishing, 2009.

Appendix 1: Biographical Sketches of Important Individuals Mentioned in the Text

Adela, Countess of Blois (ca. 1067–1137): daughter of King William I and Queen Matilda of Flanders; sister of King William II and King Henry I; wife of Stephen, Count of Blois; mother of King Stephen. Her son claimed the throne in competition with his cousin, Empress Matilda, through his mother.

Aiofe [Eva], daughter of Diarmid Mac Murchada [Dermot MacMurrough] (ca. 1145–1188): declared heir to the kingdom of Leinster after the death of her brother (a policy contrary to Irish law), Aiofe married Richard fitzGilbert de Clare ("Strongbow"), Earl of Pembroke, as part of the negotiations between Strongbow and her father to gain his support of Diarmid's campaigns to recover Leinster. As heir of Leinster, she conveyed the wealthiest and most populated portion of Ireland to her husband, and thence to their daughter, Isabella, who married William Marshal, becoming, by right of his wife, Earl of Pembroke and Lord of Leinster.

Alexander II, King of Scots (r. 1214–1249): son of and successor to King William the Lion and Ermengarde de Beaumont; supported the barons during the civil war between John and the baronage and allied with the French by invading England from the north when they invaded from the south. Reconciled to King Henry III in 1217 and married his sister, Joan. The two kings established the current boundary between England and Scotland in the Treaty of York (1237). Alexander attempted to expand royal influence into the regions of Scotland controlled by the kings of Norway, but was unsuccessful. Joan of England having died, he married Marie de Coucy; their son, future Alexander III, was his only legitimate progeny.

Alexander III, King of Scots (r. 1249–1286): son and heir of Alexander II and Marie de Coucy; became king at the age of seven, resulting in a long minority. When he reached his majority he returned to father's policy of trying to wrest Scottish lands away from Norway; succeeded in gaining overlordship of the Western Isles and Isle of Man (Treaty of Perth, 1266), which he transferred to Clan Donald as "Lords of the Isles," who controlled it largely independent of the Crown. Married [1] Margaret, daughter of Henry III and Eleanor of Provence, who had two children—Margaret, Queen of Norway, and Alexander, who died before his father; and [2] Yolande de Dreux. At his death his heir was his granddaughter, Margaret "Maid of Norway," who was three years old. Her death in 1290 precipitated the Great Cause.

Alfred, King of Wessex (r. 871–899): fifth son of King Aethelwulf and Queen Osburh of Wessex; three elder brothers succeeded their father in order and he succeeded his fourth brother Ethelred. Later referred to as Alfred "the Great," he successfully unified the southern half of England under his rule against the northern Danelaw; established nominal overlordship of the Danelaw with his victory over King Guthrum at the battle of Edington. Alfred was responsible for creating an extensive administrative reorganization of both the royal government and the military, one that survived into the early modern era, albeit with significant modifications. He also was the patron of a collection of scholars who translated essential Latin texts into Old English; he was himself responsible for some of the translations. Married Ealhswith of Mercia; they had five children including Edward the Elder, his successor.

Athelstan, King of Wessex (r. 924–939): son of Edward the Elder and his first wife Ecgwynn; grandson of Alfred the Great. Successfully unified southern England and the Danelaw after the battle of Brunanburh, although this unity did not survive his death. Responsible for extending the administrative reforms of Alfred in the development of a royal chancery that oversaw the production of writs and charters; expanded Alfred's education program to enhance learning in England, especially in vernacular. Participated in European politics at a higher level than his predecessors. He seems never to have married; his successor was his half-brother Edmund I.

Ball, John (ca. 1338–1381): English priest who embraced the doctrinal opinions of John Wyclif and preached both religious and political rebellion during the Great Rising of 1381. After the rebellion was put down, Ball was arrested and executed for treason. His head was stuck on London Bridge for years afterward.

Berkeley, Lord Thomas de (1245–1321): a prominent nobleman during the reign of Edward I; associated most with the Valence earls of Pembroke, especially Countess Joan and her son, Earl Aymer. He fought on the royalist side at the battle of Evesham and was affiliated with the royals (his mother was the granddaughter of King John by his mistress, Adela de Warenne) for his entire career. Married Joan Ferrers, daughter of William Ferrers, Earl of Derby, and third wife, Margaret de Quency; they had seven children. Although at an advanced age, he fought at Bannockburn in 1314 and was taken prisoner. After paying ransom, he died at Berkeley Castle.

Bernard of Clairvaux, St. (1090–1153): the most famous member of the Cistercian Order, even more so than Robert de Molesme, who founded the order. Abbot of the second Cistercian house of Clairvaux; theologian; preacher of the Second Crusade; avid writer of letters to royals and prominent nobles. Bernard and the philosopher and logician Peter Abelard were locked in a lifelong struggle against each other; Bernard succeeded in having Abelard's teachings condemned. Bernard supported other radical thinkers, such as Hildegard von Bingen, but was known as the proclaimer of a rigid orthodoxy in favor of the absolute liberty of the church against lay interference.

Bigod, Hugh (ca. 1211–1266): second son of Hugh Bigod, Earl of Norfolk, and Maud Marshal, Countess Marshal (eldest daughter of William and Isabella Marshal). Appointed as justiciar of England during the (Second) Barons' War. His son, Roger, eventually inherited the earldom of Norfolk and the Marshalsy from his uncle.

Bower, Walter (ca. 1385–1449): abbot of Inchcolm Abbey in Scotland and the author of one of the first comprehensive works of Scottish history, the *Scotichronicon*. This was both an adaptation of an earlier history, the *Chronica Gentis Scotorum* of John of Fordun, and a significantly new work that expanded Fordun's chronicle and extended it to 1447.

Bruce, Edward, Earl of Carrick (ca. 1280–1318): younger brother of Robert Bruce, led invasion of Ireland by the Scottish troops but was defeated and killed in battle. When Robert Bruce was crowned, he passed the earldom of Carrick to Edward.

Bruce, Robert, Earl of Carrick and King of Scots (r. 1306–1329): one of the Competitors in the Great Cause, Robert Bruce succeeded to the throne of Scotland in part through his elimination of his greatest rival, John III Comyn, Lord of Badenoch. Crowned in 1306 by Countess Isabella MacDuff at Scone, he systematically eliminated his opposition and, with his victory at Bannockburn in 1314, solidified his hold on the throne. Bruce and his followers sent the *Declaration of Arbroath* to Pope John XXII in 1320, and in 1324 the pope recognized him as the rightful ruler of Scotland. Married twice: [1] Isabella of Mar (d. 1296) and [2] Elizabeth de Burgh of Ulster; several children, among them Marjorie Bruce (founder of the House of Stuart) and King David II.

Burgh, Elizabeth de, Countess of Ulster (1332–1363): daughter and heir of William Donn de Burgh and Maud of Lancaster; through marriage to Lionel of Antwerp, second surviving son of Edward III, and Philippa of Hainault, Duchess of Clarence. Their daughter, Philippa, married Edmund Mortimer, Earl of March; their successors eventually claimed the English throne against the House of Lancaster.

Clare, Isabella de, Countess of Pembroke (1172–1220): daughter and heir of Richard fitzGilbert de Clare, Earl of Pembroke, and Eofe daughter and heir of Diarmid Mac Murchada, King of Leinster. Married, in 1190, William Marshal and through her he became Earl of Pembroke and Lord of Leinster. They had ten children—five sons and five daughters—and, despite the significant difference in their ages (over 20 years) their marriage was successful not only with respect to children, but also politically. Isabella is likely one of the patrons of the poet who wrote *The History of William Marshal*. She did not long outlive him, dying less than a year after her husband. Buried at the family foundation of Tintern Abbey.

Clare, Richard fitzGilbert de [Strongbow], Earl of Pembroke (1130–1176): through his father, Gilbert de Clare, Lord of Striguil and Earl of Pembroke and, by right of his wife, Aiofe Mac Murchada, Lord of Leinster in Ireland. Forfeited titles in 1155 because of his support of King Stephen against Empress Matilda, but recovered them during reign of Henry II because of his support of the invasion of Ireland. Alliance with Diarmid Mac Murchada, deposed King of Leinster, led to his marriage and acquisition of that region. Their daughter married William Marshal.

Cnut, King of Denmark, Norway, and England (r. 1017–1035): son of Sweyn Forkbeard, King of Norway and Denmark, and conqueror of England after the defeat of both King Ethelred II and his son Edmund "Ironside" in 1216. Married Ethelred's widow, Emma of Normandy, and ruled over a united kingdom. Carried on the administrative innovations of his Anglo-Saxon predecessors but did not try to integrate the administrations of all the kingdoms he controlled. After death, conflict between his and Emma's son Harthacnut and Emma and Ethelred's son Edward "the Confessor" led to the return of the House of Wessex on the throne.

Columbanus, St. (543–615): Irish monk and missionary notable for founding both Luxeuil Abbey in France and Bobbio Abbey in Italy. Considered one of the leaders of the revival of learning and the expansion of Celtic forms of Christian monastic practice into continental Europe.

Comyn, John III of Badenoch (John Comyn the Red) (d. 1306): one of the Competitors for the throne of Scotland; married to Joan de Valence, daughter of William and Joan de Valence of Pembroke. John Comyn's claim to the throne was considered somewhat better than that of Robert Bruce—he could claim legitimate descent through both father and mother—and this might have been the primary reason for his murder by Bruce in the Church of the Grey Friars of Dumfries on February 10, 1306. His murder precipitated the invasion of the English, led by his brother-in-law, Aymer de Valence.

Cú Chulainn: Irish mythological hero of the Ulster Cycle, also known as the *Táin Bó Cúailgne* (The Cattle Raid of Cooley).

Dafydd ap Gwilym (ca. 1315–1370): Welsh poet of both romantic and topical poetry, written in the "court" style typical of English poets such as Geoffrey Chaucer. Considered the finest medieval poet writing in Welsh and one of the finest poets of the British Isles.

David I, King of Scots (r. 1124–1153): son of Malcolm III and Margaret of Wessex; brother and heir of Alexander I; brother-in-law of King Henry I. David was responsible for the "Normanization" of the Scottish court by inviting Norman barons to hold land in Scotland in feudal tenure. He also was an avid founder of monasteries and reformed the diocesan structure in Scotland to conform more to Roman practice. Supported his niece, Empress Matilda, against King Stephen. Married Maud, Countess of Huntingdon; successor was Malcolm IV, his grandson.

Edward I, King of England (r. 1272–1307): son and successor of Henry III and Eleanor of Provence; one of the most active and successful kings—and also controversial as to his legacy—of medieval England. Before his succession he led the army against Simon de Montfort at the battle of Evesham (1265) and went on crusade with King Louis IX of France and refortified Acre (1270–1273). Upon succession, promoted significant advances in royal administration, parliamentary representation, law, and statute. Successfully annexed North Wales and intervened forcefully in the succession crisis in Scotland. Was responsible for the expulsion of the Jews from England after the death of his beloved first wife, Eleanor of Castile. Married, secondly, Margaret of France; had many children with both wives. Was succeeded by eldest surviving son, Edward of Caernarvon.

Edward II, King of England (r. 1307–1327): in contrast to his father, possibly the least successful monarch in medieval England. Inherited a war with Scotland's King Robert Bruce, which resulted in humiliating loss at the battle of Bannockburn (1314). Accusations of enriching favorites led to several baronial revolt: the Ordinances of 1311, rebellion of Thomas of Lancaster in 1322, and ultimately the revolt of the barons led by his wife, Isabella of France, and son, Edward III in 1327. Deposed and allegedly murdered at Berkeley Castle. Succeeded by son, Edward III.

Edward III, King of England (r. 1327–1377): one of the most legendary and popular kings of medieval England, although his reign was troubled by the effects of the wars in Scotland, the beginning of the Hundred Years' War, and the devastations of the Black Death in 1348–1350 and its reappearance in 1361. Declared himself King of France through his mother, Isabella, daughter of Philip IV, precipitating the Hundred Years' War; successful battles at Crécy and Poitou led to reacquisition of Normandy and Gascony. Response to the Black Death—the Statute of Laborers (1351)—led to widespread disaffection. Founded the Order of the Garter. Married Philippa of Hainault; they had 14 children of which 4 survived both parents; several children died of plague in 1348. Succeeded by grandson, Richard, son of Edward, Prince of Wales and Joan of Kent.

Eleanor of Aquitaine, Queen of England (1122–1204): daughter and heir of William X, Duke of Aquitaine, and Aenor de Châtellerault; she married, first, King Louis VII of France in 1132 but this marriage was annulled in 1152. Almost as soon as the annulment was complete, she remarried Henry, at the time Count of Anjou and Duke of Aquitaine, but who was soon to be King Henry II of England. Eleanor had two daughters with Louis and eight children with Henry. She outlived all her children except her youngest, King John, and was a significant presence in the reigns of both her husbands and her sons. She retired to Fontevrault Abbey, where she died and was buried.

Eleanor of Castile, Queen of England (1241–1290): daughter of Ferdinand III of Castile and Joan, Countess of Ponthieu, which she inherited from her mother; wife and queen consort of Edward I. A significant political figure in her own right, she was also largely responsible for the Crown's policy toward the Jews, which led to their expulsion in 1290. Eleanor accompanied her husband most of the time, including to the Holy Land on crusade, where she gave birth to their daughter, Joan of Acre (as well as another, unnamed daughter the year before). She gave birth to at least 16 children, only 6 of whom survived their mother, and only 4 of whom—3 girls and their youngest son, Edward of Caernarvon—survived both parents. After her death, Edward erected 12 stone monuments—known as Eleanor Crosses—in the procession from Lincoln, where she died, to London, where she was interred at Westminster Abbey. Three crosses still survive.

Eleanor of Provence, Queen of England (ca. 1223–1291): daughter of Ramon Berenguer IV, Count of Provence, and Margaret of Savoy; wife and queen consort of Henry III. Her eldest sister, Marguerite, was married to Louis IX of France (St. Louis); her two younger sisters, Sancha and Beatrice, married royal brothers Richard, Earl of Cornwall, and Charles, Count of Anjou, respectively. Thus all four sisters married men who ultimately became kings, as Richard of Cornwall was elected "King of the Romans" (the first step to being crowned Holy Roman Emperor) and Charles of Anjou was crowned King of Sicily following the death of Manfred, son of Emperor Frederick II. Although a very effective administrator for her husband, Henry, Eleanor was not well liked, according to chronicles, because of the advancement of her relatives, known as the "Savoyards," who accompanied her to England. She and Henry had at least five children, four of whom survived their father, but only two—their sons Edward and Edmund—survived both parents. After Henry's death, Eleanor raised several of her grandchildren and, in 1275, retired to Amesbury Abbey, a royal foundation. She was buried there; her grave is not identified.

Emma of Normandy, Queen of England (ca. 985–1052): Queen consort of both Ethelred II and his successor (after the death of Edmund Ironside, her stepson) Cnut, Emma was the daughter of Richard, Duke of Normandy, and Gunnora, his second wife; she was William the Conqueror's aunt. Emma, who was likely the patron of the paean to her titled *Encomium Emmae Reginae*, sent her children by Ethelred to Normandy, and married his successor Cnut, becoming queen consort of England, Denmark, and Norway. She seems to have supported her son Harthacnut against her son Edward "the Confessor" after Cnut's death, and negotiated their joint rule, which lasted for two years until Harthacnut's death. Once Edward became sole king of England, Emma retired to her extensive estates. She was buried with Cnut and Harthacnut at the Old Minster, Winchester.

Ethelred I, King of Wessex (r. 865–871): fourth son of King Aethelwulf of Wessex and older brother of his successor, King Alfred. Despite being victorious at the battle of Ashdown against the Vikings, he was unable to stave off further incursions and suffered several defeats at their hands. His wife might have been Wulfthryth (contested among several historians) and they had three children, two of them sons, who were passed over in the succession because they were children at their father's death. Buried at Wimbourne Minster in Dorset.

Ethelred II "the Redeless," King of England (r. 978–1016): his nickname, mistranslated as "Unready" actually means "poorly counseled"—a pun on his name, which means "wise counsel." Son of King Edgar and his second wife, Queen Aelfthryth, he succeeded to the throne at the age of 10 after the murder of his half-brother Edward "the Martyr" (his mother was possibly implicated in this murder). Ethelred's reign was fraught with problems, especially Viking invasions. He was forced to flee to Normandy in 1013 upon the invasion of Sweyn Forkbeard (father of Cnut) and returned after Sweyn's death in 1014. Married twice—[1] Aelfgifu of York and [2] Emma of Normandy—he had at least 12 children, among them King Edmund Ironside (first wife) and King Edward the Confessor (second wife). He died in the midst of the invasion of Cnut, defending London.

Gerald of Wales (1146–1223): also known as Gerald de Barri, son of William fitzOdo de Barri, Lord of Manorbier in Pembrokeshire, and Angharad fitzGerald, whose mother was Nest ferch Rhys ap Tewdwr, King of Deheubarth. Educated at Gloucester Abbey and Paris, Gerald was appointed archdeacon of Brecon but is best known as a prolific writer of both ethnographic history and travelogues of his journeys through Wales and Ireland. His works also included lives of prominent bishops and saints, and justifications for creating an archdiocese out of the bishopric of St. David's, to which he aspired. He had an adversarial relationship with the kings of England, including Henry II and, especially, John.

Glyndwr, Owain (ca. 1349–ca. 1415): claimed to be the last surviving prince of both Deheubarth and Powys and led a long-running rebellion against the English king Henry IV and English control of Wales. Although the revolt was unsuccessful, Glyndwr evaded capture and died possibly in Herefordshire, protected by his daughter and his allies.

Godwine, Earl of Wessex (1001–1053): was one of the most important political figures during the reign of Edward the Confessor; his daughter, Edith, was Edward's wife and queen, and his son, Harold, succeeded Edward after his death in 1066.

Grosseteste, Robert, bishop of Lincoln (ca. 1168–1253): one of the most prominent churchmen of medieval England, Grosseteste was likely the first chancellor of the University of Oxford, Master of the Schools, and bishop of Lincoln. He is considered by many scholars to be the founder of scientific inquiry and method in the English schools. An incredibly prolific writer, Grosseteste wrote poetry, treatises on estate management, theological texts, saints' lives, and, most importantly, several treatises on physics, astronomy, the properties of light, the tides, mathematics, and the properties of the rainbow. His most famous student, Roger Bacon, is considered the developer of the inductive method of reasoning, also espoused by William of Occam.

Harold Godwinson, King of England (r. 1066): son of Godwine, Earl of Essex, and brother-in-law of Edward the Confessor, Harold succeeded Edward in 1066 and was the last English king. He was able to repel the invasion of Harald Hardrada, King of Norway and Denmark, at the battle of Stanford Bridge, but was killed at the battle of Hastings by the invading Normans.

Gruffudd ap Gwenwynwyn (d. 1286): the Prince of Powys Cyfeilog and one of the most prominent Welsh nobles during the thirteenth century. His loyalties vacillated between the English kings and the princes of North Wales, but ultimately the barons of Powys had to throw their support behind Henry III and Edward I because of the constant pressure on their borders from the house of Gwynedd. Gruffudd released his control of Powys to King Edward, who then regranted it to him as a marcher barony. His son, Owain, who had been raised at court as a hostage for many years, changed the family name to "de la Pole" after the town of Welshpool, which became the county town of the new barony of Powys.

Henry I, King of England, Duke of Normandy (r. 1100–1135): youngest son of William the Conqueror and Matilda of Flanders, he succeeded his brother William II (Rufus) after Rufus's death in a hunting accident. Henry issued a comprehensive coronation oath, which formed the basis for notions of baronial liberties; he established the Exchequer as a royal department independent of the king's treasury (the "Wardrobe") and instituted the preservation of the "Pipe" Rolls; he expanded all levels of royal administration. The death of his only legitimate son, William, in 1120 sparked a succession crisis; he declared his daughter Empress Matilda his heir but the barons reneged on their oaths after Henry's death and chose Matilda's cousin Stephen of Blois. Henry married Edith of Scotland (whom he renamed "Matilda"), daughter of Malcolm III and St. Margaret; she was the last direct heir to the English throne, being the great-granddaughter of Edmund Ironside. The marriage was controversial because Margaret had been dedicated to the church. They had 2 children before her death in 1118; Henry, however, had at least 20 other children by mistresses. After Matilda's death, Henry married Adeliza of Louvain, but had no children with her. He died, allegedly after eating a "surfeit of lamprey eels," and was buried at Reading Abbey.

Henry II, King of England, Count of Anjou, Duke of Normandy and Aquitaine (r. 1155–1189): son and heir of Geoffrey Plantagenet, Count of Anjou, and Empress Matilda, daughter of Henry I of England; married Eleanor, Duchess of Aquitaine and divorced wife of King Charles VII of France. Henry was one of the most successful and energetic kings England ever experienced. He was instrumental in developing notions of English common law and judicial procedure; expanding the position of England in European politics; enhancing the royal administration into a professional system that could run without the physical presence of the monarch. His reign was also controversial: the conflict with Thomas Becket, archbishop of Canterbury, resulted in his death; the revolt of his sons and wife against him; and the invasion and conquest of Ireland. His marriage to Eleanor produced eight children; he also had several illegitimate children with mistresses. He died shortly after resisting yet another conflict with surviving sons Richard and John; he was buried at Fontevrault Abbey. Eleanor, his widow, survived him by 15 years and was a significant presence in the reigns of both her sons.

Henry III, King of England (r. 1216–1272): son of King John and Isabella of Angoulême; succeeded his father at the age of nine, which resulted in a lengthy period of regency. The longest reign in English history before that of Queen Victoria, Henry's period as king was marked by multiple rebellions and threats of rebellion; the legalization of Magna Carta; an impressive and important expansion of the structures of English government, judicial process, law, and administration; the creation of parliamentary representation below the level of the baronage; and consolidation of English authority in the British Isles. Henry married Eleanor of Provence; her elder sister was Marguerite, wife of King Louis IX of France, making them brothers-in-law. The French king supported Henry during the Barons War and rebellion of Simon de Montfort (1258–1265). After 1265, Henry slowly turned the reins of government over to his eldest son, Lord Edward. His and Eleanor's two sons, Edward and Edmund "Crouchback," Earl of Lancaster, both survived their father. He was buried in a magnificent tomb at Westminster Abbey, the church he spent thousands of pounds on to rebuild and beautify in order to commemorate his personal patron saint, King Edward the Confessor.

Henry IV, King of England (r. 1399–1413): son of John of Gaunt, son of Edward III, and Blanche, heir to the duchy of Lancaster; he was known as Henry of Bolingbroke. After several tours of crusading activity in eastern Europe with the Teutonic Knights, Henry usurped the crown, deposing King Richard II in 1399; his reign was punctuated by reports of Richard's survival (he is alleged to have starved to death at Henry's Pontefract Castle) as well as unrest—civil and religious—throughout the realm. He died after a long period of increasingly debilitating illness. Henry's first wife was Mary Bohun, coheir, with her sister Eleanor married to Henry's uncle Thomas of Woodstock,

Earl of Gloucester, to the earldom of Hereford; they had six children, including the heir, Henry of Monmouth. Several years after Mary's death in 1394, Henry married Joanna of Navarre; this marriage was childless. He was buried, with Queen Joan, at Canterbury Cathedral.

Henry V, King of England (r. 1413–1422): eldest son of Henry IV and Mary Bohun; often in conflict with his father during Henry IV's reign, once he became king he rehabilitated the reputation of the deposed Richard II and translated his body from the priory where he had been hastily buried to a tomb at Westminster Abbey. Henry also began a campaign against the Lollards and reawakened the Hundred Years' War by challenging the heir to the King of France, Charles VI. The ensuing campaign culminated in the rout of the French army at Agincourt (1415), several years of negotiation to conclude a truce (Treaty of Troyes, 1420), Henry's marriage to Charles VI's daughter Catherine, and his designation as successor to the French throne. His death two years later resulted in the loss of France during the reign of his son, Henry VI, who was nine months old at the time of his succession. Henry V's tomb in Westminster Abbey is one of the more extravagant tombs in the church.

Henry VI, King of England (r. 1422–1462, 1470–1471): only child of Henry V and Catherine of Valois, Henry was nine months old at his succession. The lengthy regency, headed by his large collection of ambitious uncles and cousins, resulted in the resurgence of the son of Charles VI, Charles VII, and the ultimate loss of the war in 1453. Henry VI inherited the mental illness that had plagued the Valois family for several generations, and his periods of illness were punctuated by problems at home and abroad. In 1450, the rebellion of Jack Cade gripped the kingdom; in 1461 Henry was deposed by his cousin Edward of York (Edward IV). Although his supporters returned him to the throne in 1470, he was removed in favor of Edward IV again six months later, in 1471, and he died soon after. Henry married Margaret of Anjou, cousin of King Charles VII; they had only one child: Edward of Westminster, who died at the battle of Tewkesbury in 1471 defending his father against the forces of Edward IV. An avid patron of religious institutions, Henry VI also founded Eton College; King's College, Cambridge; and All Soul's College, Oxford. He was buried at Windsor Castle.

Henry of Almain (1235–1271): son of Richard, Earl of Cornwall and King of the Romans and Isabelle Marshal, and nephew of King Henry III. He was murdered in Italy by the two surviving sons of Earl Simon de Montfort in revenge for his role in their father's death.

Hus, Jan (ca. 1369–1413): Bohemian follower of John Wyclif, Hus returned to Prague and established a Wycliffite dissenting church there, known as the Hussite movement. Although he was arrested and executed as a heretic by the Council of Constance (1414–1418), the Hussite movement persisted in Bohemia until the Reformation.

Hywel Dda, King of Deheubarth (ca. 880–950): semilegendary bringer of a systematic law code to his kingdom, Hywel Dda ("the Good") eventually extended his kingdom through almost all of Wales, from Gwynedd and Angelsey to Pembroke. He achieved a diplomatic détente with King Athelstan of England, and they maintained an alliance against other Welsh princes and in maintaining the borderlands between the two territories. Although the "Laws of Hywel Dda" were not written down until centuries later (probably in the late twelfth century), chronicle sources closer to his reign mention him as a codifier of law. After his death, his kingdom was divided among his three sons as well as portions recovered by the hereditary rulers, such as Gwynedd.

Isabelle of Angoulême, Queen of England (ca. 1188–1246): second wife of King John, after his death in 1216 she returned to France and eventually married Hugh X Lusignan, the son of her earlier fiancée, Hugh IX. With John, she had five children; with Hugh she had nine. Her Lusignan children went to England after her death, and Henry III's relationship with them—especially her youngest, William de Valence—created conflict between the king and the baronage, as well as between the king and the family of Queen Eleanor of Provence, who were also competing for patronage from the Crown. Isabelle promoted a rebellion against King Louis IX, which failed; she died at Fontevrault and was buried there.

John, King of England (r. 1199–1216): perhaps one of the most notorious kings of medieval England, John inherited the throne from his brother Richard I, possibly through nefarious means (he is alleged to have murdered his nephew Arthur of Brittany, who had a slight claim). His reign is considered to be disastrous by many historians: his military failures in France led to the loss of Normandy and Anjou and the reduction of the duchy of Aquitaine to the province of Gascony; his repressive taxation and quarreling with the church led to the First Barons War and Magna Carta. Nevertheless, John's reign also ushered in a more standardized system of judicial procedure—the courts in eyre—that expanded royal justice, and he was significantly limited by the massive debts that Richard I left when he died. John also attempted to regularize the fiscal relationship between Jewish bankers and Christian borrowers. His first marriage to Isabella, Countess of Gloucester, ended in an annulment in 1199; he married Isabelle of Angoulême less than a year later. He and his second wife had five children and he was succeeded by his nine-year-old son, Henry III, at his death. John was buried at Worcester Cathedral.

John of Gaunt, Duke of Lancaster (1340–1399): third surviving son of Edward III and Philippa of Hainault, John was one of the most important, complex, and divisive political figures in the second half of the fourteenth century. Duke of Lancaster through his first wife, Blanche, he was regranted the title after her death. His second marriage, to Constance of Castile, led to his claim to be King of Castile—an expensive and ultimately fruitless exercise. Their daughter, Catherine, became Queen of Castile by marrying the competitor to the throne, Henry III of Castile. John's long-term association with Katherine Swynford (whose sister was married to Geoffrey Chaucer) and their many children led to the creation of the Beaufort family, who were central to the politics of the next century. John fought beside his brother, Prince Edward of Wales, during the Hundred Years' War and was regent during the early years of the reign of his son, Richard II. He also was sympathetic to the teachings of John Wyclif, who was a member of his household, even serving as his chaplain. Hostility against Duke John led to the Great Rising of 1381, during which his London residence, the Savoy Palace, was destroyed. Although Richard II always expressed loyalty to his uncle, he refused to allow John's son Henry Bolingbroke to enter into his Lancaster inheritance; this led to the invasion of Henry and Richard's deposition.

Lacy, Alice de, Countess of Lincoln and Salisbury (1281–1348): daughter and heir of Henry de Lacy, Earl of Lincoln, and Margaret Longespee, Countess of Salisbury in her own right, Alice brought both titles to her marriage to Thomas, Earl of Lancaster and Leicester. The marriage was unhappy and they were separated at the time of Thomas's rebellion and death. Alice remarried a member of her household named Ebulo Lestrange; this was a love match that was very successful but did not produce children. During the later years of the reign of Edward II, Alice was targeted by the king's favorites, the Despencers (Hugh the Elder and Hugh the Younger), who extorted significant properties from her and Ebulo in exchange for her security. She might have been complicit in the final rebellion against Edward II; certainly her life in the reign of Edward III was somewhat more secure. After Ebulo's death in 1335, Alice was abducted and raped by Hugh de Freyne and forced to marry him; his death only a few months later liberated her. She took a vow of chastity and lived out the rest of her life on her estates. When she died, her estates passed to the Crown; she was buried at Barlings Abbey.

Lacy, Margaret de, Countess of Lincoln (ca. 1206–1266): daughter of Robert de Quincy and Hawise of Chester, who inherited the earldom of Lincoln, Margaret received the earldom upon her marriage to John de Lacy, Lord of Pontefract. She was a patron of Bishop Robert Grosseteste, who wrote his treatise on estate management for her when she was widowed in 1240. In 1242, she remarried Walter Marshal, the fourth son of William and Isabella Marshal and Earl of Pembroke. His death in 1245 meant that she controlled one-third of the Pembroke and Leinster estates in dower, which embroiled her in the complicated arrangements for the distribution of the Marshal inheritance among 13 different coheirs. Margaret and John de Lacy had two children, Edmund, who inherited the earldom of Lincoln after her death, and Maud, who married Richard de Clare, Earl of Gloucester and Hertford (and one of the heirs to the Marshal inheritance). When her son died, she and her daughter-in-law, Alice of Saluzzo, shared wardship of her grandson, Henry de Lacy. She was buried in the church of the Hospitallers at Clerkenwell, outside London.

Lionel of Antwerp, Duke of Clarence (1338–1368): second surviving son of King Edward III and Queen Philippa; married Elizabeth de Burgh, heir to the earldom of Ulster in Ireland. He was appointed as governor of the Lordship of Ireland and was responsible for trying to enforce the Statutes of Kilkenny of 1366. His daughter Philippa married Edmund Mortimer, Earl of March and conveyed her mother's earldom of Ulster to him; the Mortimers were identified as potential heirs to the throne in the reign of Richard II and became embroiled in the conflicts of the Wars of the Roses in the fifteenth century.

Llywelyn ab Iorwerth (1173–1240): also known as Llywelyn Fawr (Llywelyn the Great), he was one of the most significant princes of Gwynedd of the pre-Edwardian Conquest. Llywelyn cleverly manipulated competing alliances and interests between the English kings and the Welsh princes in order to amass power and authority. He was able to secure the homage of the Braose lords of Bergavenny and was able to invade Powys as an ally of King John, who had arrested Gwenwynwyn. This alliance, despite the marriage of Llywelyn and Joan of England, one of John's illegitimate daughters, broke down, and Llywelyn sided with the barons and was a Magna Carta signatory. He fought against the marcher barons consistently throughout the early years of Henry III's reign but also formed alliances with them through the judicious use of marriages of his children. His political and diplomatic abilities secured the survival of Gwynedd until the Edwardian conquests. He was buried at Aberconway Abbey.

Llywelyn ap Gruffudd, Prince of North Wales (ca. 1223–1282): also known as "Llywelyn the Last," he was the grandson of Llywelyn ab Iorwerth. By engaging in a deliberate campaign to eliminate all his brothers and rivals for control of Gwynedd, Llywelyn succeeded in gaining that control. He was able to capitalize on the Barons War and the rule of Simon de Montfort to negotiate a treaty, making him the overlord of North Wales and to gain control of Powys, whose lords were allied with the royals. Continuing conflict with his brothers Dafydd and Owain led to Edward I's intervention and the eventual invasion of Wales. Llywelyn was forced into concessions with King Edward in order to have his betrothed, Eleanor de Montfort, released—she had been captured on her way to Wales to marry him, and was living with the royal family. Although Edward permitted Llywelyn and Eleanor to marry, this did not end the conflict. When his brother Dafydd rebelled against the royal officials controlling Gwynedd,

Llywelyn joined him. He was killed in an ambush and the rebellion collapsed. Although his place of burial is not known, it is traditionally claimed to be at the Cistercian Abbey of Abbeycwmhir, in Brecon.

MacAlpin, Kenneth, King of Scots (810–858): King, according to tradition, of Dál Riata and conqueror of the Picts; he is usually referred to as the first King of Scots as a united kingdom.

MacDuff, Isabella, Countess of Buchan (d. ca. 1313?): daughter of Donnchadh III, mormaer of Fife and one of the Guardians of Scotland following the death of Alexander III, and Johanna de Clare, daughter of Gilbert de Clare and Alice de Lusignan. Although her husband, John Comyn, Earl of Buchan, supported King Edward against Robert Bruce, Isabella supported Bruce. According to chronicles (and possibly a legend), Isabella assumed the right of the mormaers of Fife to crown the king at Scone. It is certain that she actively engaged in resisting the English invasion that followed the murder of John III Comyn of Badenoch, and this resulted in her capture and imprisonment in 1306, first at Berwick Castle and then at the Carmelite friary at Berwick. Many legends have arisen regarding her captivity. She seems to have died in captivity possibly around 1313, because the other women captured with her were redeemed after the battle of Bannockburn (1314).

Mac Murchada, Diarmid, King of Leinster (ca. 1110–1171): deposed by the "high king" of Ireland, Ruaidri Ua Conchobhar, because of his abduction of Derbforgaill, wife of the King of Brefne, Diarmid secured the assistance of Richard fitzGilbert de Clare to reattain the throne. The result was the invasion of Ireland by the Anglo-Normans, the marriage of his daughter, Aiofe, to de Clare, and the reduction of Leinster to a lordship under the rule of the kings of England. Diarmid had been a controversial monarch in a region—Ireland—that was known for internecine squabbling on a grand scale. He was deposed several times, in part because the titular High Kings, who were also the kings of Connacht, worried about him claiming the title. He was an avid patron of monasteries and churches, and was buried in the precinct of Ferns Cathedral, his royal seat. His reputation among Irish historians has suffered because he is blamed for inviting the Anglo-Normans into Ireland.

Malcolm III Canmore, King of Scots (r. 1058–1093): heir to Duncan I and possibly the killer of his father's enemy and usurper, Macbeth (of Shakespeare fame), Malcolm succeeded to the throne by eliminating most of his rivals and formed an alliance between himself and King Edward the Confessor. He protected members of the Anglo-Saxon royal family exiled after the Norman Conquest and married, as his second wife, (Saint) Margaret of Wessex, daughter of Edward the Exile, in 1070. His first wife (or mistress) is identified as Ingibiorg Finnsdotter of Orkney. Malcolm's reign was marked by almost constant warfare along the border between Scotland and England, especially after the conquest; he was killed in a skirmish near Alnwick, Northumberland. He was eventually buried at his foundation, Dunfermline Abbey, which became the traditional resting place of medieval kings of Scotland. Five of his sons succeeded him as king.

Margaret, Maid of Norway, heir to the throne of Scotland (1283–1290): the granddaughter of King Alexander III and Queen Margaret of England, and daughter of King Eric II of Norway and Margaret of Scotland, Margaret was three years old when her grandfather died and she was declared heir to the throne. She was betrothed to Edward of Caernarvon (Edward II), a marriage that would have joined Scotland and England into a single polity, but she died in Orkney on her way to Scotland, at the age of seven.

Margaret of Wessex, Queen of Scots, St. (ca. 1045–1093): daughter of Edward the Exile and granddaughter of Edmund Ironside; wife of King Malcolm III; mother of

Edith/Matilda, wife of King Henry I. Margaret's reputation for both piety and goodness—as well as her fertility, having given birth to eight children—led to her being canonized in 1250. She is the only Scottish royal saint.

Marshal, William, Earl of Pembroke (ca. 1144–1219): youngest son of John Marshal and Sibylla of Salisbury, his prospects were limited until he was taken up by Queen Eleanor of Aquitaine and entered royal service. The result, in large part because of his intelligence, diplomacy, and unswerving loyalty to the Crown, was marriage in 1190 to the most notable heiress of the age, Isabella de Clare, Countess of Pembroke and Lady of Leinster, when he was about 45 and she was 18. Their 30-year marriage was extremely successful, resulting in 10 children and an apparently mutual devotion. Earl Marshal accompanied King Richard I on crusade, acted as regent in the minority of Henry III, and gained the reputation of being "the most perfect knight." He was the most important nonroyal political figure during the entire period of Angevin rule, including overseeing the presentation of the first legal form of Magna Carta.

Empress Matilda: daughter and heir of King Henry I (r. 1100–1135), who was his chosen successor. She was the widow of Holy Roman Emperor Henry V and then the wife and widow of Geoffrey Plantagenet, Count of Anjou. The English barons reneged on their promise to crown Empress Matilda and instead elected to crown Stephen of Blois; the result was a civil war that was fought between the two contenders and their allies from 1135 to 1155.

Montfort, Simon de, Earl of Leicester (ca. 1208–1265): the son of the leader of the Albigensian Crusade, Simon successfully claimed the earldom of Leicester as the heir of his grandmother, Amicia de Beaumont, in 1239. He had eloped with the widowed sister of King Henry III, Eleanor, whose first husband was William II Marshal, Earl of Pembroke, the previous year and became embroiled in an argument with successive earls and, after 1245, the 13 coheirs, over Eleanor's dower assignment. Simon created a baronial party, mostly of younger generation barons and heirs to baronies, and in 1258 led the rebellion known as the (Second) Barons War. Between 1258 and his death at the battle of Evesham in 1265, Simon was largely in control of the government, with King Henry III and his family often in virtual—or actual—captivity. Lord Edward, with a coalition of followers including Roger Mortimer of Wigmore and William de Valence, his uncle, defeated the baronial forces at Evesham. Simon and his eldest son were killed and the former's body was horribly mutilated. Simon is commonly credited with the first summons to parliament that included representatives from towns and nonnobles from the counties.

Paris, Matthew (ca. 1200–1259): one of the most famous of the medieval chroniclers centered at the abbey of St Albans. Matthew was very opinionated and his assessment of historical figures is both very entertaining and very biased. What makes his manuscripts most unusual is that he not only acted as his own scribe, but that he also illustrated them with plentiful drawings and color-wash paintings. In his *Chronica Majora*, although technically a continuation of the chronicle of Roger of Wendover (known as the *Flowers of History*), he actually reworked a great deal of Roger's work in his own compilation. Matthew's dislike of Henry III, his affection for Richard of Cornwall and Richard's first wife, Isabelle Marshal, and his support of Simon de Montfort and the baronial party form an important component to understanding popular attitudes about the events of the era.

Richard I, King of England, Duke of Normandy and Aquitaine, Count of Anjou (r. 1189–1199): although a highly romantic figure, Richard I was a problematic king. Second son of Henry II and Eleanor of Aquitaine, he gained a reputation for audacious bravery in battle, which carried over to his reign, which was punctuated by crusades, numerous expensive wars and campaigns, and little administrative innovation. Richard spent a total of 6 months in England during his 11-year reign (2 of those months were at the time of his coronation) and usually left his mother, Queen Eleanor, and a series of royal officials, most important among them William Longchamp, to rule in his stead. His marriage to Berengaria of Navarre was unproductive; contemporary chroniclers and modern historians are conflicted as to his sexual preferences. Although he had declared his nephew Arthur of Brittany as his heir, his brother John attained the throne at his death.

Richard II, King of England (r. 1377–1399): son of Edward "the Black Prince" of Wales and Princess Joan of Kent; succeeded his grandfather Edward III at the age of 10. The regent of the kingdom was his uncle John of Gaunt, Duke of Lancaster, who headed the official council. Richard's reign was problematized by popular hostility to John of Gaunt; his lack of power during his minority and the difficulties of attaining sovereign authority after reaching his majority; and several revolts, including the Great Rising in 1381 (the English Peasants' Revolt) and a revolt of barons who established control of the government as Lords Appellant for two years, in 1387–89. Growing discontent and poor diplomatic choices led to Richard being deposed by his cousin, Henry Boling-broke, son of John of Gaunt. His marriages, to Anne of Bohemia and to Isabella of Valois, produced no children. Richard was imprisoned in Pontefract Castle and, according to contemporary chronicles, was starved to death. He was buried in the church of King's Langley, Hertfordshire, but Henry V disinterred his body and reburied it in an elaborate tomb at Westminster Abbey.

Rollo: Rollo the Viking (ca. 846–ca. 932) was the first Duke of Normandy, after King Charles the Simple, sometime around 918, ceded a portion of the old Roman province of Armorica to him in exchange for protection from other Viking raids. This created the duchy of Normandy and the county of Brittany. Rollo was William the Conqueror's great-great-great grandfather.

Stephen, King of England (r. 1136–1155): son of Adela, daughter of William the Conqueror, and Stephen, Count of Blois, Stephen invaded England as soon as his uncle Henry I died; despite the barons' oaths that they would adhere to the dead king's desire to have his daughter, Empress Matilda, crowned as his successor, many of them revoked their oaths and crowned Stephen. The result was a 30-year civil war between Stephen and his allies and Empress Matilda and her allies, sometimes referred to as the Anarchy. When Matilda's son Henry, Count of Anjou and Duke of Normandy, was old enough to lead an army, he invaded and fought Stephen's forces to a standstill. In the Treaty of Winchester (1153), Stephen agreed to pass over his surviving son, William, and declare Henry his heir. His wife was Matilda, Countess of Boulogne, who is often credited with being one of the most important strategists in Stephen's administration. They had five children, only two of whom survived their parents: William, Count of Boulogne, and Marie, Countess of Boulogne.

Straw, Jack (d. 1381?): possibly legendary coleader of the Great Rising of 1381, along with John Ball and Wat Tyler. Nothing is known about his life, and reports in chronicles of his death by beheading in 1381 are likely invented. The name might have been one of the pseudonyms used by Wat Tyler.

Thomas, Earl of Lancaster (1278–1322): son of Edmund Crouchback (second son of Henry III and Eleanor of Provence) and Blanche of Artois; married to Alice de Lacy, Countess of Lincoln and Salisbury; was one of the baronial leaders against the rule of Edward II, both in the early years of the reign, as one of the Lords Ordainer who demanded that the king abide by the "Ordinances" of 1311, and as leader of a revolt in 1322. Captured after the battle of Boroughbridge, he was executed at his estranged wife Alice's Pontefract Castle. His reputation historically is conflicted: there is not only the recognition that Edward II was a problematic king, but also that Thomas of Lancaster was himself power-hungry and a problematic leader.

Tyler, Wat (d. 1381): one of the coleaders of the Great Rising. He led the delegation that met King Richard II at Mile End in London and was killed there by the mayor, William Walworth, and one of the king's attendants, John Cavendish. His head was displayed on London Bridge along with those of other executed rebels.

Valence, Joan de [Munchensy], Countess of Pembroke (ca. 1230–1307): daughter of Warin de Munchensy and heir of her mother, Joan Marshal; inherited one-fifth of the earldom of Pembroke and the county of Wexford in Ireland in 1245. Married in 1248 to Henry III's half-brother, William de Valence, the couple weathered the storms of the reign, including William's exile during the Barons War, to emerge as major political players in the reign of Edward I. After William's death in 1296, Joan remained politically involved, especially because her daughters were married to people who could potentially claim the throne of Scotland; her daughter Joan married John III Comyn of Badenoch, and grandmother Joan had to take charge of her orphaned and at-risk grandchildren. She and William had seven children; only two survived their mother: Agnes and Aymer.

Valence, William de, Earl of Pembroke (ca. 1228–1296): youngest son of Hugh X Lusignan and Isabelle of Angoulême; married to Joan de Munchensy and through her became Earl of Pembroke and Lord of Wexford. William became the target of baronial anger because of his marriage to Joan as well as (at least according to Matthew Paris) his difficult personality; this led to his exile in 1258 during the Barons War. He was instrumental in freeing Lord Edward from his imprisonment and participated in the battle of Evesham. He went on crusade with Edward and became a prominent member of his court when he succeeded Henry III as king. William died because of wounds received in a skirmish in France; he was survived by his wife, Joan, and four of his seven children. His and Joan's youngest son, Aymer, ultimately inherited both parents' estates. William was buried in Westminster Abbey.

Walsingham, Thomas (d. ca. 1422): monk of the Benedictine abbey of St. Albans and one of the writers of the multigeneration chronicle maintained by that abbey (another was Matthew Paris). His *Chronica Maiora* traced the history of the reigns of Edward III and Richard II in the fourteenth century, and of Henry IV and Henry V in the fifteenth. He was highly critical of the Lancastrians, but approved the usurpation of the throne by Henry Bolingbroke.

William I, Duke of Normandy, King of England (r. 1066–1087): conqueror of England at the battle of Hastings; sometimes referred to as William "the Bastard" because his father never married his mother (or, indeed, any of the mistresses who provided children for him). William consolidated English rule despite numerous revolts and conflicts, especially along the borders of Scotland and Wales. Although he spent a great deal of time on the continent in his French possessions, through an effective administration and a heavy hand he was able to retain control. The comprehensive survey of land in England, known as Domesday Book, was produced in 1086. Married Matilda of Flanders, who proved to be an effective regent and administrator in his absence; they had at least nine children; succeeded by Robert "Curthose" as Duke of Normandy; William II as King of England.

William I, "The Lion," King of Scots (r. 1165–1214): brother and successor of Malcolm IV, grandson of David I. His lengthy reign spanned those of Henry II, Richard I, and John in England. William was focused on reappropriating the earldom of Northumbria, which he ultimately had to give up in the Treaty of Falaise (1174), after he was captured by the English at the battle of Alnwick. This humiliating treaty remained in place until the reign of Richard I, who released him from the treaty in exchange for a cash payment of 10,000 marks to help fund his crusade. He married, at the instigation of Henry II, Ermengarde de Beaumont; they had four children but William had many more illegitimate children by various mistresses. He was active in expanding the administration of his grandfather and continuing the practice of "Normanization" of the southern Scottish provinces and counties. He founded Arbroath Abbey, where he was buried.

William II, King of England (r. 1087–1100): known as "Rufus" because of his florid complexion, succeeded his father as King of England, but not as Duke of Normandy; seized the latter from his brother, Robert "Curthose" when he went on crusade in 1096. William's reign was marked by conflicts with the church and also with some of the barons, as he reportedly ruled with a heavy hand; he never married; it was rumored that he was a religious skeptic, which was why his conflicts with churchmen were so heated. William was killed in a hunting accident; it is not clear whether his brother Henry, who was present, was implicated in the accident. He was buried in Winchester Cathedral.

Wyclif, John (ca. 1331–1384): dissident theologian and preacher, Wyclif was a lecturer and master at Oxford University, where his theological stance, opposed to some of the basic precepts of the medieval church, came to the notice of religious authorities. His writings, which renounced the luxury and decadence of the church and its officials, advocated the translation of the Bible into English, and questioned the legitimacy of some of the sacraments, were condemned, but he was protected by John of Gaunt from prosecution. He retired to the parish of Lutterworth, where he died. His followers were known as "Lollards"; their movement and Wyclif's teachings were condemned at the Council of Constance in 1314.

APPENDIX 2: GLOSSARY OF TERMS MENTIONED IN THE TEXT

aldorman: also spelled *ealdorman*; in the Anglo-Saxon period, the military and administrative leaders of a shire, or county

amercement: see **mercy**

appeal: in English law, a charge made against an individual

approver: a criminal who testifies against his or her fellow-perpetrators

assize: a court of law, or certain kinds of litigation heard in a court of law

attach[ed]: if a litigant failed to answer the sheriff's summons, the sheriff was commanded to "attach" him or her: arrest him and remand him temporarily to prison

baillie/bailly: in England, Wales, and Ireland, the estate under the control of a bailiff; in Scotland, a royal official charged with administering a district or county

bailiff: an estate official in charge of a particular portion of the estate, such as a manor or castle; he answered to the seneschal and was the overseer of all local activities on the estate

bailiwick: the precinct of a baillie

bard: in Celtic courts, a professional poet and singer who created and performed poetry for the court; Anglo-Norman aristocrats also employed bards, especially in Wales and Ireland

Black Death: the endemic disease that ravaged Europe between 1347 and 1350 and revisited, in various forms, every 7 to 11 years thereafter until the eighteenth century. The initial infection was a combination of bubonic plague, and two variants, pneumonic plague and septicaemic plague.

brideprice: in Anglo-Saxon England and other Germanic kingdoms, prospective groom or his parents negotiated a kind of "purchase" of a bride, giving an amount of cash, movables, and land appropriate to the bride's status. This brideprice was sometimes paid to the bride's family and sometimes directly to her as a form of "reverse dowry." The brideprice also factored into the property a woman controlled if she outlived her husband.

burgage: a house and its land in a town or urban area

calends: in the Roman calendar, the "calends" is the first day of the month

cantref/cantred: in Wales, an estate similar to an "honor" or lordship in England, held by a nobleman; in Ireland, a region or specifically delineated geographical area

Carolingian Renaissance: the period of educational and artistic revival popularly attributed to the court of Charlemagne and those of his son, Louis the Pious, and grandson, Charles the Bald. The focus of the Carolingian Renaissance was the revival of classical

Latin and the educating of clergy. This "revival" flourished from the mid-eighth century to the end of the ninth century.

carucate: see **hide**

Chamberlain: the highest official in a royal, or, sometimes, in a magnate household. The Chamberlain controlled access to the king and oversaw the running of the household.

charter: a formal document that operates as a contract in which one party is transferring, donating, or conveying some form of property—movable or immovable—to another party. Charters were witnessed by at least one other person besides the creator of the charter and were also sealed with the seals of the parties involved.

chirograph/cyrograph: see **indenture**

churl: also spelled, in Old English, *ceorl*; this is a free peasant who has the ability to own land in Anglo-Saxon England

clipped coin: coins that had been in circulation for some time experienced the eroding of their outer edges, either through wear and tear or through deliberate shaving of the edge, called coin clipping

cloister: the square or rectangular open atrium, surrounded by a covered walkway known as an "ambulatory," that separated the monastery's church and the other buildings, such as the dormitory and refectory (dining hall)

commote: a political and administrative district in Wales, similar to a county

constable: an official in charge of the militia housed in a fortified manor or a castle; in the royal administration, the constable was a largely honorific position for an elite magnate, but still performed a similar function as the leader of the defense troops

corn: a generic term for any cultivated grain. In England, corn usually referred to wheat, barley, and rye; elsewhere it could also include oats and other grains. It never referred to what is now called "sweet corn" or "maize," as this was brought to Europe from the New World after 1500.

deed: any kind of written agreement; **—of covenant:** an agreement to enter into a partnership

default: in legal terms, a failure to appear when summoned to court; in fiscal terms, the failure to pay a debt

demesne: the arable land controlled directly by the lord of an estate, rather than distributed to tenants or villeins

distrain/distraint: if a person failed to appear in court despite the sheriff's summons, he or she was arrested and his or her possessions to the value of the case being decided were taken in to the sheriff's hand as collateral

dorse: the back side of a parchment membrane from a roll; in books this is known as the verso page

draper: a seller of cloth

dykes/dykeworks: raised earthwork fortifications that were used defensively to provide extra security to a manor or castle, and also built as seawalls in order to expand arable land in low marshy areas, such as East Anglia

enrolled: a procedure of registering a writ in the royal chancery by submitting it to be copied into a "roll" or register of writs; such rolls were also maintained by elite households, monastic houses, and the church

esquire: see **squire**

exacted: assessed a monetary penalty that must be paid to the king

Exchequer: the office of the treasury in England, Ireland, and Wales. The term refers to the accounting method used, in which a checkerboard cloth and wooden counters were employed to add and subtract daily tallies of debts and payments. The system was also adopted by towns and cities, guilds, and elite households.

eyre: literal meaning is "itinerant" or "traveling," but refers specifically to royal courts that were sent on a circuit throughout the kingdom to hear and judge cases that would normally have been heard either at the central court at Westminster or in the county courts.

farm: the grant, by charter, of the income from a property in exchange for a percentage of that income. Grants in farm (or "fee-farm") were not permanent or inherited and the terms of the grant could change depending on the terms of the contract.

farthing: a coin worth one-quarter penny

fealty: the oaths taken by a vassal at the receipt of a fee or fief—a grant of land in exchange for military service

fee: also known as "fief," this is the basic unit of land tenure at the knightly level or above. A knight's fee was the property given to someone in exchange for service and it included a dwelling, arable land, pasture, woods, and other "appurtenances" proportionate to the value of the fee. The average value of a knight's fee was assessed as 20s per year in the thirteenth century.

feudal tenure: the form of land-holding held according to feudal obligations. Feudal tenures required a reciprocal relationship between the granter of the land—such as a king or baron—and the holder or "tenant" of the land—such as a knight or free person; the form of the land was known as a "fief."

fine: an agreement, made with a chirograph or indenture, relating to a financial arrangement

fortnight: two weeks

Fourth Lateran Council (1215): one of the most important church councils of the Middle Ages, presided over by Pope Innocent III. There were many changes to doctrinal positions made at the council, including the reduction of "degrees of consanguinity" (levels of relationship in which people were not supposed to marry) from seven to four, a demand that all priests should abandon wives and concubines (a persistent problem in the church), and forbidding priests to preside or participate in "ordeals" (a form of legal dispute resolution involving presumed divine intervention), which led to the rapid growth of jury trials in England and its subject territories.

franchise: connected to landholding, this refers to any rights and privileges provided to the landholder by specific grant or by charter

Friars Minor: members of the Franciscan Order

fripperer: someone who sells used clothing

gage: the collateral paid in cash for a promise or loan

geld: a payment of a tax in cash or kind

gentry: a landed social class above the level of the peasantry but below that of the knights. The gentry developed as an identifiable group in the later Middle Ages and formed a significant component of the professional administrative class, including membership into the parliamentary knighthood.

grange: the portion of an estate in which the storage barns were built and maintained

Great Cause: the name assigned by chroniclers for the competition among the potential successors to the Scots' throne after the death of Margaret of Norway in 1290. The candidates were known as the Competitors.

heriot: the death duties, or death payment, owed to the king or the lord in Anglo-Saxon England in order for the heir(s) to receive his/her/their inheritance

hide: a unit of arable land, originating in the Anglo-Saxon period, that corresponded to the amount of farmland thought to sustain a family and household. The number of acres varied over the years, but in the later Middle Ages the "hide" and the "carucate" came to be considered equivalent and were counted as about 120 acres.

homage: an oath sworn by a vassal or subordinate to his or her lord in which she or he pledges eternal loyalty. Women as well as men could swear oaths of homage.

honor: a particular kind of lordship that conveys to the holder special privileges and liberties

hundred: an administrative and judicial unit—all counties in England were divided into hundreds (in the Anglo-Saxon period these were called "wapentakes"), which formed the basic unit of citizen obligation of free men in the county. Hundreds were assigned to make up juries and were obligated to engage in the view of frankpledge several times a year.

indenture: a particular kind of bipartite or tripartite document, also known as a chirograph (or cyrograph), that recorded an agreement between two or more parties. Two or three exact copies of the agreement were written on a single piece of parchment: two ran vertically and the third ran horizontally along the bottom of the parchment membrane—the "foot." Seals were attached to all three copies, and the copies were separated by cutting a sawtooth (in Latin, *indentata*) seam between them, which prevented forgeries from being created because all copies could be tested by lining up the jagged edge. The two parties to the agreement received one of the upper two copies; the "foot" was enrolled in the royal chancery.

inquest: a generic term for all inquiries or investigations made by any official body, from the king to individual estate managers

inquisition: any investigation by an official body; —**of the country:** an inquisition conducted by a jury appointed to investigate a particular dispute

issues: refers to profits made in cash or kind; —**of pleas** issues of pleas refers to the profits made by litigants purchasing writs to introduce litigation in the king's or local courts.

justiciary/justiciar: a royal official who acts as the head of the judicial system, overseeing the central courts of law

livery: a kind of uniform, beginning in the thirteenth century, that identified the wearer as connected to the household of a particular nobleman or noblewoman, or to the royal household. Liveries usually included a particular color or set of colors, a badge with the family heraldic standard inscribed, and other identifiers.

Lollard: a follower of the religious teachings of John Wyclif; after 1400, any person who espouses forms of religious dissent or anticlericalism; an ignorant, uncouth person

mainprise: the process of acquiring "sureties"—people who will swear to take responsibility for an accused prisoner, or for someone being sued in civil court, or for someone involved in a law case who must be summoned in order for the case to continue

march: the border between two independently ruled regions, such as between Wales and England, and between Scotland and England. Lords of the marches gained special privileges in exchange for their obligations to defend the border.

mark: another unit of currency, equal to two-thirds of a pound sterling

marriage-gift: in Anglo-Saxon England, the property granted a bride by her family upon her wedding; also known as a "dowry"

marshal: a high-ranking household official in charge of the stables and maintenance of the military and defensive structures of the estate

mercy/in mercy/amercement: an admission of guilt or a guilty decision in a civil court resulted in the payment of penalties owed to the king through his representative the sheriff, and damages awarded to the plaintiff. The penalty owed to the king was called an "amercement" and the guilty party was "in mercy" to the sheriff—in Latin, *misericordia*.

Michaelmas: the feast of St. Michael the Archangel, on September 29. This was the beginning of the fiscal, law-court, and chancery year in the British Isles and it still marks the beginning of the university school year in the United Kingdom.

minster: a cathedral church or important parish church

moors: in northern England and southern Scotland, the terrain, known as the moors, is marked by low rolling hills, few trees, and native grasses and shrubs

mormaer: independent lord of a region in Scotland; in Latin the term used for this was "comes," which came to be translated in English as "earl." The Anglo-Saxon term "thane" is also sometimes used in place of mormaer.

morning gift: known in Old English as *morgengab*. This is a grant of land and movables that the new husband grants to his bride on the morning after the wedding (and the wedding night). An important component in the wife's property were she to be widowed, the morning gift was considered her own property, which she could will to anyone she chose.

octave: in the medieval chancery and law court calendar, a week was counted from Monday to Monday: eight days, or an octave

outlawed: literally, removed from the protection of the common law. When a person accused of a crime flees rather than appears at the court of law, he or she is declared "outlaw": that is, outside the law.

papal bull: the term used for an official document from the papal chancery, sealed with the pope's lead seal (unlike the wax seals usually used), known as a *bulla* in Latin

pipe: 1. also known as a "butt," this is a wine barrel that holds one-half a tun; 2. the colloquial term used for the exchequer account rolls, known as the "Great Rolls of the Pipe" or "Pipe Rolls"

Poitevins: the family of Queen Eleanor of Provence, who settled in England after her marriage to King Henry III

poll tax: a tax levied on every adult person; the word "poll" in Middle English meant "head"

porter: a household official in charge of protecting and overseeing the main gate and the entrance and egress of people into the household

pottage: a kind of stew or soup that was the staple of medieval diets. It was made of a combination of grains plus vegetables and different kinds of animal proteins—fish, meat, poultry, meat juices—depending on the wealth of the household. For peasants, pottages replaced almost all other cooked food except at special holidays. For elites, pottage was also a daily dish, but it was far more complex and the contents related to the times of the week and year when Christians were instructed to "fast" (not eat meat) or "feast."

Preaching Brothers: Friars of the Dominican Order

Prime: the third of the eight canonical hours of the church, a system of telling time before the invention of clocks. It usually was called, or tolled, at around sunrise.

privy seal: The royal administration used two different kinds of seals for "signing" documents. The Great Seal, which was used for official documents coming out of the government departments of chancery, exchequer, etc., and also for royal proclamations and statutes, was kept at Westminster. The privy seal was the king's private seal, which he kept with him and used to seal correspondence, orders, and other documents.

prisage: a customs duty paid on wine

purgation: in church courts, the process by which a member of the clergy was punished by receiving penance for crimes committed

put oneself upon the country: to subject oneself to a jury trial in which the jurors investigate the crime or dispute and decide on the person's guilt or innocence

raise the hue and cry: the obligation of every man in a community to announce, loudly and in public, when he witnesses a crime being committed, or discovers that a crime has been committed

regrator/regratress: a person—usually a woman—who sold cooked food from a cart. Regrators were the sellers, not the preparers of the food, which they usually purchased from the makers.

replevy/replevin: the act of pleading for return of distrained property following the successful removal of a penalty for default

Saint Hillary, Octave of: the second of four sessions of the legal and administrative year began on the feast of St Hilary, January 13.

scrivener: a professional scribe who belonged to the scrivener's guild

scutage: monetary payment owed in lieu of military service for a knight's fee

seisin/disseisin: the legal right to land is known as "seisin"; when someone who has a rightful claim to a piece of property is forcibly removed from it, this is called a "disseisin"

seneschal: an estate official in charge of overseeing the daily workings and production of an estates or estates. The seneschal was usually the highest official of an elite household and reported directly to the lord or lady.

serjeanty: a military position, akin to knighthood, but owing different kinds of services. Lands held in serjeanty were of lesser value than those held as knights' fees and required payment of different kinds of customary services, but it was often difficult to distinguish between them. When referring to royal service, the serjeant often was in charge of mustering troops or overseeing certain kinds of courts of law.

shire-moot: a court of law in the Anglo-Saxon period, overseen by the sheriff of a county and attended by the ealdormen, abbots, bishop, and other elites. The court was held in the open in order for anyone who wanted to attend to be able to do so.

shire-reeve: the original term in the Anglo-Saxon period for a sheriff: a royal official in charge of a shire or county

squire/esquire: a military soldier below the level of knight, who could fight both on foot or on horseback. Squires also acted as servants of knights and were "knights in training" with the expectation of being raised if they performed particularly well in feats of arms or battle. In the later Middle Ages, a landed position below that of knight was the "esquire." Latin word for squire was *armiger*, which simply meant a soldier.

tallage: a tax on land

tenement: a generic term for any landed property held through rent or as a portion of a knight's fee

thane/thegn: in Anglo-Saxon England, a nobleman who controls an inherited estate, and who owed military and administrative service to the king. The term is also sometimes used to describe mormaers in Scotland.

tithe: literally, one-tenth of one's annual income; the basic level of gifts to the church required of all Christians

tithing-men: men registered in a hundred who were responsible for the view of frankpledge

tourneying: the travel by young knights around the country to attend tournaments and conduct feats of arms

tun: a large cask for storing and transporting wine

usher: a household official in charge of overseeing visitors' access to the lord, lady and family

view of frankpledge: the meeting of all men in a given community to present to the sheriff or court official a list of all crimes that had been committed since the previous view

villein: a peasant of servile status, also known as a "serf." The term "villein" was used in legal documents; the status was known as "villeinage."

wardrobe: refers not only to the chests in which the family's clothing was stored, but also to the movable wealth and treasure of the family. Also, in the Middle Ages, referred to as a "garderobe," in this instance it includes not only the storage of clothing and other movables, but also the room in which the toilets were built.

wardship: the guardianship over a property during the minority of the heir or the absence of the lord or lady

wimple: a wrapped head covering worn by all adult women and now associated with nuns' habits

writ: a formal and official document, thought to have been invented in Anglo-Saxon England, that is written in the form of a letter and that conveys instructions, information, and commands of the sender of the writ to the recipient and "all present who see and hear this letter"; **—of *bono et malo*:** rather than a general writ of gaol delivery, this as a special writ relating to a specific prisoner

BIBLIOGRAPHY

GENERAL TEXTS ON MEDIEVAL BRITISH ISLES

Bartlett, Robert. *England under the Norman and Angevin Kings, 1075–1225*. Oxford: Clarendon Press, 2000.

Carpenter, David. *The Struggle for Mastery: The Penguin History of Britain, 1066–1284*. London: Penguin Books, 2003.

Cosgrove, Art, ed. *A New History of Ireland II: Medieval Ireland, 1169–1534*. Oxford: Oxford University Press, 1993.

Crick, Julia and Elisabeth Van Houts, eds. *A Social History of England, 900–1200*. Cambridge: Cambridge University Press, 2011.

Davies, R. R. *Conquest, Coexistence and Change: Wales 1063–1415*. Oxford: Clarendon Press/University of Wales Press, 1987.

Davies, Wendy, ed. *From the Vikings to the Normans*. Oxford: Oxford University Press, 2003.

Fleming, Robin. *Britain after Rome: The Fall and Rise, 400–1070*. London: Penguin Books, 2011.

Griffiths, Ralph, ed. *The Fourteenth and Fifteenth Centuries*. Oxford: Oxford University Press, 2003.

Harvey, Barbara, ed. *The Twelfth and Thirteenth Centuries*. Oxford: Oxford University Press, 2001.

Horrox, Rosemary and W. Mark Ormrod, eds. *A Social History of England, 1200–1500*. Cambridge: Cambridge University Press, 2006.

Ó Cróinín, Dáibhí, ed. *A New History of Ireland I: Prehistoric and Early Ireland*. Oxford: Oxford University Press, 2005.

Pryor, Francis. *Britain in the Middle Ages: An Archaeological History*. London: Harper-Collins, 2006.

Rigby, S. H., ed. *A Companion to Britain in the Later Middle Ages*. Chichester: Wiley-Blackwell, 2008.

Rubin, Miri. *The Hollow Crown: A History of Britain in the Late Middle Ages*. London: Penguin Books, 2005.

Stafford, Pauline, ed. *A Companion to the Early Middle Ages: Britain and Ireland c. 500–1100*. Chichester: Wiley-Blackwell, 2013.

Thomson, John A. F. *The Transformation of Medieval England, 1370–1529*. London: Longman, 1983.

Walker, David. *Medieval Wales*. Cambridge: Cambridge University Press, 1990.

USEFUL WEBSITES

British History Online. http://www.british-history.ac.uk/

Castles of Wales. http://www.castlewales.com/

CELT: Corpus of Electronic Texts. http://www.ucc.ie/celt/

The Cistercians in Yorkshire. http://cistercians.shef.ac.uk/

English Heritage Archaeological Monographs. http://archaeologydataservice.ac.uk/archives/view/eh_monographs_2014/

Epistolae: Medieval Women's Letters. http://epistolae.ccnmtl.columbia.edu/

Henry III Fine Rolls Project. http://www.finerollshenry3.org.uk/home.html

Internet Medieval Sourcebook: England. http://legacy.fordham.edu/Halsall/sbook1n.asp

Internet Medieval Sourcebook: Celtic States. http://legacy.fordham.edu/Halsall/sbook1o.asp

Medieval Genealogy Resources. https://sites.google.com/site/cochoit/home

INDEX

ABOUT THE EDITOR

Linda E. Mitchell is the Martha Jane Phillips Starr Missouri Distinguished Professor of Women's and Gender Studies and Professor of History at the University of Missouri—Kansas City. She is also senior editor of the international journal *Historical Reflections/Réflexions Historiques*. Dr. Mitchell is the author of numerous books and articles on medieval history, in particular focusing on the British Isles, women, families, and gender. Her publications include *Portraits of Medieval Women* (Palgrave Macmillan, 2003), *Family Life in the Middle Ages* (Greenwood Press, 2007), *The Ties That Bind: Essays in Medieval British History in Honor of Barbara Hanawalt* (co-editor, Ashgate, 2011), and *Joan de Valence: The Life and Influence of a Thirteenth-Century Noblewoman* (Palgrave Macmillan, 2016).